GM's
Motorama

The Glamorous Show Cars of a Cultural Phenomenon

David W. Temple

Edited by Dennis Adler
Foreword by Chuck Jordan
Introduction by David E. Davis Jr.

Dedication **To Dad for teaching me how to write the dreaded essay assignments of grade school.**

On the cover:
Clockwise from top left: 1956 Buick Centurion Rusty Thompson, 1961 Impala Special convertible GM Media Archive, 1956 Oldsmobile Golden Rocket Photo by Yann Saunders, courtesy Cadillac Studio, 1994, 1954 Chevrolet Corvair GM Media Archive, GM Firebirds GM Media Archive, 1954 Cadillac La Espada Photo by Yann Saunders, courtesy Cadillac Studio, 1994, 1954 Oldsmobile F-88 Dennis Adler, 1959 GM Motorama matchbook cover Charles D. Barnette collection

Center: 1958 GM Firebird III. *Bruce Berghoff collection*

On the frontispiece:
Program guide from the 1955 GM Motorama at the Waldorf-Astoria. *Author collection*

On the title page:
1957 Chevrolet Corvette. *David Temple*

On the back cover:
Top Left: Bonneville Special. *Dennis Adler*

Top Right: GM has reconsidered the fate of its legendary Camaro and has produced a retro-styled concept car that has a few design cues reminiscent of the 1969 version. *GM Media Archive*

Bottom: At the 2003 North American International Auto Show, Cadillac took the spotlight with its concept car dubbed simply and elegantly "Sixteen." The name emphasized the 830-ci V-16 of 1,000 horsepower and 1,000 ft-lbs of torque under the car's long hood. *GM Media Archive*

First published in 2006 by Motorbooks, an imprint of MBI Publishing Company, Galtier Plaza, Suite 200, 380 Jackson Street, St. Paul, MN 55101-3885 USA

MBI Publishing Company titles are also available at discounts in bulk quantity for industrial or sales-promotional use. For details write to Special Sales Manager at MBI Publishing Company, Galtier Plaza, Suite 200, 380 Jackson Street, St. Paul, MN 55101-3885 USA

ISBN-13: 978-0-7603-2826-2
ISBN-10: 0-7603-2826-9

Acquisitions Editor: Lee Klancher
Designer: Jennifer Bergstrom

Printed in China

Library of Congress Cataloging-in-Publication Data
Temple, David W., 1964-
   GM's Motorama : the glamorous show cars of a cultural phenomenon / David W. Temple ; foreword by Chuck Jordan ; introductions by David E. Davis, Jr.; edited by Dennis Adler.
      p. cm.
   ISBN-13: 978-0-7603-2826-2 (hardbound w/ jacket)
   ISBN-10: 0-7603-2826-9 (hardbound w/ jacket) 1. Motorama (New York, etc.) 2. General Motors Corporation—Exhibitions. 3. Experimental automobiles—United States—Exhibitions—History. I. Adler, Dennis, 1948- II. Title.
   TL7.U62N489 2006
      659.19'6292220973—dc22
                              2006018154

CONTENTS

Foreword

The General Motors Motorama was an "automotive happening" during an era when people were crazy for cars. Motorama visitors lined up, sometimes for hours, to see many of the same cars that were in their local showrooms. The difference was the elegant setting, a spectacular stage show and, most of all, the mouth-watering Dream Cars which provided visitors a peek into the future. People loved it.

General Motors pioneered the Dream Car concept. Harley Earl, the head of GM Styling since its beginning in 1927, introduced GM's first Dream Car—the 1938 Y-Job. In 1951, Harley Earl's Le Sabre was unveiled and created a sensation. So in 1952, Earl, always the showman, proposed a new and expanded Motorama which would feature a series of Dream Cars, one for each car division, with spectacular stage shows spotlighting these cars. Corporate management agreed, Mr. Earl made the studio assignments, and a new era was born.

I was a young designer at GM at the time and I vividly remember the excitement. With less than a year to create, refine, and fabricate finished interior and exterior models, we were under the gun. Production design may have suffered somewhat, but with the Motorama cars, the creative juices were flowing. The pace was fast, the atmosphere was free, and our heart and soul plus many long hours went into our work. In the end, the cars made it to the Motorama opening—but just barely.

The 1953 Motorama was a resounding success and the cars were indeed the stars. In fact, one concept car, the Chevrolet Corvette, was so enthusiastically received that it immediately went into production. But 1953 was not the end. During the next three years, GM Styling continued to design and build new concept cars with more variety, more innovation, and more design excitement. Motorama visitors continued to come in record numbers.

After the 1956 Motorama, things changed. Because of continually increasing costs and new corporate marketing opportunities, the 1957 Motorama was canceled. GM Styling's annual crop of Dream Cars also came to an end because, as the style leader, GM was giving away too many valuable design ideas to our competitors. GM Styling's program of concept cars continued, but now in secret behind locked doors. One fact was certain—our Motorama experience had taught us the importance of creativity and the value of advance design as we charged ahead.

The Motorama produced many benefits for GM, not the least of which was increased sales and a brighter image. To GM Styling it was a priceless experience. In my 43 years at GM Design, I have never known a time that was more exciting, more creative, and more productive than the Motorama years. I believe the design of our Motorama cars had a profound influence on America's golden era of automobile design of the 1950s and 1960s.

Chuck Jordan

—Chuck Jordan, retired GM vice president of design and
design chief of the 1955 Motorama GMC L'Universelle and 1956 Motorama Buick Centurion

Editor's Note Looking Back to the Future

Every so often you stumble across an idea that makes you stop and ask, "Why didn't I think of that?" For the better part of my 30 years in automotive publishing I have been an editor for *Car Collector* magazine, and back in 2003 one of my contributing editors, David Temple, came to me with an idea to do a series of articles on the missing GM Motorama cars. I liked it, and I knew no one could research a subject like David. He had proven that time and again with incredible articles such as the piece he wrote on the loss of the Chrysler Norseman when the Andrea Doria sank in 1956. The result of David's "idea" turned into a series of three articles that received more letters and comments than any article in years. David had struck a nerve with collectors and enthusiasts born in the 1930s and 1940s who had attended the GM Motorama in the 1950s, I among them, having seen two with my parents at the Pan-Pacific Auditorium in Los Angeles, before the age of 12. I was hooked on dreams of super-sleek rocket cars and the promise that one day automobiles would be propelled by nuclear power. Fortunately, the use of jet engines was as close as we ever came to that realization!

As it did for many Americans in the early postwar era, the GM Motorama left a lasting impression on those who attended, and for numerous reasons. For my parents, it marked the beginning of a new era: the country having just come out of a world war, the nation was shifting its focus from the conflict and such necessary frugalities as gas rationing, war bonds, and driving on bald tires, to tens of thousands of soldiers returning home, women putting down their work gloves, renewing relationships, and beginning life again in a world that would be forever changed. For children born during and shortly after the war, the Motorama was a vision, a fantastic world where the dreams of a nation were taking shape, and at the same time, shaping the impressions of that future we would carry with us into adulthood. When Disneyland opened in 1955, one of the first attractions was the Carousel of Progress, which mirrored many of the futuristic themes and cars shown in the Motorama. Walt Disney put it best when he described Tomorrowland: "Tomorrow can be a wonderful age. Our scientists today are opening the doors of the Space Age to achievements that will benefit our children and generations to come . . . The Tomorrowland attractions have been designed to give you an opportunity to participate in adventures that are a living blueprint of our future."

For me, much of this became second nature by the time I was a teen, but for David, who was born years after the last Motorama exhibit closed and its Dream Cars sent off to be crushed, this was the past, the past that he had to research and rebuild from old files at General Motors and through interviews with the designers who created many of the Dream Cars we treasure today. To that end, David has done a remarkable job of gathering not only historic photographs but firsthand knowledge from the people who were there. One of the most intriguing aspects of this book, as I am certain most will find, is the tales of the lost cars, those which either *were* destroyed, as was intended, or vanished never to be seen again. This is part of the mystique that still surrounds the Motorama Dream Cars half a century later. Today, those that survive are among the most valued collectible automobiles of the mid-twentieth century; an interesting end for cars that were never meant to be.

—Dennis Adler

Preface and Acknowledgments

Special cars fascinate enthusiasts. That's a very straightforward premise for a book. And it is as true today as it was when the first special cars were built in the 1930s. What makes a car special can be a combination of characteristics. Rarity can be one of those traits. Unique styling can be another. Certainly, there are no cars rarer or more uniquely styled than the Dream Cars of the 1950s. The modern term for such cars today is "concept car." Ford, Chrysler, Packard, and GM built many of them in the decade of the 1950s, but those of the latter company are the subject of this book, and arguably the most significant of the era.

I became fascinated by Dream Cars many years ago. Two events helped spark this particular interest. First was discovering photographs my dad had taken at the 1953 GM Motorama held at the San Francisco Civic Center—one of which is shown in this book. I first saw them in the mid-1970s. The second event came soon after when reading an article in the August 1976 issue of *Motor Trend*. It was titled "The Case of the Lost Albanita—And Other Cars That Have Mysteriously Disappeared." It told the tales (some rumor, some factual) of numerous concept, exotic, and unusual cars that had been lost over the years. The article began with author John Pashdag relating a dream in which he comes upon a junkyard aglow in moonlight while ". . . driving along a two-lane road through the semi-urban sprawl on the outskirts of—where? I'm never quite sure. Sometimes it looks like Detroit. . . ." The sight of a giant tarp flapping in the gentle breeze captures his attention. Curious, he walks over to the edge of the tarp and in his own words, " . . . with one quick motion, [I] whip it into the air like a magician uncovering his rabbit-bearing hat, and fall back in awe as I see . . . a boat-tailed Duesenberg, a brace of 1939 Pierce-Arrows, a 1904 Royce, a dozen Chrysler Dream Cars, two dozen Ferraris, an Italian Mustang, three Hudson Italias, a fiberglass Cadillac. . . ." The story ended with, "For every historic automobile found, two more seem to vanish, and by the time they're found, the one that was found when they were lost has been lost again. It's a vicious circle, a losing battle for the collector and a winning battle for time." The images of Pashdag's dream produced in this author's mind were captivating. The cars of which he wrote are not only mechanical devices, but works of art.

When I asked my dad about his photos and he explained what these cars were and how they were later destroyed, I was both fascinated and appalled. "How could they create these amazing cars and then just scrap them?" I thought to myself. For many years most enthusiasts, as well as GM officials, assumed that most of these cars were destroyed. Fortunately, the last paragraph quoted from John Pashdag's article is now known to be no longer altogether true, and the dream of which that author wrote three decades ago foreshadowed the future. Many of the cars somehow escaped the destruct order, though some did not. Several have been fully restored or are under restoration at the time of this writing, others are confirmed to have been scrapped, and a few more are rumored to be hidden away.

These Dream Cars are not fascinating only for their peculiar history; they are also compelling because of their styling. Futuristic styling moved people, possibly because the cars seemed to embody freedom itself, and provided a sense of a bright future ahead. Probably the best definition of a Dream Car was provided by Charles Barnette, a Cadillac-LaSalle Club member and contributor to their publication, *The Self-Starter*, when he wrote that "[It] is the pure realization of human imagination and enthusiasm expressed in its most free form."

Another reason for this book is that what little is written about the Motorama show cars tends to give the impression to the reader that they were nothing more than wildly designed shells built to wow the crowds who saw them. These cars were much more substantive than that. In some way each was a "laboratory on wheels," even though many of them did not actually run. Furthermore, over the years, erroneous information has been perpetuated about these show cars. I am aware of having done so myself. My three-part series for the September, October, and November 2003 issues of *Car Collector*, titled "Fate Unknown," has a few errors picked up from various sources. This book corrects those mistakes. Much original source literature such as official press releases and brochures from GM, contemporary articles in magazines like *Motor Trend*, *Cadillac Craftsman*, *Automobile Topics*, etc. were used to research this book. People who were involved in the Motorama in some way were interviewed, too. Unfortunately, there are few participants remaining.

Hopefully, this book will be as much an adventure to you as discovering my father's photographs of the '53 GM Motorama cars and reading the article in *Motor Trend* was to me so many years ago. Maybe someone who reads this book will even find a missing piece of the puzzle regarding the lost Motorama Dream Cars; there are still a few of these special cars with an unknown fate. This book, therefore, cannot represent the total history of these amazing cars, as their stories continue to unfold. Unfortunately, the passage of time has erased some information, but there are undoubtedly more stories to be discovered and told. Fortunately, a few mysteries regarding the four 1953 Cadillac Le Mans were solved while researching this project thanks to the help of members of the Cadillac-LaSalle Club.

A book such as this does not get written without the cooperation of many people, a great deal of research, and even a significant amount of serendipity. The author acknowledges the valuable assistance of Buddy Abell (Capitol Cadillac, retired), author and historian Dennis Adler (editor of this book), Mark Auran, Charles D. Barnette (Cadillac-LaSalle Club), Don Baron, Dick Baruk, Bruce Berghoff (H. B. Stubbs, Company, retired), Susan Black (Longview Public Library), Joe Bortz (Bortz Auto Collection), Darlene Browers (adult services librarian, Ronald J. Norick Downtown Library, Oklahoma City, OK), Donna Christian (Toledo Library, Toledo, OH), Andrew Clark (Alfred P. Sloan Museum), Linda Cobon (manager, Records & Archives Exhibition Place, Toronto, Ontario), Cathy Conrad (legal assistant to Charles D. Barnette), Stuart Blond, John Crowell (Cadillac-LaSalle Club), Gil Cunningham, David E. Davis Jr., Bernie DeWinter, IV (Cadillac-LaSalle Club), Richard Earl (www.carofthecentury.com), Wayne Ellwood (former editor, *SHARK Quarterly*), Dave Fabian (H. B. Stubbs, Company), Don Far (GM Shows and Exhibits Group, retired), Tomajean Haugerud, Daniel Jobe (Capitol Cadillac, Cadillac-LaSalle Club), Fred Joliet (GM, Cadillac Division, retired), Chuck Jordan (GM vice president of design, retired), Jim Jordan (Cadillac-LaSalle Club), Dan and Fred Kanter, Lon Keathley (Director, GM Shows and Exhibits Group, ret.), Donald Keefe, Scot M. Keller (GM, staff director, Corporate Brand Communications), Homer LaGassey (stylist, ex-GM Design), Matt and Michaline Larson (Cadillac-LaSalle Club, Classic Car Club of America, GM Heritage Center), Todd Lemmons (technical advisor for www.Buicks.net), Kevin Lowery (www.ridedrive.com), Mary Lusk (adult reference librarian, Pleasanton Library, Pleasanton, CA), Charles Marshall, Keven McConnell, Fred Miller, Kim Miller (AACA Library and Research Center, Hershey, PA), Doug Mitchell, Larry Muckey (former member of Eldorado Brougham Owners Association), Danny Page (Tex-Ark Antique Auto Club), Tim Pawl (Cadillac-LaSalle Club), Prof. James Perkins, John Perkins (GM, Oldsmobile Division, retired), Edward Poole (Cadillac-LaSalle Club), Bill Pozzi, Yann Saunders, Donald Schwarz (GM Design, Industrial Design, retired), Richard Sisson (Cadillac-LaSalle Club), Vince Taliano (Cadillac-LaSalle Club, newsletter editor for Potomac Region), Barbara Thompson (National Automotive History Collection, Detroit Public Library), Rusty Thompson, Wayne Turner (Cadillac-LaSalle Club), Carla Tynes (legal assistant to Charles D. Barnette), Kirk Vangundy, Peggy Vezina (GM Media Archive), Ken Wallace (RM Auctions), Harry Warholak Jr. (Warhoops Used Auto & Truck Parts, Sterling Heights, MI), Bill Warner (Chairman, Amelia Island Concours d'Elegance), Joe Whitaker (editor, *Classic Chevy World*), Heather Wilson (research specialist, Toronto Public Library), Steve Wolken (GM Tech Center), and Richard A. Wright. To all of you, I extend my sincere appreciation.

—David W. Temple, March 24, 2006

Introduction

Capturing the Hearts and Minds of Impressionable Male Adolescents

The General Motors Motorama shows ran from 1950 to 1961, starting at New York's Waldorf-Astoria and spreading to cities such as Los Angeles, Miami, San Francisco, etc. They became cornier, more grandiose, and more expensive with each passing year. It was as though the lobby of the General Motors building had been keelhauled through Disney's Magic Kingdom. The dreadful all-singing, all-dancing road shows that were fixtures in the domestic industry's dealer conventions, new product reveals, and metropolitan auto shows, which occurred up through the 1970s, were also part of every Motorama. It is worth noting that by the time the plug was pulled on Motorama, GM sales had fallen precipitously, and one might ask, "What was the point?" But Motorama did accomplish the goal that GM styling chief Harley Earl probably most wanted to achieve—it captured the hearts and minds of impressionable male adolescents around the country, and those adolescents, a few decades older, still talk about it.

Bill Warner is a collector who conceals his serious intent beneath an eternally cheerful "What, me worry?" demeanor, and is the force behind the Amelia Island Concours d'Elegance every March. His take on Motorama: "In my desire to own a Motorama car, I've spent a good portion of my adult life chasing rumors and dead ends, hoping to find one of GM's holy grails at a price I could afford. In the absence of finding one, I've bought and restored a 1954 Corvette, a 1955 Corvette, a 1953 Oldsmobile Fiesta, a 1958 Cadillac Eldorado Brougham, and a 1957 Cadillac Eldorado Biarritz (with parade boot). When you are bitten early in life, it can cost you dearly. Some years ago, my search for Harley Earl's Oldsmobile F-88 III ended when an acquaintance in GM's design department confirmed that Irv Rybicki, former VP of design had had the car scrapped. Scrapped! Was he crazy? The car had a neat stainless roof that disappeared under the rear deck like a Mercedes SLK, and an aluminum Olds V-8 with four side draft carburetors, and exhaust tips that exited in front of the front wheels. It had a low, Ferrari-like grille and a wraparound windshield. I had seen Harley Earl in it at the Daytona Speedway sometime in '59 or '60.

"In truth, it wasn't a Motorama car, but a one-off special, given to him upon his retirement. After his death, it was in storage somewhere on the Speedway grounds, where a rodent ate up the interior. Returned to GM, no funds would be allocated for its restoration and it was scrapped. Many Motorama cars met similar fates: the Waldorf Nomad, the Corvette Corvair fastback, and the Cadillac La Espada and El Camino (Yes folks, the name El Camino first appeared on a Cadillac). Most of the 1956 cars were scrapped at War Hoops, a scrap yard near the GM Tech Center. But as the late Bill Mitchell once told me, some of the GM employees couldn't bear scrapping the cars and they sort of disappeared out of the back gate."

Author collection

Author collection

Harley Earl and Big Bill Knudsen (William S. Knudsen, Henry Ford's production wizard, later president of General Motors, and later still war production czar for the government during World War II) used to attend the Paris Automobile Show together. On several occasions they were accompanied by Knudsen's young son, Bunkie (Semon C. Knudsen, who had a brilliant career of his own at GM before jumping ship to become president of Ford, only to be undermined and destroyed by Lee Iacocca's Machiavellian paranoia). Harley and Big Bill and Bunkie would roam through the Paris Show arguing about styling concepts and mechanical innovations. Bunkie Knudsen recalled, before his death in 1998, that they'd return to their hotel after dinner and at about two in the morning the telephone would ring. It was invariably Harley Earl, ready to fire some new ammunition in the resumption of that day's automotive quarrels. It would be nice to know that today's American automotive leaders cared as passionately.

It is pure speculation, but one does get the feeling that Motorama and its smaller-scale predecessors sprang from Harley Earl's wish to have his own Paris Automobile Show: something elegant, something special, something open to the public but exclusive in its way, an event where Harley could get up close and personal with the public as they sampled his wares.

Bill Davis, a serious collector, past president of the Classic Car Club of America, a trustee of the CCCA Museum in Kalamazoo, Michigan, and a past president of the Rolls-Royce Owners Club, gave us his views. "I was sixteen years old and car crazy, going to high school in New Jersey. I was amazed that just one company was doing this, as opposed to some sort of joint effort by the whole industry. I could just get on the train and go up to the Waldorf, and it just blew my mind!

"I remember the first hardtop sedan—the 1953 Cadillac Orleans. I also remember a 1954 Buick Roadmaster, which was done as a landau car with a leather-strapped trunk on the back. Later, I saw that car on the street in front of Bergdorf-Goodman. I remember an Olds Super Eighty-Eight convertible, red, and I remember thinking how super it really was. The whole ambiance of the show was just amazing. There were all sorts of dancers and actors, but more than anything it enabled GM to test the waters for these cars."

To the vast horde of insiders and contract workers who performed the actual labor of creating the show at each venue around the country, then knocking it down again,

Motorama Program

PLACE
Dinner Key Exposition Hall, S. Bayshore dr., at Coconut Grove.

TIMES
Wednesday, 4 to 7 p.m. Special invitational preview for civic, business and social leaders of South Florida.
Wednesday, 8 to 11 p.m. Open to the public.
Thursday through Tuesday. Open to the public daily from 10 a.m. to 11 p.m., except Sunday, when the hours are from 12 noon to 11 p.m., and Tuesday, when the doors will open at 10 a.m. and close at 10 p.m.

ENTERTAINMENT
GM's "Motorythms," which includes a ballet, choral group, orchestra and other acts, and "Fashion Firsts," a style show of new automobiles and women's gown fashions, will be presented on the exposition hall stage daily at 2:10, 3:20, 4:30, 7:30, 8:50 and 10 p.m.

Motorama was a giant boondoggle. There are still houses in the suburbs of Detroit with carpet and drapes straight off the trucks that brought Motorama exhibits back to Detroit. One didn't have to be a GM vice president to enjoy these benefits. Carpenters and electricians had equal opportunity to share the spoils. If your next-door neighbor worked on the show, a discreet word might furnish your basement recreation room. If you spoke to the right guy, and you were the right size, you could show up at the office wearing the very same electric blue gabardine suit that the actor who played the sales-manager wore in the showroom skit. Large crews of middle-level executives and support people a long way from home with liberal expense allowances had all kinds of adventures that somehow never surfaced in the accounting process.

Most of the cars in any given Motorama were extravagant Harley Earl and Bill Mitchell comic-book fantasies, except 1955, which featured a "Powerama" that was the showcase for all of GM's off-road industrial/commercial/agricultural vehicles, and 1961, which was devoted entirely to production cars. Five new models were introduced at that final Motorama, but production cars were never what the show was about. Someone must have expressed a concern that an entire show based on production vehicles would lack pizzazz, because the Batmobile-like Firebird III was resurrected from the 1959 show and parked rather self-consciously among all the bread-and-butter coupes and sedans.

It all came to an end in 1961. The executives who'd started it all in the 1950s had either moved on or become bored with Motorama, and a new generation of bean counters was expressing concern about these large

Author collection

"show business" expenditures in a period of GM car sales decline. Also, by 1961, Detroit's executives were beginning to think about the 1964–1965 New York World's Fair. Ford and Chrysler had made big commitments, along with a number of imported carmakers, and General Motors had to be there. Obviously, Motorama and some very similar extravaganza across the bridge at the World's Fair would be wasteful and redundant.

Like Bill Davis, quoted above, my memory is selective. I only attended one or two early Motoramas, and like most of America's growing minority of imported car enthusiasts, I only paid close attention to those show cars that appeared to lean toward the imports—the Corvette, the Corvair, the Buick Wildcats, the Olds Starfire, and the Pontiac Bonneville Special. I hated all the stuff that borrowed from the Lockheed P-38 and various military jets. The psychological implications of all those chrome breasts and enameled phalluses gave me the creeps. There was something else. Harley Earl's celebrated 1938 Buick "Y-Job," the father and mother of all American show cars, was still the most beautiful concept car ever to emerge from a Detroit design shop. Nothing in any of the Motoramas was ever able to eclipse the Y-Job, the cherry on top of the whipped cream on top of Harley Earl's illustrious career.

Obviously, a large slice of the American car-buying public was bowled over by Motorama. Say the word *Motorama* in any group of retirement-age Americans this weekend, and they'll bend your ear for an hour about the great cars that were introduced there. I find that memory plays us false in these discussions, however. Motorama is often credited with the introductions of cars and features that never saw the inside of the Waldorf-Astoria's ballroom, or that came along long after Motorama had become a historical oddity.

Some of us cannot understand why so little attention was paid to the imported car revolution that was taking place in the streets right outside the doors of Motorama. The people who designed the Motorama displays, the people who designed the cars themselves, were driving to work in MGs and Jaguars and Porsches and Austin-Healeys. There were even Ferraris in the styling department garages. Why didn't Motorama address this growing threat to Detroit's traditional supremacy? Only 10 years after that final 1961 Motorama, Volkswagen had established a solid beachhead with the Beetle, and Toyota and Datsun were coming ashore to start mopping up.

—David E. Davis Jr.

Author collection

PART I

The Beginning

Earl (seated at right) had great influence at GM in the early postwar era. His control over styling at GM was unprecedented; his protégé and ultimate successor, William Mitchell, standing to Earl's right, continued that tradition from 1958 to 1977. *Dennis Adler collection*

Chapter One

Birth of the Experimental Car and the GM Motorama

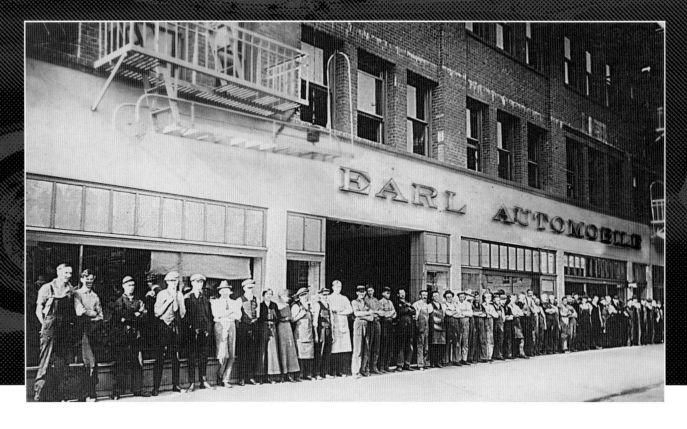

The General Motors Motorama was created to showcase the products of the corporation, which included not only automobiles from Cadillac, Buick, Oldsmobile, Pontiac, Chevrolet, and GMC, but also its auto parts and nonautomotive divisions. More notably, it featured experimental, or "Dream Cars," created to test public reaction to new ideas. These cars also exposed the public to advanced concepts, a simple but effective way to introduce features that would be found on automobiles in the near and distant future.

GM styling engineer Harley Earl knew the public did not respond well to too much change too soon, but he knew people could, and would, regard many changes as desirable by the time they went from Dream Cars to production cars. GM's traveling extravaganza spotlighted the company's many products through interactive exhibits, orchestras, and troupes of dancers who performed at half-hour intervals, amid lavish décor. It was a spectacle unlike any in the history of the automobile.

The Earl Automobile Works emerged from The Earl Carriage Works after the founder's son, Harley Earl, took over the business. Earl's shop turned out as many as 300 custom bodies a year. *Earl Family collection*

The Y-Job, seen here in a rare photo with the top raised, became the styling model for a number of later GM designs, both before and after World War II. *GM Media Archive*

Some regard the Cadillac V-16 Aero Dynamic Coupe, first seen at the 1933 Century of Progress World's Fair Exposition, as the earliest GM concept car. It was later put into limited production. *Dennis Adler*

The roots of the Motorama can be found as early as 1928, the year GM hosted an all-GM auto show in the Astor Hotel in New York City. This was repeated in 1929 and the following year GM began hosting what were known as Industrialist Luncheons at the new Waldorf-Astoria on Park Avenue. This invitation-only event showcased the products of the company against a backdrop of Persian rugs and landscape paintings. These shows continued until World War II interrupted automobile production. During the 1939–1940 New York World's Fair, General Motors set up sophisticated displays under the banner of "Futurama." These shows and others gave GM experience in producing attractive and entertaining displays to draw interest in its products.

Prior to these early events, GM hired a styling engineer who would become legendary in the automotive world. His name was Harley Jefferson Earl. General Motors' rise to leadership in the area of styling throughout the 1930s, 1940s, and 1950s can be largely credited to Earl, who spent his early years in the Hollywood, California, area. His father, Jacob W. Earl, owned a carriage works business in which Harley became heavily involved after recovering from an illness that had interrupted his studies at Stanford University. Jacob gradually placed his shop under Harley's leadership and the firm later evolved into the custom car business.

The Earl Carriage Works transformed into the Earl Automobile Works and its clientele consisted of the rich and famous—from wealthy businessmen to the stars of the new movie industry in Hollywood. Earl's shop produced about 300 custom bodies a year. Some of Earl's creations were shown at the Los Angeles Auto Show.

The *Los Angeles Times* found those at the January 1919 event to be newsworthy and reported that "the most startling local models at the show are those built by the Earl Auto Works, whose sensational Chandler and Marmon are attracting huge crowds. These cars are designed by Harley J. Earl, a local man . . . who has sprung into prominence as a maker of motor fashions almost overnight."

Earl sold his company to Cadillac distributor and custom car builder, Don Lee, in July of that year. It was a convenient arrangement; Don Lee's Los Angeles Cadillac agency and Harley Earl's shop, which had done bodywork and customizing for Lee, were less than a block apart. Harley became chief designer and director of the custom department of what was renamed The Don Lee Coach and Body Works.

The new company became newsworthy, as well. The *San Francisco Chronicle* reported the change: " . . . this is the largest plant of its kind west of Chicago, and for several years Earl's has been one of the six largest builders of custom bodies in the United States. . . . It is Don Lee's intention to turn out in this plant the very best coach work obtainable anywhere. With this idea in view, he will send one of his designers to New York twice a year, and as soon as European manufacturers are once more in production, [after recovering from World War I] a Don Lee designer will make a yearly trip abroad . . . "The designer sent to study styling trends in New York and abroad was Harley Earl.

Between 1919 and 1920, Don Lee Coach and Body Works produced hundreds of custom cars. This success was due in part to Earl's approach to customers—he

not only showed them drawings of his proposals, but also full-scale clay models. Clay models and trips to Europe would be valuable tools to Harley Earl. Modeling concepts in clay was something as revolutionary as the moving assembly line for automobile production and like the moving assembly line, spread to automakers everywhere. Earl reportedly said, "A picture is worth a thousand words, but a model is worth a thousand pictures."

Earl's work at Don Lee's shop gave him access to the upper-level managers of Cadillac. In 1921, Cadillac president R. A. Collins asked Harley Earl to create some clay concepts for Cadillac sport sedans; these concepts were completed within a couple of months, but by then Collins had moved on to Peerless. However, Alfred P. Sloan Jr., president of GM, learned of Earl's work as did the Fisher brothers of Fisher Body. Sloan and Lawrence Fisher would both remember the name Harley Earl.

By 1925, Lawrence Fisher was the president of Cadillac and during the latter part of the year he visited Don Lee's shop and met Harley Earl; the two became good friends and played golf together. They also discussed the subject of styling automobiles—something Fisher and Sloan had discussed in the past. They recognized that styling could be a great sales tool and Harley Earl clearly knew how to style cars.

Late in 1925, Fisher, who wanted Earl to do some design work for a new model called LaSalle, summoned him to Detroit. On January 6, 1926, Earl boarded a train to Detroit, a trip that ultimately resulted in a remarkable career that lasted over three decades and changed the way automobiles were made. In short, Harley Earl developed the concept of automotive design through his skill and his philosophy

GM's 1949 show dubbed "Transportation Unlimited" toured two cities, New York and Detroit. Shown here is a scene at the Waldorf-Astoria where an array of GM's cars, including the prototype Chevrolet Bel Air, was displayed. The Bel Air was Chevrolet's first hardtop model, which became available the following year. GM Media Archive

Pontiac's prototype Catalina two-door hardtop was shown at "Transportation Unlimited." *GM Media Archive*

A modified Series 62 convertible named El Rancho featured a western-themed interior. *GM Media Archive*

that art had a place in the products of industry. Furthermore, he came to the attention of Sloan as well as Fisher at a time when the latter two had recognized the need to consider the value of styling as a tool to sell cars.

During an early 1954 interview, Harley Earl noted how cars were designed in the days prior to the "Art and Colour Section." He said, "Fisher Body would draw up the body and the hood, and then they would model the body, and it would end up on sawhorses, maybe two or three feet high—no wheels or anything. And then the divisions would take that drawing and they would put on their front end and their fenders and wheels, and they . . . would put them together. Well, when I worked on the LaSalle, we didn't do it that way. We made it all one—built it right together as one unit rather than separate it."

Harley Earl created and became head of the "Art and Colour Section" of General Motors soon after being hired by Alfred Sloan Jr. The GM styling department began with about 50 people, but grew to about 1,100 by 1957. (Some of those included for a time, Gordon Buehrig, Franklin Q. Hershey, and Virgil Exner, who went on to leave their own mark upon automotive history.) Earl's Art and Colour Section blended well with Sloan's philosophy of planned obsolescence. Model year changes were meant to entice the public to buy new cars through just enough changes to make the next new model seem better. Another aspect of that philosophy was to not make too radical a change too soon.

In his book, *My Years With General Motors*, published in 1965, Alfred Sloan Jr., explained, "The prominence of styling in the automobile market in recent years is the outcome of the

Many special Cadillacs were exhibited throughout the Motorama years. This one, the 1950 Debutante, is shown receiving some attention from the GM staff. The unusual car featured gold-plated interior components and leopard skin upholstery. *GM Media Archive*

GM specifically built five show cars for its display at the 1950 Canadian National Exhibition in Toronto. The Chevrolet Royal Canadian, in the center of the brochure, featured gold-plated exterior hardware and a plaid interior. *Author collection*

evolution of the annual model and the high state of the art of automotive engineering. Styling, as an organized staff activity, was first undertaken in the automobile industry by General Motors in the late 1920s. Since 1928, styling and engineering in the corporation have evolved together in a continuous interaction that brought about the modern General Motors style. Throughout the first three decades of the industry, until the late Twenties, the engineer dominated the whole design. . . . At the close of World War II, we made the projection that for an indefinite period the principle attractions of the product would be appearance, automatic transmissions, and high-compression engines, in that order, and that has been the case."

Sloan also wrote of Harley Earl's approach: "Harley Earl had no doubts as to what the main line of development in car styling should be." He said in 1954: "My primary purpose for twenty-eight years has been to lengthen and lower the American automobile, at times in reality and always at least in appearance. Why? Because my sense of proportion tells me that oblongs are more attractive than squares."

In 1937, the Art and Colour Section became GM Styling and as such, its initial assignment was a first in the automobile industry. Harley Earl was responsible for creating the experimental car at GM. (For the 1933 World's Fair, a Cadillac V-16 show car built by Fleetwood and named the Aero Dynamic Coupe was exhibited. The body style, which later went into very limited production, was unique in its fastback styling, and some experts reasonably argue it was the first concept car.)

The first acknowledged concept car, the 1938 Buick Y-Job, served as Earl's "laboratory on wheels." The Y-Job had many advanced features—both in terms of styling and its mechanical systems, which included hidden headlights, horizontal grille, wraparound bumpers, prototype "Dynaflow" torque-converter transmission, electric power windows and top, power steering, 13-inch wheels, and no running boards. It was very low for the time. From the ground to its peak, the Y-Job measured only 58 inches. The length stretched 208 inches and the width reached 74 inches. Lower, longer, wider, in the Earl idiom. The car was radically different for the day and predicted many styling cues that would later be adopted by GM.

With the backing of company president Alfred P. Sloan Jr., and Buick Division head Harlow H. Curtice, Earl was able to get his Y-Job, or "semi-sports car" as he called it, built to his specifications. Earl drove it as his personal transportation for years, and the car served as the basis for styling the 1942 Buick as well as early postwar models.

In 1940, Earl was appointed to vice president; no automaker to that point had elevated styling to such a high management level, and Earl made the most of it.

By 1946, the Y-Job was beginning to age, but it had been the basis for so many designs that the car had earned its place in history. Buick's chief engineer since 1936, Charles Chayne (pronounced "chain") and Harley Earl got together to discuss what they had accomplished with the Y-Job. As Chayne reported in an article about the XP-300 he wrote for the February 1952 issue of *Motor Trend*, "We decided that it was time to build a successor to the Y-Job to see if we could better our mark of 'good after ten years' by doing one that would be still fresh and new after fifteen years. We weren't very far before it was clear to us that one car could not possibly contain the things we wanted to try, so we worked out a program for two cars."

Thus, during the last part of 1946, Earl and GM executive vice president and general manager of Buick, Harlow Curtice, began discussing successors to the Y-Job. Several months later, two cars were agreed upon with the internal designations XP-8 and XP-9. Ultimately, the XP-8 became the LeSabre and the XP-9 became the Buick XP-300. Though Buick would later use the moniker, LeSabre, the XP-8 did not officially have a specific association with any GM division; it was simply the General Motors LeSabre. The formal approval of the LeSabre

Above
Dated August 1, 1949, this photo shows the clay mockup of the XP-8 wearing a plate with "Chevrolet" identification. *Steve Wolken collection*

Below
This photo, dated November 29, 1949, associates the XP-8 LeSabre with Buick as indicated by the identification on the grille. Ultimately, the car was the General Motors LeSabre. *Steve Wolken collection*

21

Here is the LeSabre's supercharged, aluminum 215-ci V-8 as it appeared in May 1954. *Steve Wolken collection*

This photo dated January 14, 1952, shows the fuel cell in the right side quarter panel. This tank held the methanol that fed one of the two carburetors. Note the tank says, "Buick Motor Company" and the date of manufacture is given as November 1950. *Steve Wolken collection*

and XP-300 projects happened in May 1951. A newly created studio dubbed Special Automobile Design and headed by Ed Glowacke (from the Chevrolet Division) immediately began the styling of the LeSabre. Interestingly, photos taken on August 1, 1949, reveal that "Chevrolet" appeared on a mock license plate attached to the rear of the plaster model. As the design progressed, the Chevrolet reference was removed and Buick lettering appeared (late 1949) on the front of the car, but that is as close as the LeSabre got to being division specific. Chayne was given the responsibility for the XP-300 project. The designers of this car and the LeSabre were instructed to create both a styling and engineering masterpiece.

Harley Earl had discovered a fresh source for inspiration by the time these two projects were initiated—aircraft like the P-38 Lightning (which served as the basis for the tail-fin age that began with the 1948 Cadillac) and the new marvel of aviation known as the jet plane. (With GM's Allison division building the engines for the P-38 and other World War II–era aircraft, as well as building other engines, Earl had the opportunity to stay up-to-date on the newest trends in aviation.) Even boats provided influence in the design of the cars.

Enter Ed Glowacke—one of GM's most talented designers. Glowacke raced cars and boats and also piloted his own private airplane and gliders. He contributed much to the aviation-themed look of the LeSabre— the distinctive oval grille (that actually is not a true grille—more on that in a moment), the so-called "Dagmar" bumper bullets (named for a shapely actress of the era), gull-wing bumpers, and the interior or cockpit filled with aircraft-style gauges.

The styling of both cars as explained in Chayne's article for *Motor Trend* was dictated primarily by the "decision to build them just as low as possible. Doing this, pretty well forced the cars into being two-passenger convertibles, since with the necessary mechanical parts ahead of and behind the passenger space we would have been forced into an excessively long wheelbase had we attempted to use a second seat." Another key aspect of the two cars' designs was that they must be "complete in every sense of the word and still be capable of really terrific performance."

The structural aspects of the LeSabre were as radically different as the styling. Most of the body panels were of lightweight cast magnesium. Magnesium was being used in aviation applications like the first intercontinental range bomber, the massive Convair B-36; its use in an automotive application certainly added a flavor of the exotic to what was an astonishing car for the time. The front fender valance, cowl, door lock pillars, and deck lid were single large castings of magnesium. The remaining panels were of sheet aluminum. Ribs were cast into the deck lid to add strength to this large piece. Casting these members in magnesium was a difficult achievement; multiple attempts were required to get the correct shape for adjoining panels to align perfectly. The floors were aluminum honeycomb sandwiched between aluminum sheets. Magnesium and extensive labor were partly responsible for the staggering price tag for this one-of-a-kind car, which sources state as being approximately $500,000 to as much as $1 million (which is today roughly the equivalent of $5 million and $10 million).

Perhaps the car's most unusual visual feature was its wraparound windshield. The LeSabre and the XP-300 were the first cars to have a wraparound or as GM called it "Panoramic" windshield. (These, by the way, were *tinted* windshields—another Harley Earl innovation.) Earl had first tried to have wraparound glass created in 1918, but the glass maker simply could not find a way to bend a large pane of glass without breaking it. Many years later, GM's glass supplier, Libby-Owens-Ford, was finally able to give Earl what he wanted after extensive development between 1946 and 1950, and the wraparound windshield, like tailfins, got widespread use throughout the 1950s and into the early 1960s.

The complex body with stiff sills and driveshaft tunnel was set upon a ladder-type frame made of chrome-moly steel; wheelbase measured 115 inches. The parallel wishbone front suspension was atypical, too. The A-arms were cast alloy with the upper A-arm pivot rod being imbedded in a solid piece of cylindrically shaped rubber which itself was encased in a steel casting. Hydraulic tubular shock absorbers were attached to the steel casings and the lower A-arms. With the rubber in torsion, it acted as an effective springing medium—at least for a while. Eventually, the rubber began to lose its elasticity. When that became a problem, Chayne replaced the setup with torsion bars. The rear of the chassis received a transaxle comprised of a modified Buick Dynaflow with a de Dion differential attached to it. (However, at some point a four-speed Hydra-matic replaced the Dynaflow.) The de Dion setup is a

Harley Earl is shown examining the full-size clay model of the LeSabre. Earl pioneered the concept of modeling automobiles in clay. *Steve Wolken collection*

type of semi-independent suspension with a drop-center beam axle connecting the two driving wheels aft of the open, double-jointed driveshafts; it is separate from the final drive unit, which attached to the frame. A transaxle combines the final drive unit with the transmission, which is located between the driving wheels; it separates the transmission from the engine, thus moving a significant portion of the weight toward the rear to provide improved weight distribution in rear-wheel-drive cars. The rear-mounted torque converter was driven at engine speed, which made possible the installation of a generator and hydraulic pump in the rear of the chassis. Each was driven by the input shaft of the transaxle. The hydraulic pump operated four built-in jacks (one at each corner) to raise the car when needed (i.e., changing a flat tire). The double-jointed axle shafts were made of magnesium and the rear suspension was a tapered single-leaf spring mounted transversely. Thirteen-inch wheels helped make the car low, but to get adequate braking, 3 ½-inch-wide, 9-inch-diameter finned brake drums with four brake shoes per drum were used. The overall height with the top up measured just 50 inches; the cowl height as measured from the ground peaked at a mere 36.25 inches.

The engine was yet another amazing piece of engineering for the day. It was an experimental V-8 with aluminum block and heads displacing 215 cubic inches—a volume obtained with a square bore and stroke (3.25x3.25 inches). The block extended below the crankshaft centerline; its main caps were cross-bolted. Wet cylinder

Above
The LeSabre was sent to the Paris Salon aboard the "DeGrasse" inside a special aluminum container built by Alcoa Aluminum. Later, General Dwight D. Eisenhower had the opportunity to take a ride in the experimental car that absolutely amazed many thousands of Europeans. When Ike became president of the United States, his inaugural parade car was a 1953 Cadillac Eldorado. *Earl Family collection*

Letters of praise regarding the LeSabre poured into General Motors. *Steve Wolken collection*

liners were centrifugally cast of Ni-Resist iron. Problematic at first was the intake manifold design. Before the actual engine was constructed, a mockup was made and sent to GM Styling.

Joseph Turlay, who was in charge of engineering the special V-8, was told by Harley Earl to make the engine at least 6 inches lower. Turley's initial thought was that his boss's order was impossible to accomplish. However, with some ingenuity he did it. He reduced the height of the oil pan and added a windage tray to keep the crank throws from aerating the oil. The flywheel size was reduced without sacrificing the mass required by substituting bronze in place of iron. A Roots-type supercharger was neatly packaged just above the intake manifold, which doubled as the valley cover. The chain-driven camshaft was suspended from the bottom of the intake. Combustion chambers were hemispherical with the intake and sodium-filled exhaust valves mounted at a 90-degree angle to each other. The intake rocker arms were mounted transversely on the engine, while the exhaust rockers pointed fore and aft. This unusual arrangement allowed for a more compact engine to fit within the limited space of the engine compartments of the LeSabre and XP-300. Valve seats were stainless-steel inserts. The compression ratio of the engine's cylinders fitted with domed pistons was high for the day at 10.0:1. Both hydraulic and solid lifters were tried in the experimental V-8.

Two aircraft type Bendix-Eclipse two-barrel carburetors feed the fuel supply to the engine of the LeSabre and XP-300. On the LeSabre, one carburetor received premium gasoline from the left side aircraft-type fuel cell and the other got methanol from the right; the cells of 20-gallon capacity each were located in the quarter panels with their respective filler door located on the inboard side of the fins within the chrome molding. Each filler door was labeled with embossed letters (spelling out "GASOLINE" and "ALCOHOL") and each filler cap was made integral with the filler door. When the methanol fuel cell was filled, a special funnel with a petcock and overflow tube was used to keep the liquid from spilling onto the paint. The methanol-fed carburetor was engaged via progressive linkage and a valve in the methanol fuel line. Mashing the accelerator pedal opened up the flow of methanol to the rear carb and activated the blower. The LeSabre then roared with 335 horsepower or about 1.56 horsepower per cubic inch—an astonishing figure for the day.

There were more mechanical marvels to the LeSabre. The oval grille in front, as stated earlier, is not really a grille, but rather a door which hides and supports close-set headlights. When the headlight switch was set to "on" the door moved inward, rotated 180 degrees, and then moved outward with both headlights aglow. The instrument panel, as well as the rest of the interior, was clearly inspired by the aircraft of the day. Among the instruments present were an altimeter, compass, clock, ammeter, gauges for oil pressure and temperature, engine coolant temperature, and a digital speedometer. Between the black leather-covered bucket seats was a console housing a chronograph, radio controls, and a rain sensor to automatically raise the top in the event rain began to fall when the car was parked with the top retracted. Reportedly, Earl preferred to leave the LeSabre parked with the top down, especially if the strong possibility of rain was in the forecast. Crowds tended to gather around the car, so when the first drop of rain struck the moisture sensor the convertible top began to raise itself automatically, much to the surprise of the crowd. The convertible top retracted into

a well that was covered by a pivoting lid much like the Y-Job and the Corvette that followed. Its seats were electrically heated; the temperature could be controlled with a rheostat. All the gadgetry was powered by a 12-volt electrical system.

The XP-300 was similar mechanically to the LeSabre, but the former had torsion bars in front from the start, a different de Dion axle design, 1-inch-longer wheelbase, methanol and gasoline fuel tanks mounted behind the seat, a single fan in the engine compartment, coil springs all around, and other suspension and steering component differences. Its hydraulic system was more complex than that in the LeSabre; it operated the hood, windows, seats, locking devices for the doors, cowl vents, and jack system. The hood and fender tops were an integral unit that flipped forward for access to the engine compartment. Moreover, there were notable differences between the two cars' braking systems. The XP-300's body was of heat-treated aluminum panels painted Venus White. The styling of this car was somewhat similar to that of Earl's LeSabre, but the two were clearly distinguishable from each other. Both had the panoramic windshield, a simulated jet exhaust nozzle at the rear and, of course, both were low in height. Each also had bucket seats and a console. The similarities in appearance ended there, though. The XP-300 had chrome louvers extending down the side of its fenders (with the fender-mounted ones and forward one-third of those on the doors serving as engine compartment heat vents), an opening in the center of the massive bumper to allow air to reach the radiator, a sealed-beam, floodlight-type back-up lamp mounted in the simulated rear jet exhaust, a chrome fin down the rear deck center-line (which concealed the hinges for the

This photo of the XP-300 shows its construction well underway. *Alfred P. Sloan Museum*

GM's chief engineer, Charles Chayne, was in charge of the XP-300 project. Reportedly, Chayne once drove the experimental car at 140 miles per hour! *GM Media Archive*

General Motors displayed its production and experimental cars at the Canadian National Exhibition. The Buick XP-300 can be seen near the center of this photo from late August 1953. A Cadillac Le Mans is also visible in the background. *CNE Archives, Alexandra Studio Collection, Neg. 5888*

deck lids that could be opened from either side), and its interior was more spartan in appearance than that of the LeSabre—it was actually more like that of a sports car.

Though it had the appearance of a sports car, the XP-300 was certainly more comfortable. The finely pleated blue leather-covered seats had bladders that could be inflated with a squeeze-bulb to change their contour and could be adjusted in the fore/aft and up/down directions. Its steering column was telescopically adjustable as well. The console housed most of the gauges and controls, though the speedometer was combined with the tachometer and mounted on the dash directly ahead of the driver's position. A soft top could be installed; when not in use it was folded and stored in a compartment behind the front seat. The backlight (called a Riviera-type) was retractable and could be lowered even with the top in place. The cockpit could also be covered with a detachable hardtop (though it may never have been used; no photographs of it in place could be located by GM Media Archive).

The 1951 Buick XP-300 can be seen at the Alfred P. Sloan Museum in Flint, Michigan, when not being exhibited at a special event. Note the XP-300's exhausts, which exited through ports in the rear bumper; Cadillac would pick up this feature for the 1954 models. *Rusty Thompson*

The body and frame of the XP-300 were welded together into one solid unit. When the doors were closed, hydraulically operated steel bars slipped into place like the bolts of a vault door, thus making the doors a structural part of the body. The XP-300 weighed only 3,125 pounds. Its light weight and high horsepower engine translated into excellent performance. Reportedly, Charles Chayne once drove the XP-300 at 140 miles per hour!

LeSabre was the first of the two experimentals to be shown to the public. The December 1950 issue of *Life* magazine featured the car using photography of the mockup. In February, the XP-300 was shown at the Chicago Auto Show (though it was not quite finished). Both cars were then shown to members of the press at the GM Proving Grounds several months later. Earl also drove the experimental car in the 1951 Watkins Glen race-day parade. The race car drivers and a crowd of 100,000 fans were suitably impressed with the uniquely designed automobile. The LeSabre then went overseas for exhibit in Paris, where it drew large crowds. During its stay there, the chief mechanic for the LeSabre, Leonard McLay, took General Dwight Eisenhower for a ride in the experimental car. Eisenhower was impressed with the LeSabre and said so in a letter he wrote to Harley Earl.

Both cars were shown on the 1953 GM Motorama tour, though the LeSabre by then had been updated with new wheels, deleted fender skirts, and additional air intakes and outlets to improve engine compartment cooling.

Harley Earl drove the LeSabre frequently; for him it was Y-Job number two. He eventually put about 45,000 miles on the complex car. During that time, it was pictured on the cover of many automotive publications and, in that alone, the LeSabre probably more than paid for itself in terms of advertising for GM. The Buick XP-300 logged nearly 10,400 miles.

Both the LeSabre and XP-300 exist today and are displayed at various events from time to time. When the two cars are not on the show circuit, the LeSabre is kept at the GM Heritage Center, while the XP-300 can be viewed at the Alfred P. Sloan Museum in Flint, Michigan, where it has been since about 1966. Before sending it to the museum, GM Styling refurbished the car.

Though its interior had the look of a typical sports car, the XP-300 was certainly much more comfortable. Its finely pleated, blue, leather-covered seats were adjustable in four directions and had bladders that could be inflated with a squeeze-bulb to change their contour. The steering column was telescopically adjustable, as well. Console housed most of the gauges and controls. *Rusty Thompson*

Stage shows were used to introduce the cars at the GM Motorama; on stage is a 1953 Chevrolet sedan. *Bruce Berghoff collection*

In the near term, the frontal styling of the XP-300 predicted the look of the 1953–1954 Buick line and the LeSabre's fin shape can be seen in the 1953 and 1954 Pontiacs as well as the 1957 Cadillac. The gullwing bumper of the LeSabre showed up on other GM Dream Cars as well as production Cadillacs. The LeSabre's influence went beyond American automobiles; European designers were at least as awestruck by this car as their counterparts in the United States. The car even inspired a few semi-replicas during the 1950s.

Years after the LeSabre and XP-300 experimental cars were built, Buick and Oldsmobile offered aluminum engines, and bucket seats and consoles were in widespread use on cars like Buick's Wildcat of the 1960s, as well as competing makes. Pontiac made use of the transaxle in the early 1960s in its Tempest/LeMans series. Jordan tends to downplay the influence of the LeSabre on these cars, yet each new car that came along during this time was built upon a foundation of the cars that came before it. Both the successes and the failures offered insight into designing the next automobile. Harley Earl pushed his stylists "to go all out" and without him, the cars of the 1930s, 1940s, 1950s, and even the 1960s would all have been very different.

While the design work was being done on the LeSabre and XP-300, General Motors was starting what would soon become the extravagant auto show known as the GM Motorama. The term *Motorama* may or may not have its origins with General Motors. The term *ama* means spectacle and GM's first "ama" was the Futurama. From there, perhaps, the terms *Motorama* and *Autorama* came into being. The title Motorama had been in use for other auto shows involving customs and sports cars for some time

The XP-300's detachable hardtop still exists and is in storage at the museum.

The legacies of the two experimental cars differ. The LeSabre greatly influenced car design while the XP-300 had little influence.

Retired GM stylist and vice president Chuck Jordan explained the impact of the LeSabre. "The LeSabre had dramatic proportions and shape. The LeSabre really knocked us for a loop. It represented Harley Earl's design philosophy and it influenced all of us; it was a very exciting car. We knew we had to go all out."

Jordan had been with GM only a short time when he got his first look at the LeSabre. He started designing trucks, but was told if he ever wanted to get anywhere in the business, he needed to design cars. He was later in charge of two Motorama vehicles—the 1955 GMC L'Universelle and the 1956 Buick Centurion, and much later, the 1985 Buick Wildcat concept car. He retired from GM at the end of 1992. Under Earl, Jordan learned the value of having a place where a stylist "could design freely and take risks to develop new ideas."

Above
The first production Cadillac Eldorado in Artisan Ochre (left of center), the Oldsmobile Fiesta (lower right), the Pontiac Parisienne (upper left), and the 1951 Le Sabre (on stage) were just a few of the highlights of the 1953 GM Motorama. This view is inside the Waldorf-Astoria, where every Motorama made its debut. *GM Media Archive*

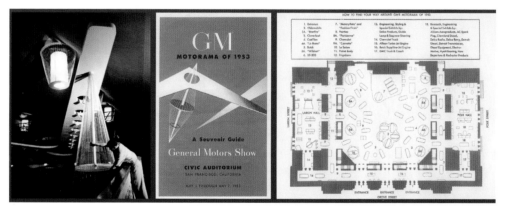

Left
One of the props used during the 1953 GM Motorama resembled an aircraft wing. A worker sets up the stage props inside the Shrine Convention Hall. The program guide, in this case for the show in San Francisco, reflects the design of the stage décor. Inside the handout, show attendees could see the floor plan, which helped attendees find the many exhibits of the Motorama. *Author collection*

when GM's version began. In fact, GM was a participant in the Los Angeles Motorama in 1952, when they displayed the XP-300 amid a wide variety of automobiles including vintage Duesenbergs, customs by George Barris, and foreign sports cars like Jaguar.

GM first used the name Motorama for the company's spacious exhibit at the Chicago Museum of Science and Industry in 1947. General Motors also staged other shows in the mid-1950s like the Wonderama in Dayton, Ohio, and one in Chicago called Powerama.

The first major postwar GM show named "Transportation Unlimited" occurred in New York City in January 1949, then again in Detroit in April. At the Waldorf, GM introduced its Buick Riviera two-door hardtop (which was ahead of its official release), prototype two-door hardtops—Chevrolet's Bel Air, Pontiac's Catalina, and Cadillac's Coupe de Ville—and three modified production Cadillacs. These modified Cadillacs were a Series 62 convertible named El Rancho and two altered Fleetwood Sixty Specials dubbed Caribbean and Embassy. As reported in the February 1949 issue of *General Motors World*, Cadillac described the four special Cadillac show cars as "sleek sybaritic specimens of automotive splendor."

The prototype two-tone Coupe de Ville differed from what actually went into production later. It was built on the Fleetwood's 133-inch wheelbase chassis and had hydraulically

Workers can be seen installing the facade in front of the Automobile Building at Fair Park in Dallas, Texas, in May 1953. *H. B. Stubbs Co.*

operated windows (including the vent windows), a simulated rear fender air scoop (as did the Embassy), a 1950-style Series 75 backlight, a one-piece curved windshield, short-wave telephone, and a pull-out desk. Upholstery for the seats and headliner for the Coupe de Ville was gunmetal leather.

A western-themed interior was the main attraction of the "Mexican Dawn" brown El Rancho convertible. Upholstery was of waxed saddle leather trimmed with dark suede kip's hide and saddle-stitched in white cord. Interior hardware consisted of antiqued and hand-engraved silver.

The black Embassy was fitted with a leather-covered roof and a toolkit of chrome-plated tools. Its luxurious interior had silver hardware, pearl-gray clipped sheepskin carpet, hydraulically operated divider between the front and rear compartments, tubular storage pocket for an umbrella, vanity case, and a shortwave telephone. The Caribbean Daybreak green Caribbean sedan was outfitted inside with kip's hide suede and antiqued silver hardware.

The next big event, General Motors' "Mid-Century Motorama," which occurred in New York City in 1950, featured specially trimmed cars in addition to the regular line of automobiles to impress the 320,000 visitors who came to the event between January 19 and 27. The one from Cadillac was named the Debutante; it had leopard skins covering the upper portion of the front and rear seat backs, the upper side panels, and the complete floor in the front and rear compartments. Its armrests were covered with iridescent gray leather and every unpainted metal surface within the interior was gold plated. The exterior was just as exotic. A special paint called Tawny Yellow Buff was said in a GM press release to "complement the

Rufous Buff color in the leopard skins." The pearl luster of the exterior was achieved by overlaying the base paint with a sprayed layer of miniature, moon-shaped fish scales obtained only through a special process that required dissolving the larger portion of a fish scale leaving only the tiny pearl essence. The car reportedly inspired the 1956 comedy, *The Solid Gold Cadillac*.

Five cars were built specifically for the Mid-Century Motorama at the Canadian National Exhibition (which incorporated multi-make autos) in Toronto—two Oldsmobiles dubbed Golden Jubilee and Westward-Ho, a pair from Pontiac named Magnificent and Fleur de Lis, plus the Chevrolet Royal Canadian.

For 1951 and 1952, GM did not sponsor similar shows, though they did have interesting cars to present to the public—the LeSabre and the XP-300 of course—plus prototypes, the 1952 Cadillac Eldorado and the 1952 Buick Skylark; and the 1952 Cadillac Townsman, which was a 50th Golden Anniversary model built using a Series 60 Special. These cars were shown at various events during the year.

By the time the 1953 model year arrived, sales of General Motors' automobiles were on a two-year decline, thus something was needed to boost sales. Showing GM's products in a dazzling, spectacular way in high-population centers was seen as a means to attain greater sales. With the experiences from past auto shows and Harley Earl's imagination and show-biz influence, GM was set to produce an auto show on a grand scale.

The first GM Motorama with Dream Cars was in 1953. The extravagant show began its national tour in January in the Waldorf-Astoria. The one-week shows went on to Miami (February), Los Angeles

(April), San Francisco (early-May), Dallas (mid-May), and Kansas City (June). Dallas and Kansas City were dropped from future tours after 1953. The display of new GM automobiles, mildly modified production vehicles, and Dream Cars, along with Broadway-style stage shows, brought 1.5 million visitors to the tour.

General Motors spared no expense in bringing its show to these cities; over $5 million was spent for the shows and exhibits in addition to the cost of the Dream Cars like the Wildcat and Le Mans, which could cost six figures to design and build. (The respective GM divisions were not responsible for the Dream Cars; the projects were assigned to the advanced studio sections from each division.)

No admission was charged, which would have helped cover or at least reduce the cost of moving the cars and equipment with hired carriers (consisting of roughly 125 trucks) from city to city, the cost of local advertising, the one-week rental of convention halls, stage shows, special décor, and maintenance of the show cars. Cutaway cars and engines added another $100,000 or so to the cost of the show, and then there was transportation and lodging for the crew, staff, and cast members, totaling about 1,000 people.

In Miami, the large Dinner Key Auditorium provided three times the space of the Waldorf. GM took advantage of this space by displaying many more cars and other exhibits. The larger show required 300 carpenters, 200 exhibit demonstrators, 100 ushers, 35 guards, and 30 members of GM's public relations department. Another 60 dancers, singers, musicians, and models were part of the cast of the stage show, "Motor-Rhythms and Fashion Firsts."

Of course, back then General Motors could afford such expenditures. By 1955, the company operated 119 plants in 65 communities in 19 states, six plants in Canada, and manufacturing facilities in 18 foreign countries. General Motors had clearly become a giant since it was organized in 1908. The company would become so successful—acquiring a 49.9 percent market share according to the November 1, 1954 issue of *Time* magazine—that some in the U.S. Congress were thinking GM should be broken up.

One way that GM actually did save on costs, or at least make the most of its concepts, was to show the Dream Cars at venues beyond the Motorama, such as the Chicago Auto Show and dealerships across the country. Some of the cars like the 1953

The regular line of cars displayed by GM at its Motorama had better fit and finish than those in dealers' showrooms. Here a 1953 Olds Ninety-Eight convertible is seen receiving attention from a worker prior to the GM Motorama in Dallas. Another worker stands on a ladder to make adjustments to the "cloverleaf" platform, which held a car from each GM automobile division. *H. B. Stubbs Co.*

This beautiful color ad for the 1954 GM Motorama at the Dinner Key appeared in the *Miami Daily News. Author collection*

One of the many advertisements for the 1955 GM Motorama was this eye-catching illustration published in the *Los Angeles Times. H. B. Stubbs Co.*

Le Mans were even used in parades in various parts of the country.

The GM Motorama was said to be "General Motors' top salesman, its best prognosticator and barometer of business." The unfortunate drawback was that it also told the competition what GM was thinking in terms of future styling. Still, the GM Motoramas were a great success in bringing attention to the company and sales soared for 1953 and continued to climb during most of the Motorama years.

During the 1953 show at the Waldorf, GM president Harlow Curtice told *The New York Times*, "Public response to the Motorama, as indicated by the crowds that are filling the exhibition, is extremely gratifying. I am sure from former experience with General Motors' shows, that this early public enthusiasm confirms our feeling that 1953 will be a very good year for our business."

Halfway through that inaugural Waldorf show, GM had taken approximately $600,000 in orders from show attendees. Harley Earl was quoted as saying the Motorama "was like picking up a lucky horseshoe. We didn't know how good it was until later."

Indeed, over 2.3 million people attended the 1956 GM Motorama in the five cities it visited, making it the most successful of all. As reported in the May 1956 issue of *Auto Age*, GM received $1.3 million in orders for its cars at the New York City showing alone. Despite this, the 1956 tour was the last of its kind, and the Firebird III would be the only Dream Car exhibited for the 1959 and 1961 shows.

Eventually, the increasingly high cost of the Motorama and the popularity of television helped put an end to the grand spectacle. Management found that, with more and more people owning a TV set, advertising through television was more cost effective. Additionally, GM's ideas were essentially being given away to its competitors for free. Anyone, including stylists from Ford Motor Company and Chrysler Corporation, could attend the Motorama.

In fact, in an interview conducted under the sponsorship of the Edsel B. Ford Design History Center in 1985, Bill Mitchell said, "We made about four specials—Olds, Buicks, Pontiacs—and we noticed, somebody did, that Ford engineers came in there after the show and were taking dimensions, which is all right, but, by God, out comes the Thunderbird." Mitchell was referring to the 1958 Thunderbird.

The success and spectacle of GM's Motorama did not go unnoticed by the people at FoMoCo. In 1956, one of Ford's designers suggested to George Walker, the vice president and general manager of Ford's Styling Center, that several show cars should be built to be shown at various points in the country and Canada. This show, to begin in 1957, would be called "Stylerama" and would represent Ford's version of GM's Motorama. Company boss Henry Ford II was very receptive to the idea. However, the Stylerama was canceled after many clay model designs were completed. The Edsel fiasco, which cost Ford Motor Company a few hundred million dollars, and the high cost of everything associated with staging the shows, proved to be the undoing of the project. Furthermore, some of the concepts coming from the design studio were judged as simply too futuristic to appeal to the public. (For example, the Nucleon proposed a nuclear-powered automobile!)

Incidentally, the Futurliner and Streamliner buses are often associated with the Motorama, but that was a separate program called the Parade of Progress, which occurred annually from 1936 to 1941, and then started up again for a time in 1953.

The Numbers

Throughout this book the reader will see each Motorama car's "EX", "XP," and/or "S.O." number. Former stylist Chuck Jordan believes the system was employed simply to help keep track of the costs associated with each prototype project; accountants for GM used such identifications when logging the expenses incurred. Why some numbers jump out of sequence is not evident. For instance, the 1956 Chevrolet Impala was assigned XP-101 and the 1956 Buick Centurion was XP-301, while the 1958 Firebird III was XP-73. Some XP cars did not get beyond the drawing board or clay stage such as the XP-30 design from 1954, which helps explain skips in the sequence.

The S.O. (Shop Order) numbers were also used for accounting purposes, according to retired Oldsmobile engineer John Perkins. These S.O. numbers were assigned to "bucks" or functional mockups such as experimental convertible tops, as well as experimental cars. Hence, while the 1954 Olds F-88s were all an XP-20, they each received their own shop order number. These numbers were sometimes used as a VIN—something that could be useful in authenticating a genuine experimental car.

Broadway singers Priscilla Gillette, David Atkinson, The Ashtons, The Cabots, and others performed on stage at the 1955 GM Motorama at the Waldorf-Astoria. This is a program guide for the event. *Author collection*

Crowds can be seen gathering around the stage at the Waldorf to see the spectacular 1956 Oldsmobile Golden Rocket, left, and the 1956 Pontiac Club de Mer, right. *GM Media Archive*

The Cadillac Eldorado Brougham, Pontiac Strato-Star, and the Oldsmobile 88 Delta are shown in this 1955 photo. At lower left is the Cadillac Celebrity. *H. B. Stubbs Co.*

PART II

The Motorama Cars—
Stars of the Show

Among the prototype Corvettes built, the 1954 hardtop model was the one that should have been put into production alongside the roadster. A closed coupe might have sold better after folks got a taste of the roadster's features, or lack thereof. *Dennis Adler archives*

Motorama Cars of Chevrolet

A fiberglass prototype Chevrolet named Corvette made its debut during the 1953 GM Motorama. The sporty roadster, EX-52, Shop Order 1737, created quite a stir at Motorama shows across the country. Allegedly, the crowd pleaser was secretly wired to record the comments of people, so Harley Earl and his team could hear honest reactions to the Corvette. Whether or not that was true, GM personnel were stationed around the Dream Cars to witness the public's reactions.

Responses to the Corvette were almost unanimously favorable. Many believe that this resulted in the decision to begin production of the car, but actually the decision had already been made prior to the public unveiling. The only major aspect that was undecided was whether to build the two-seater from fiberglass, like the prototype, or tool up to build the cars out of steel. When production was pushed ahead of the original schedule, due to the public's response to the prototype, the first Corvettes rolled off the Flint assembly line on June 30, 1953, with fiberglass bodies.

The Corvette legend began with the first show car prototype, which made its debut at the Waldorf-Astoria in New York City, the first stop of the 1953 GM Motorama. Pictured with the car are Ed Cole (then Chevrolet's chief engineer and later to become president of General Motors). Standing next to the car is Thomas Keating, Chevrolet's general manager. *Dennis Adler archives*

The Corvette was one of Harley Earl's ideas; he wanted GM to produce an American sports car to rival those being imported from Europe after World War II. Sports cars were becoming increasingly popular, and Earl recognized the need for America to enter the potentially lucrative market. However, he wasn't the first.

Nash began offering a Healey in 1951 with an aluminum body built in Italy by Pininfarina atop a chassis designed in England by Donald Healey, and powered by a Nash engine and driveline. American sportsman Briggs Swift Cunningham also built some two-seater sports cars starting in 1951; his C-4R finished fourth at Le Mans in 1952. Other sports car choices included the Kurtis and Crosley's little Hotshot. Even so, there were still few alternatives to rival the MG, Jaguar, and Alfa Romeo.

However, as popular as they were to American sports car enthusiasts, only little more than a quarter of one percent of new car registrations in this country were for sports cars in 1953. These cars had a number of undesirable characteristics to the majority of Americans. Zora Arkus-Duntov told a group at an SAE meeting in 1953 that statistics showed that the American public did not want a sports car, but went on to question if the statistics gave a true picture. He noted the market for such a car was an unknown quantity and that perhaps a sports car designed to American tastes and roads might have a significant following.

Chrysler Corporation and Ford Motor Company also investigated the sports car market. Dodge built a prototype called the Storm Z-250, but found the costs of production too high to make it marketable; the

same was true of Chrysler's 1955 Falcon. Even Ford chose to make its Corvette-fighting 1955 Thunderbird a sporty boulevard cruiser rather than a true sports car.

Harley Earl's interest in producing a sports car coincided with the refinement of a still relatively new material —glass-reinforced plastic or GRP—which would soon become very important to the Corvette project, as well as most of the Motorama Dream Cars.

The Corvette and Corvette-based show cars pose together in Miami during February 1954. The "hardtop" car joined the Motorama at this time. Note that the fastback Corvair is painted light green. A deep red Corvair was exhibited at the preceding Motorama in New York City. *Wayne Ellwood collection*

The Corvette fastback was another version of the car that might have had more initial success than the roadster. Another decade would pass before Chevrolet offered two versions of the Corvette. *Dennis Adler archives*

The brilliant red Corvette Corvair sits on its turntable at the Waldorf. *GM Media Archive*

One of the earliest uses for GRP was for aircraft radomes during World War II. After the war, aircraft were built with an increasingly greater number of fiberglass pieces. Civilian uses included storage tanks, pipes, laminates, sports gear, etc.

The Glasspar Corporation, which manufactured fiberglass boats, was experimenting with the material; it built a prototype fiberglass sports car body, which was evaluated by GM officials. Howard "Dutch" Darrin had been working with the material to build a sports car for Henry Kaiser. His Darrin was revealed to the public in 1952, which was about the time that work started on the Corvette project.

But even Dutch Darrin's car was not the first to be built of GRP. As early as 1944, Owens-Corning was working with Kaiser in developing GRP bodies for automobiles. With the Korean War underway and certain metals being rationed, automakers began investigating alternative materials. After an article arranged by U.S. Rubber about the new material appeared in a February issue of *Life* magazine, a Chevrolet production engineer called the company to learn more. Technicians from the Mishawaka, Indiana, plant went to Detroit to show how a mold could be made from a fender to make an identical part from fiberglass. GM Styling and Chevrolet Engineering immediately began experimenting with GRP.

In September 1951, Earl attended the sports car races at Watkins Glen and watched the MGs, Allards, Ferraris, and Cunninghams speed around the track. Briggs Cunningham is reported to have good-naturedly ridiculed Harley's LeSabre, which he drove to the event, by suggesting to Earl he should have brought a car he could race. This may have been the trigger that fired Earl's thoughts (or at least to take the idea more seriously) of building a sports car at GM, although seeing all those sports cars on the track certainly had much to do with Earl's vision of an American rival.

Earl once said the idea for the Corvette was born while driving the LeSabre as the pace car for this race. Regardless of the exact moment he started thinking of the Corvette, it was a turning point in automotive history. The project began under the designation of Opel Passenger Car Development Project. Opel, incidentally, was a name borrowed from GM's German division. (In 1968 Opel introduced a sports car called the GT, which looked like a smaller version of the Corvette. The Opel GT was produced through 1973.)

Amazingly, the time to bring the car from a paper proposal to the mockup stages, and then finally to a functional prototype, was accomplished in about eight months. One of the requirements for the proposed sports car was that it be economical to build so as to meet a selling price of around $1,850. A relatively low price would be one of the important factors that would make the car acceptable to the target market. This directive meant that as many already existing components as possible had to be incorporated into the design. One of those was the Chevrolet chassis. Other items already in use by Chevrolet were the straight six and "Powerglide" two-speed automatic transmission (two decisions that would cost Chevrolet dearly after the 1953 model year). A Chevy V-8 was two model years away, and a manual transmission befitting a sports car was further in the future than that, so the 'Vette would have to settle for a hopped-up "six banger" and an automatic transmission.

One of the people assigned to make the Corvette a reality was Robert McLean, who had both an engineering and industrial design degree from Cal Tech. His work helped to establish the basic dimensions and proportions of the car—a wheelbase of about 102 inches, low center of gravity, and a weight distribution of about 53/47 (front/rear). The stock Chevrolet chassis already in use would need to be modified, which added to the expense of production; Maurice Olley, director of Chevrolet Research and Development, was responsible for the chassis layout. Disappointingly, even with the use of off-the-shelf parts, the price for the production car would become nearly double that of the original goal.

Fiberglass construction was originally seen as a way to expedite the process of building the prototype. A steel production car was actually planned, using Kirksite tooling. Such tooling would allow about 10,000 bodies to be built in a year, which happened to be the

The Corvair's dash did not receive any obvious modifications, but the upholstery and door panels were different than those of a stock Corvette. *Detroit Public Library National Automotive History collection*

The prototype hardtop Corvette appeared at various shows, including the GM Wonderama in Dayton, Ohio. *H. B. Stubbs Co.*

Commemorative albums were made for GM president Harlow Curtice. This page shows the 1954 Corvair in artist renderings with upholstery and paint samples of the actual car. *Photo by Yann Saunders, courtesy Cadillac Design Studio*

anticipated demand for the car. As things progressed, the demand appeared to be so great that the decision was made to get the car into production as soon as possible by building 300 units in fiberglass. Chevrolet's experience with fiberglass soon revealed the tooling would be good for much longer than the Kirksite dies, and less costly, thus the decision was made to retain fiberglass construction for the Corvette.

The production version differed in numerous details from the prototype, though not much visually. Prototype 'Vettes, which were heavier than the production type, were constructed with thicker fiberglass and formed with a one-piece body. For production, the upper front and lower front, upper rear and lower rear body sections were joined, and the rocker panels were glued and riveted to the assembled body. The resulting seam was covered with chrome trim. This revised design reduced the number of compound curves in the molds. Hydraulically operated hood and trunk lids were installed on at least the first prototype for display purposes; these panels opened and closed as the show car was revolved on its turntable. The published horsepower rating for the Waldorf 'Vette was 160, while the production car was officially given as 150.

Two more Corvette prototypes were built (see Chapter Ten for further details) and apparently the body of the first prototype was destroyed in one final test of the car.

From Corvette Dream Car to reality; around the time of the 1954 GM Motorama in New York City, GM made the decision to proceed with a production Nomad based on the Bel Air. Interior views of the Nomad show car are seldom seen. This photo shows that the dash appears to be identical to that of a Corvette. Manual windows were employed as evidenced by the crank on the door panel, though the tailgate window was power operated. *Author collection and GM Media Archive*

Road test reports regarding the 1953 Corvette were generally favorable, but the first 300 cars, which were built at Flint, went to VIPs or were retained by GM for further testing. (According to the September 1953 *Motor Trend—Spotlight on Detroit*—Corvette number one went to Harlow Curtice, though that statement is probably erroneous.)

When the general public discovered that they could not just go to the local dealership to purchase one, they began to lose interest in the car. Moreover, the lack of roll-up windows and other little conveniences made the car somewhat of a disappointment to many potential buyers. Quality control was another issue. Panel fit was generally poor and stress cracks appeared fairly quickly. A price tag of $3,490 was certainly a deterrent to ownership as well. Hand finishing the cars like the show cars would have clearly improved the early panel fit problems, but would have pushed the price much higher. The lack of sales of the 1954s would seriously impact planning for the Corvette, at least for a while.

Motor Trend judged the new Corvette to be "an exciting car to drive" but noted it would "barely nose out an average [Buick] Century on an unobstructed freeway." The 'Vette's top speed was found to be about 108 miles per hour. The automatic transmission was anemic, the brakes inadequate, and the lack of simple conveniences, like exterior door handles, quickly diminished general interest in the Corvette. Harley Earl's Dream Car was becoming a nightmare.

Even with the praise from the road testing types and its advanced features, the Corvette barely survived. It would not have had a chance without the support of key people within Chevrolet like Ed Cole and Zora Arkus-Duntov, who was hired just about the time Corvette production started.

Chevy's Golden Anniversary 1955 Bel Air two-door hardtop (lower right) is seen here during the GM Motorama in Boston. It was GM's 50-millionth production automobile. The green and white Bel Air sedan near the center of this photo has a see-through hood so visitors can see the new compact air conditioning system which fit completely within the engine compartment. *GM Media Archive*

Duntov's work in refining the Corvette into a true sports car, as well as the enormous money flowing into GM at the time, is how the car survived past 1955 and ultimately became an automotive icon. Ford's two-seater Thunderbird probably had some impact on Chevrolet's determination to make the Corvette a success, too, as it quickly surpassed Corvette sales in 1955.

Today the Corvette is into its sixth generation and a museum is dedicated solely to this fiberglass sports car. The new C-6 has a top speed of 186 miles per hour thanks to a low coefficient of drag (0.286) and a new LS2, 6.0L V-8 delivering 400 horsepower. Chevrolet's C-5R racer provided valuable lessons on how to make the

Many cut-away displays were created during the Motorama years. This one is a 1955 Bel Air four-door sedan. *GM Media Archive*

The frontal design of the 1955 Biscayne Dream Car was this model's most unusual exterior feature. Rear styling of the Biscayne was similar to what appeared on the 1960 Corvair. *GM Media Archive*

The frame of the Biscayne was nearly fully custom fabricated. *GM Media Archive*

new 'Vette better and faster—a familiar theme to 'Vette enthusiasts.

For a while, GM was considering a line of Corvettes, thus two Corvette-based prototypes—the Nomad station wagon (Shop Order 1954) and the Corvair fastback (Shop Order 2071)—were created for display alongside a mildly modified Corvette wearing a prototype detachable hardtop (Shop Order 2000), for the 1954 GM Motorama. Neither the Corvette "Corvair" nor Corvette-based Nomad went into production.

Carl Renner was put in charge of styling the Nomad. The frame from the EX-52 prototype, according to a GM work order, was modified as needed for use on the Nomad. Work Order #19100 dated October 8, 1953 specified, "Using Chassis components available from the Waldorf Show Corvette Car 852, rebuild Chassis to drawings supplied for a steerable, but not necessarily runable, Nomad Body to be supplied by Styling." The Nomad was assigned

the number 857 for "records purposes." Modifications made to the frame included lengthening, reshaping, and adding pieces; the wheelbase was stretched 13 inches to 115 inches. New front and rear springs were installed and the front crossmembers were revised. This same work order also specified the chassis was to be "finished in show quality."

Chevrolet issued a brochure explaining the virtues of both the Nomad and the Corvair. About the Nomad, it said, "Here for the first time is an experimental model combining the sleek styling of a sports car with the versatility and utility of a Station Wagon. The glass fiber reinforced plastic body affords unusual visibility and seating space for six passengers. The electrically operated rear window automatically retracts into the tailgate as it is unlocked, and may also be controlled by a pushbutton on the instrument panel." This concept would eventually be adopted for Chevy's 1959 wagons. The center window directly behind the main roof support on each side did not roll down, but instead slid fore and aft.

The side trim of the Nomad was similar to the 1953 Corvette prototypes but extended to the doors. Conventional door handles, rather than pushbuttons, were attached and the exhausts exited through a port on each quarter panel. Simulated versions of these oval exhaust ports would later be offered as extra-cost accessories on Chevrolets starting in 1958. The two-tone paint appears in some color photographs to have been a blue-tinted gray metallic lower body with possibly Polo White or India Ivory upper body; the colors could have been entirely custom mixed. Since the overall height of the Nomad was low, the top of the roof was visible. Harley Earl saw a need to give this expanse of fiberglass some sort of visually interesting detail; ultimately, a series of grooves running side-to-side on the roof, aft of the B-pillars, was the result. Overall height stood at just 54 inches while overall length and width measured 191 and 71 inches, respectively.

Door panels and seating of the Nomad show car differed completely from that of the Corvette. Upholstery was in a combination of blue, white, and silver leather and fabric. The front seat cushion extended the full width of the passenger compartment and the seat backrest divided with one-third on the driver's side; both sections of the split backrest were hinged so they could be tilted forward to allow access to the rear seat, which could be folded forward to sit flush with the cargo floor. With the rear seat folded, the distance from the back of the front seat to the tailgate extended 75 inches. The headliner was white and had chrome bows applied—a feature that would be used for the production Bel Air–based Nomad the following year. Dashboard and instrumentation appears to have been left unaltered from that of a Corvette with the exception of the rearview mirror being relocated from the top of the dash to the windshield header; this modification shows the attention to detail given to this car. A dash-mounted rearview mirror in the relatively long car would not have provided a clear view for the driver, thus it was relocated to the higher location. Embossed stainless steel covered the rear compartment floor. The lower rear panel under the tailgate was hinged to open downward and allow access to the spare tire; this feature would also be seen on other Motorama cars.

Two Nomad show cars may have been built; at least one may still exist. Over the past several years, the Nomad has inspired

a number of semi-replica street rods as well as a couple of GM concept cars.

Chevrolet said its 51-inch-high Corvair brought "new aerodynamic design to the closed sports car." Its name was a contraction of Corvette and Bel Air. The distinctive Corvair featured a panoramic windshield slanted back at a 55-degree angle, a fastback roof that swept back to a jet exhaust-type opening, a trio of small rectangular vents on the fenders for interior ventilation, and twin bulges with chromed, slotted vents on the hood, to let the heat escape the engine compartment. Exhaust vents for the interior air were mounted on the swept C-pillars and were controlled with manual buttons inside the car. The so-called jet exhaust opening housed the

The interior of the Biscayne featured thin-shell, swiveling, front bucket seats to aid in entry/exit of the driver and front passenger. Its dash was conventional in appearance. The steering wheel was a modified production item from the all-new 1955 Chevrolet passenger car line. *GM Media Archive*

The Biscayne would be the only pillarless four-door Chevy Dream Car built for the Motorama. *GM Media Archive*

The 1956 Impala Dream Car featured Corvette attributes such as the "toothy" grille. This photo was taken in Miami just prior to the opening of the Motorama. *GM Media Archive*

fiberglass top in addition to roll-up windows. (Production 'Vettes had snap-in panels.) A taller windshield and frame assembly was installed on a 1953 Corvette painted a pale yellow (similar to Harvest Gold or Fiesta Cream) and the interior was outfitted with non-production upholstery and door panels with waffle-pattern inserts, as well as a small glove box on the right kick panel. A similarly patterned upholstery and door panel design, along with the hardtop, would appear for the 1956 Corvette, though the latter item would of course be offered as an extra-cost option. Two Corvette hardtop cars appear to have been built as well.

For 1955, Chevrolet's Motorama Dream Car entrant was the Biscayne (XP-37, Shop Order 2249) described by GM as "an exploration in elegance." Like all Motorama experimental cars, the Biscayne dramatically exhibited the freewheeling kind of thinking of its designers.

The four-passenger, pillarless, four-door hardtop, painted Atlantic Green, featured side coves and suicide doors; this was the only Motorama Chevrolet to have pillarless styling and suicide doors. The side coves which wrapped around the back of the Biscayne would be seen on the following year's Corvette though reversed from that of the Biscayne (with the point facing rearward and appearing on the front fenders and doors rather than the doors and quarters). A stylish chrome-plated Chevrolet script was mounted in the cove section of the front doors. Otherwise, side trim was nonexistent.

The frontal design was the Dream Car's most curious exterior feature. What likely served as the inspiration for the arrangement of the headlights and unusual grille was the Kurtis sports car. Long fairings for the headlights each ended just ahead of an inlet

license plate mounting, license plate lamp, back-up lights, and a bright metal plate embossed with Chevrolet emblems.

The Corvair was seen in two colors—a pale blue-green (similar to Cadillac's Newport Blue or Chevrolet's Sea Mist Green) and a deep red. Changing the color of a Motorama car was not common, but it did happen. However, in the case of the Corvair, almost certainly two examples were built.

Regardless of the light blue-green or red exterior color, the interior was upholstered in light beige leather; the pattern on the seats and the door panels differed from that of a regular production Corvette. A bulkhead, as on the Corvette, sat directly behind the bucket seats while a filler plate covered the area from the bulkhead all the way back to the bottom of the backlight.

The Corvair was said by GM to be powered with a 150-horsepower engine joined to a Powerglide, which of course was a stock Corvette driveline.

The other special Corvette displayed during that year's Motorama (starting with the Miami show) tour had a prototype that allowed cooling air into the interior. Vertical grille elements of chrome décor gave the unique-looking car something else for Motorama attendees to gaze at in wonderment. Grille openingswere covered with a fine mesh, which is a detail that does not show very well in the more commonly seen photos of the car. The end of each front fender wore an anodized gold "V" logo to emphasize the presence of the new V-8. Two recesses on the hood ran length-wise all the way to the cowl where fresh air intakes were built in. A so-called "Stratospheric" wraparound windshield curved upward into the roof; its upper portion was tinted to reduce reflections from the sun. The roof itself attached at the rear to virtually triangular C-pillars; the rearward part of the door opening cut into this triangular shape. A touch-type fuel filler cap was located just behind the rear window. The taillight shape and panel was similar to what appeared on the 1960 Corvair, the 1961 Corvette, and later the Sting Ray. Clare MacKichan (pronounced MacKeekan), who headed the Chevy Studio from 1953–1961, is credited with the styling of the Biscayne.

This model sat on a mostly custom-fabricated frame with the front portion of the structure essentially that of a stock 1955 Chevrolet. Use of a perimeter frame allowed for the floor to drop below it, thus a relatively low roof height was achieved while still allowing plenty of headroom. Overall height of the Biscayne was 52 ½ inches.

Interior appointments were special as well. Thin-shell, swiveling front bucket seats aided in entry/exit of the driver and front passenger. The rear seats were bucket type as

The Impala's five-passenger interior was attractively executed in blue vinyl and fabric with bright metallic surface tinted silver-blue. Both front seat backrests tilted forward, and the seat would slide forward for easier access to the back seat. *Author collection*

The 1956 Chevrolet Impala represented a family car version of the Corvette and in fact its full name was Corvette Impala. Some of its features were adopted for the production Impala that debuted for 1958. The spear molded into the body sides of the show car was probably inspired by that of Ghia's 1954 Fiat V-8 coupe. This feature found its way onto the 1958 Impala as a stainless-steel molding, rather than as a stamping into the sheet metal. *GM Media Archive*

well and were separated with a small console that served as a storage area and armrest. All four seats were trimmed with chrome and covered in green leather. The instrument panel and tri-spoked, chrome-trimmed steering wheel were conventional in their appearance with the latter being a modified production item from the all new 1955 Chevrolet passenger car line. Instrumentation including a 110-mile-per-hour speedometer was centered directly ahead of the driver's position.

The Biscayne was fitted with a 215 horsepower version of the new "Turbo-Fire" V-8 from Chevrolet, which in its inaugural form displaced 265 cubic inches. Its modified Turbo-Fire engine had a high-lift cam and a four-barrel carburetor.

General Motors stored the Biscayne in a warehouse until late 1959. At that point, it was supposed to have been destroyed at Warhoops Used Auto & Truck Parts in Sterling Heights, Michigan, along with at least three other Motorama cars. Though seriously mutilated, the Biscayne was not damaged to the point of being beyond repair; the "destruction" was actually done with some care.

The story about what happened to the Dream Cars at Warhoops as explained to collector Joe Bortz, was that on December 23, 1959, GM sent the LaSalle II Roadster and the Biscayne along with a representative to the salvage yard. The GM representative was given the duty of witnessing the destruction of the cars. These four Dream Cars were to be cut into pieces and their remains crushed. The representative, as the story goes, stayed around long enough to see these two cars cut into pieces; he then told the yard owner, Harry Warholak, Sr., "I want to get home. Just put'em in the crusher." The next day, two more Dream Cars were hauled into the yard with the same instructions being given. He again wanted to go home and told Warholak to "just cut'em up and crush'em and I will mark down I saw everything." Not only did Mr. Warholak not "cut'em up and crush'em," he left those two cars completely intact. The doors of the Biscayne were cut away at the hinges and the roof was detached at the pillars!

Today, the Biscayne has its body parts joined together. Many of the unique parts of the car were found with it, but the frame and engine were somehow lost. The frame was handcrafted from scratch (though its front portion is from a 1955 Chevrolet) by Kerry

Hopperstad Custom Shop. Also, a date-matching 265 V-8 and Powerglide now sit in the engine bay. Photos and other documents necessary to re-create the frame were thought to have long been discarded, but instead were discovered at the GM Tech Center in 1999; these were valuable references. The rebuilt car was mated to its frame on November 7, 2005, and it is now a running vehicle. At the time of this writing, the Biscayne is expected to be ready for public showing during 2007.

Parked on another turntable for the 1955 GM Motorama was GM's 50-millionth production automobile, which was assembled on November 23, 1954. The special car was a Chevrolet Bel Air two-door hardtop. It was painted Anniversary Gold and adorned with a reported 716 gold-plated trim parts along with a duplicate set of replacement parts for repairs if necessary. Chevrolet offered the Anniversary Gold paint color as a limited option (reportedly just 5,000) for four-door models only. The gold Chevy not only made appearances at the GM Motorama, but also at other special events commemorating the achievement such as the "Golden CARnival" in Flint. The keys to the special Bel Air were ceremoniously handed over to Harlow Curtice as part of the festivities.

The unique Anniversary Gold Bel Air two-door hardtop became privately owned at some point after its days of generating publicity for GM came to an end.

According to *Classic Chevy World* magazine editor Joe Whitaker, the car is owned by a North Carolina resident. According to the owner (who prefers his privacy, so he will be called "Mr. Gold"), he also owned a different 1955 hardtop he was planning to restore. Mr. Gold learned of some garage owners who were building another 1955 hardtop into a race car, which he examined. The body was close to being extensively modified by the garage owners,

The details of the 1956 Impala were settled by late August 1955. This full-scale clay model has the crossed-flag emblems seen on some production Impalas. *GM Media Archive*

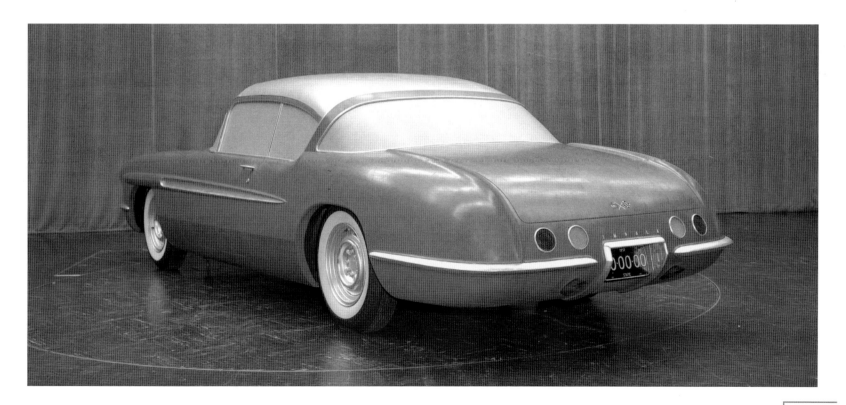

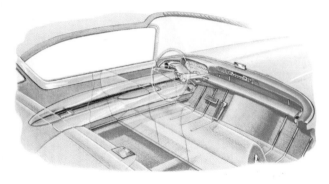

This brochure about the 1956 Impala explained the details of what made the car special. *Author collection*

but inspection of it showed it to be in better condition than the car Mr. Gold was about to restore. Since this car was about to get major modifications, Mr. Gold suggested swapping it for his car. The offer was accepted.

After getting the car home and beginning the dismantling process, Mr. Gold noticed lots of gold plating and gold paint inside the car. He also found a special plate on the firewall, so he called Tom Trainor, who had worked for GM for 30 years and was a Chevy hobbyist. Tom checked the VIN and verified the car was indeed the actual 50 millionth GM car. As of 2005, it was still in the process of being restored.

Added to the line in 1955 was the Nomad two-door station wagon. An example was prominently displayed on a turntable with a banner above announcing the "Motoramic Chevrolet" at this year's GM Motorama. Its forward-leaning B-pillars, chrome-trimmed tailgate, and open rear wheel cutouts probably looked familiar to anyone who saw the 1954 Nomad. However, this Nomad was based on the Bel Air rather

than the Corvette. From the beltline up, the production Nomad bore a strong resemblance to the Dream Car.

Chevrolet also exhibited a cut-away Bel Air as well as a Bel Air sedan with a clear plastic hood showcasing the new air conditioning unit that the division offered for the first time this model year.

The 1956 Impala (XP-101, Shop Order 2487) was the embodiment of what a Corvette as a five-passenger sports car could have been. Corvette styling cues included the "toothy" grille and sloping shape of the quarter panels. In fact, its full name was Corvette Impala. A brochure said the car "incorporates wholly new considerations in fine passenger car design from the standpoint of sleekness, safety, and luxury."

Named for the fleet African antelope, the fiberglass experimental car designed by Bob Cadaret (later to assist in penning the Chevrolet Camaro) and Carl Renner had a 225-horsepower Super Turbo-Fire V-8 engine; "Powerglide" transmission; power windows; integral bumper and grille; tinted "Panoramic" wraparound windshield that curved up into the pale, blue-tinted, brushed, stainless-steel roof; wraparound rear windshield; beltline dip near the reverse slant C-pillars; and chrome-plated wire wheels with knock-off hubs. Its nose emblem was close to the production type applied to the 1958–1960 Corvette and read "Corvette Impala." A rear plaque mounted on the license plate area said "Chevrolet Corvette Impala." The Impala's dual exhaust pipes passed through the driveshaft tunnel into a transverse mounted muffler and the dual outlets from the muffler projected through the rear body panel.

Exterior dimensions of the Corvette Impala were 74.4 inches wide, 53.7 inches high, and 202 inches in length; its wheelbase spanned 116.5 inches and road clearance measured 6 inches. A few of its external features predicted the styling of the production 1958 Chevrolets—even more so than the previous year's experimental Biscayne. Curiously, when *Motor Trend* ran an article on the all-new '58 Impala, it appeared on the cover with the '55 Biscayne, a '58 Corvette, and the Corvette SS; the '56 Impala was not pictured with the group. Both the Impala and Biscayne names would be adopted for full-size 1958 Chevrolets. Furthermore, the show car's color was at least similar to Aegean Turquoise Metallic, which was a color offered for the 1958 model Chevrolets.

Inside the Impala, a padded cornering bar of airfoil shape emerged from the steering column and angled upward to flatten into a horizontal plane that spanned the entire width of the interior; teardrop shaped heater outlets were mounted at each end of the cornering bar. Controls for the heater/defroster, headlights, and windshield wipers fit flush with the surface of the bar. A radio and a drum clock were recessed into the center section of the padded cowl. A speed warning system, consisting of ten circular windows across the instrument panel, were said to light up progressively in more intense shades of red as higher road speeds were attained. Its seats were covered in a combination of silver-blue vinyl and crosshatch pattern nylon; the front seat would slide forward when being tilted for easier access to the rear seat. French stitching was used throughout and the front seat was equipped with a fold-down center armrest with a map case, while the rear seat featured a fixed central armrest with power window switches,

courtesy light, and ash tray. (A fixed rear center armrest appeared on the production Impala two years later.) Front seatbelts were stored in the recesses between the backrests and seat cushion. A sloped and recessed package shelf and a padded rear window header served as another safety measure. Three bright metal strips running lengthwise adorned both the driver and passenger-side floors in front; the floor covering material was similar to that of a Corvette. The blue-tinted metal door panel inserts mirrored the concave shape of those of the exterior. Within them were long armrests for maximum comfort.

Ultimately, among GM divisions, Chevrolet left a lasting mark on the history of the Motorama, creating some of the most interesting Dream Cars of the era, many of which led to production cars of similar design or cars incorporating features first seen on a Motorama turntable.

This is how Chrysler 300 enthusiast Gil Cunningham found the Biscayne and the LaSalle II roadster on a visit to Warhoops Used Auto & Truck Parts in the 1970s. He was searching for the remains of a rare fuel-injected 300-D when he stumbled upon this sight and took this photo. *Gil Cunningham*

Chapter Three
Motorama Cars of Pontiac

P ontiac's Dream Car for the 1953 Motorama tour was a steel-bodied, two-door, chauffeur-driven town car dubbed Parisienne, or La Parisienne, according to a few references (Shop Order 1759), and said to represent "a neo-modern extension of the traditional landau town carriage, a nostalgic excursion into the future."

The car had a deeply hand-lacquered exterior finish fascinatingly described as "black-black." In sharp contrast, the interior's front bucket seats were upholstered in high-luster Roulette Pink cowhide, and the rear bench seat covered in beige and black button-tufted nylon. To aid entry into the rear, the right front seat automatically moved forward via a hydraulic system when the passenger door was opened. In between the bucket seats was a silver vanity compartment, and temperature controls. Continuing the color scheme, the steering wheel had a pink leather rim with black spokes and column. Carpeting was black broadtail.

The Parisienne made its debut inside the "Jade Room" of the Waldorf-Astoria. *GM Media Archive*

The Parisienne was built from a very early production 1953 Pontiac Chieftain two-door hardtop with a straight-eight engine and Hydra-matic transmission. Modifications to the body were extensive, yet subtle. They were done under the supervision of Paul Gillan, who was assisted by stylist Homer LaGassey. The result of the makeover was a lower, sleeker-looking car. Overall height of the Pontiac was reduced from 63 to 56 inches. Its hood was sectioned, the cowl lowered and shaped to accommodate a wraparound windshield, the front fenders and doors cut down, the door handles shaved and replaced with pushbuttons, and the rear deck and quarters lowered. The roof was completely different from production hardtops. A fixed landau-style top covered the passenger compartment, while the chauffeur's position was left open. Press releases stated that a "plexiglass dome" could be installed over the chauffeur's compartment, though it appears that the car was never shown with the cover in place. However, according to Homer LaGassey, the "plexiglass dome" was actually made. The landau design eliminated the use of quarter windows; however, the backlight wrapped around to provide modest side vision. The landau-style roof was fitted with a pink headliner and a vanity light on each side was "calculated to provide a flattering glow of candlelight."

The Parisienne also wore special exterior trim. Its hood ornament was a nonproduction item, as was the wheel cover design. The three, four-point stars on the front fenders would be seen on the all-new 1955 Pontiacs. A beltline chrome molding intersected the bottom of the windshield frame and wrapped all the way around to the other side. The leading edge of the landau-type roof was also dressed in a chrome band.

The Parisienne was given a mild restyle to update it to 1954 standards, given a new color scheme, and placed on the show circuit, though it did not appear at a Motorama again. Charles D. Barnette collection

A little-known car dubbed the Pontiac Avalon also toured with the 1953 GM Motorama. It featured a nonproduction color scheme of chartreuse and black. *Author collection*

The Parisienne got extended show duty after the 1953 GM Motorama tour. For 1954, the Dream Car was updated with a new color scheme—this time silver-blue paint covered the exterior and the pink leather was removed in favor of white. The freshened car made appearances at various auto shows (but not the 1954 GM Motorama) and was likely displayed at various dealerships around the country.

This Dream Car managed to get away from GM when it was sent to a Pontiac dealer in Pontiac, Michigan. The dealership, which was owned by the Pontiac Division, loaned the Parisienne to VIPs for a few years. In 1959, the Dream Car was sold to a local resident who eventually had some restoration work performed on it. This owner then sold the car in 1981 to a New Jersey antique dealer. Eventually, the existence of the Parisienne became a news story in *Old Cars Weekly*. Joe Bortz learned of the car's existence through that article and later made arrangements to buy the one-of-a-kind automobile. It is now restored to its 1953 configuration.

Another Pontiac showpiece for the 1953 GM Motorama was the production-car-based Avalon, which featured "Catalina styling," according to a GM press release. The four-door sedan was painted in a nonproduction color scheme of chartreuse with a black top. Chartreuse leather and black waffle-patterned nylon upholstery matched the exterior colors. Chromed window moldings and ribbed steel plates on the door panels were used to brighten the luxurious customized interior.

One other dramatic display from Pontiac was its cut-away car. The complete rear deck and panoramic rear window, the full one-piece windshield, and the complete front end were retained. The drivetrain was completely exposed. All exposed parts and edges were finished in "brilliant duco and chrome so as to make the car a show model as well as an engineering display," according to a press release.

Pontiac maintained its fifth place sales ranking for the 1953 model year with 418,619 cars sold under the ad banner of "Dual Streak." The lack of a V-8 would catch up to Pontiac the following year. However, the chassis of the 1953 was designed to accommodate Pontiac's forthcoming V-8, which was originally planned for 1953 but was finally introduced two years later.

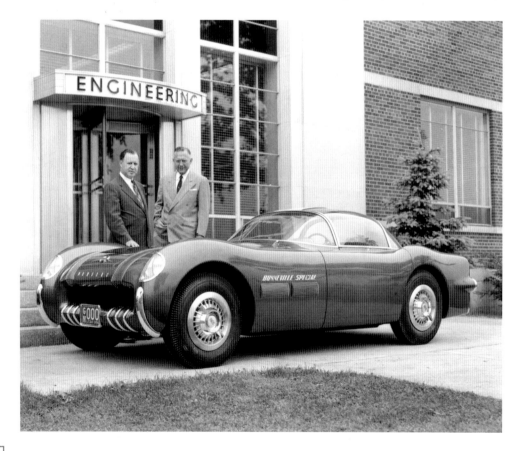

The 1954 Bonneville Special number one is shown in front of GM's Engineering building. Standing with the car are Pontiac's sales manager Frank Bridge (at left) and GM vice president and Pontiac general manager Robert M. Critchfield. *GM Media Archive*

An immense crowd has filled the Waldorf-Astoria in this view showing the Bonneville Special on its platform. In the background appear the GM Firebird, Chevy Nomad, and Cadillac El Camino. The inside joke among the stylists was the cars arrived at the Waldorf with the paint still drying. Generally, five months of 12- to 24-hour work days were spent bringing the cars from drawing-board concepts to show-ready hardware. Homer LaGassey, who assisted Paul Gillan on the design of the Bonneville Special, said, "Thank God I was young," in reference to the fast pace of the schedule required to fully develop a show car. *GM Media Archive*

An ad in *Fortnight* displayed the Bonneville Special, Strato-Streak, and all-new 1954 Star Chief that would be among the automotive stars of the San Francisco Motorama. *GM Media Archive*

The original Bonneville Special (two were built) is shown on the beach in Miami prior to the opening of the Motorama there on February 6. *GM Media Archive*

For 1954, GM Styling offered a pair of Pontiac Dream Cars—one was its version of the Corvette, called the Bonneville Special, a name instantly associated with speed thanks to the records set by racers at Utah's Bonneville Salt Flats. The label for this experimental car is credited to Harley Earl. In fact, the Bonneville Special wore a special set of Utah license plates issued by the state at the request of Earl.

Inspiration for the design of the sports car came from Eddie Miller's Pontiac-powered racer, which set speed records at the Salt Flats in 1950. Show attendees might have been somewhat unimpressed by the choice of a 268 straight eight to power the car, if they had known a V-8 was in the wings, but at least the engine did have four side-draft carburetors and was claimed to produce 230 horsepower. The choice of a straight eight may have been made so as not to reveal the still somewhat secret V-8 scheduled for 1955. Suggesting to the general public that a V-8 would be offered in the coming year might have hurt Pontiac's sales even more than they suffered in 1954, as some potential buyers would have waited for the more powerful engine. The V-8 was somewhat of an open secret by the latter part of 1953 and enthusiasts who read the trade journals had learned about the planned 1954 release of Pontiac's V-8, but of course, that plan was delayed.

The Bonneville Special project (Shop Order 2026) was designed by Paul Gillan and Homer LaGassey. They styled the car with only a few features recognizable as Pontiac themes—the silver streaks on the hood and the taillights and their housings. The curves of the front fenders and the recessed headlights bore a resemblance to the Corvette, but other than those familiar features,

The Bonneville Special is seen here being loaded onto its transport vehicle. Pontiac sponsored traveling exhibits to dealers and auto shows across the country. *Charles D. Barnette collection*

The Bonneville Special was on the cover of this fold-out brochure about the 1954 Pontiacs. *GM Media Archive*

the low and racy Bonneville Special was unique. A long hood was mandated by the straight eight, followed by a two-passenger cockpit and short rear deck, which altogether resulted in a well-proportioned compact sports car. The fiberglass body was sprayed with red-copper paint and the interior was upholstered to match.

The body sported a number of interesting visual details, including the conspicuous absence of a grille. The Bonneville Special had a wide opening roughly the size and shape of the early Corvette's grille opening; below it were mounted six thin bumper guards in sets of three per side. The leading edge of the hood had two chrome-trimmed air vents and the pontoon-like fenders wore crescent-shaped bumpers. The headlights were covered with clear bubbles—a feature originally envisioned for the Corvette. Among the car's most distinctive styling cues were dummy oil coolers machined from solid aluminum and mounted to the fenders. The chrome "silver streaks" each met a functional scoop at the cowl that funneled air into the small interior. (Flow-through ventilation for cooling was featured on many of the Motorama cars; air conditioning was an expensive and seldom-ordered option at the time.) The obligatory wraparound windshield was in place, as was a wraparound backlight. In between the two were transparent flip-up counter-balanced panels. The result of

The second Bonneville Special differed in a number of features and was a road-ready driver. Like the first, this example has survived. This car is now in a private collection. *Dennis Adler*

all the clear pieces was the look of a bubbletop with only thin chrome framing and a narrow center section between the flip-up panels to disturb the view.

From the aft end, the quarters hopped up over the rear wheels and ended in a blade-like shape with a chrome cap fitted at the lower portion to serve as a bumper. The final touch was a built-in Continental kit, creating a dramatic visage for the exotic-looking experimental sports car. In the Bonneville's case, it actually served as a place to store the spare tire, as there was no deck lid. Originally, the Bonneville was designed without the Continental spare, but at the direction of Bill Mitchell, one was included in place of the central blade first proposed.

Even though the engine had a single exhaust, twin exhaust exits in a flat oval shape slipped through cutouts in the lower valence; the other outlet was a dummy. The two-bar spinner, vented wheel covers were especially attractive and relatively complex multi-piece units that added to the car's custom appearance.

The exterior styling was exactly what Harley Earl had demanded from the start. The Bonneville Special, which stood only 48.5 inches high, added a racy image to the Pontiac Division, which was not keeping up with the successful pace of other GM divisions and needed all the help it could get until the V-8 arrived.

Inside, the Bonneville Special was equally racy, with bucket seats, center console, and instrumentation that included a tachometer. A clock and compass sat at the forward end of the brushed aluminum panel between the lift-up panels of the canopy. The array of instruments said to be black-lighted from a source mounted on the canopy center panel

Pontiac displayed this "X-Ray" car at the 1954 GM Motorama. *Author collection*

certainly looked impressive, but most if not all of them were nonfunctional. To meet the show circuit's tight schedule, LaGassey and Gillan went to an aircraft salvage yard in Detroit to buy various tachs, clocks, and altimeters. This avoided the time-consuming tasks of designing and building the instruments. Adding to the sophisticated look was a set of levers protruding from the ribbed console, one of which served as the shifter for the four-speed Hydramatic transmission. Contrasting with the copper-red upholstery was a pewter-colored lower dash, console, and door panels; the latter were recessed for a little more elbow room. A large tool compartment occupied the space behind the seats. The floor had no carpeting, but instead was of brushed aluminum with nonslip rubber strips applied through slots. A competition-style, spring-steel, three-spoke steering wheel along with lap belts, and a 120-mile-per-hour speedometer rounded out the racy theme within the Dream Car. The spectacular experimental car went from the styling team's collective imagination to a complete vehicle in only six months!

The car was extremely popular. In an article about Dream Cars that appeared in *Automobile Quarterly*, Paul Gillan said, "People were spellbound by the fact it was a Pontiac. . . . Everyone liked it." *Motor Trend* was also impressed. The highly favorable publicity led to a second Bonneville Special being built; and this example is detailed in Chapter Ten.

After the national tour ended for each Bonneville Special, the two cars somehow went their separate ways into clandestine ownership. The copper car stayed in storage for several years before it slipped

The Strato-Streak can be seen in the background to the right, sitting on its turntable platform during the Motorama in Miami. *GM Media Archive*

This view of the Strato-Streak was taken during a show in Canada. *Author collection*

out the door surreptitiously. According to an article written by Jay Lamm for the December 1991 issue of *Corvette Fever*, this car "was sold to an anonymous engineer in 1959 who was taking stock of what GM Styling (by then renamed GM Design) had ferreted away in its many warehouses. One day he came across a warehouse filled with dusty, forgotten Dream Cars. The Pontiac Strato-Streak was there, and a

Buick adopted Strato-Streak's three-piece backlight for 1957. This photo was taken at the Motorama in Chicago. *Author collection*

The Strato-Streak shows off its pillarless design and "suicide" doors. GM would later adopt the concept for its limited production Cadillac Eldorado Brougham, but never for a Pontiac. *GM Media Archive*

This photograph dated November 21, 1955, shows the interior of the retrimmed Strato-Streak. The show car was repainted in a brilliant metallic red and reupholstered accordingly. In this scheme, it was rechristened "Strato-Streak II." *GM Media Archive*

A full set of gauges was individually mounted on the center of the Strato-Streak's padded dash. *GM Media Archive*

number of others—the Chevrolet Corvair (Corvette fastback) wasn't there, or the engineer would have gone after that one, too. He had to 'settle' on taking the Bonneville Special and how he managed even that he won't say." Sometime later the original Bonneville Special was sold to a Michigan collector and then to its current owner.

Joe Bortz now owns the first Bonneville Special. The beautifully preserved car is fully original down to the paint and even "the 1954 air in the tires," according to Mr. Bortz. This car stands as an enduring monument to a long-gone era in automotive history.

The other Dream Car that year from Pontiac was a four-passenger 1954 Strato-Streak (Shop Order 1953), said to be a "spectacular sports car," designed under Paul Gillan and Homer LaGassey. It was equipped with "suicide" doors and lacked B-pillars; the doors latched into the sill and the roof. This concept had appeared in production on some European cars in the mid-1930s, but those cars were much smaller than the Strato-Streak. Even though it lacked a B-pillar, the frames around the windows were fixed thus with the doors closed so that the Strato-Streak had the appearance of a four-door sedan. Since the rear doors opened into the airstream, special locks were installed to prevent them from being opened, except when the car was stopped and the Hydra-matic gear selector placed in neutral.

A Pontiac press release pointed out many of the interesting features of the show car; these included "aerodynamic lines" and "vertical twin taillights," giving the car in each rear fender "a jet exhaust effect." A panoramic windshield and "multiplicity of glass" provided all-around vision.

The overall height (54.7 inches) of the experimental car was 8.7 inches lower than a production Pontiac. A modified regular production 124-inch wheelbase Star Chief chassis supported the fiberglass body of the Strato-Streak; the modifications allowed for ample head and legroom even with the considerably low overall height.

The front of the car had a grille and headlight design that looked surprisingly similar to that of the 1954 Kaiser Manhattan! Below the grille, however, was a distinctive gullwing-style bumper that foretold the general appearance of the one that would appear on 1956 Pontiacs. A pair of cowl air intakes and elliptical air outlets above the backlight provided ventilation for the passenger compartment and a projectile-shaped bulge on the side of the front fenders appears to have had engine compartment heat vents. The pattern of the vent was continued on the front doors. A short spear extended from the top of the bulge, while a full-length body spear extended from the lower edge. Though fins were very much in style, this Pontiac lacked them. Instead, the rear profile of the quarter panels tapered into a projectile shape, which ironically predicted the styling of the quarters for the 1957 Cadillac, with the exception of tail fins being grafted in place. The wheel covers looked only slightly similar to those of the Bonneville Special.

During the Motorama tour the Strato-Streak was shown painted light metallic green (similar to a couple of Cadillac colors offered two years later) with a beige leather interior and nylon upholstery intertwined with metallic gold threads; the dash was body color. Late in 1955, this car was repainted metallic red and reupholstered with a two-toned interior (possibly red and black). In the latter guise it was referred to as the Strato-Streak II.

A large nacelle housed some of the instrumentation directly ahead of the driver with other gauges suspended beneath the dash in smaller pods. Also inside were

The undercarriage of the Strato-Star was finished to show quality. Color of frame, differential, and driveshaft appear to be something other than the usual chassis black. Note the presence of chrome-plated rocker arm covers on the 287 V-8. Author collection

four bucket seats; the front ones swiveled a full 90 degrees to help ease entry and exit. A console, which was decorated with chrome and housed the controls for the heater, windshield wipers, and other devices, ran between the seats. Though GM installed swivel seats in several of their Motorama cars, the feature was not offered for any of their production cars until about the mid-1970s. Chrysler Corporation evidently found the concept appealing, as it began offering swiveling seats on its cars beginning with the 1959 model year.

Pontiac did, however, finally offer a four-door hardtop in 1956 (though it would not be the suicide-door, pillar-less type). Furthermore, Oldsmobile and Buick would pick up the roof wind splits and three-piece backlight for their 1957 models, but the feature would prove to be unpopular.

The engine of the Strato-Streak was also a straight eight. No specifications for this engine were located during research

This brochure about the 1954 Pontiac show cars stated that the four-door Strato-Streak was inspired by the Pontiac Catalina two-door hardtop. Author collection

A colorful brochure giving the basic details of the Strato-Star was produced. Author collection

The Strato-Star was painted in silver lacquer with Vermillion Red inner wheelwells. *Author collection*

This squirrel's eye view of the Strato-Star provides an interesting perspective on the gullwing front bumper and the unusual parking light pods. *Author collection*

Rear end styling of the Strato-Star was dramatic. A chrome visor and frame integrated the taillights and exhaust pipes. *Author collection*

for this book, though one can reasonably assume it had modifications.

Along with the Strato-Streak and Bonneville Special Dream Cars was a two-toned Chieftain four-door sedan "X-Ray Car." See-through panels allowed viewers to see the inner mechanical and structural details of a Pontiac. With it was a large banner that said, "Inside Story of Pontiac Quality."

The division built its five-millionth car (a Star Chief Custom Catalina) on June 18, but sales for the model year sank to 287,744 units. The much-needed V-8 would arrive at Pontiac just in time to power completely redesigned cars for 1955 and be dubbed the "Strato-Streak V-8."

The stylists under Paul Gillan experimented with a new type of roof construction when they designed the 1955 Strato-Star (XP-36). Its roof utilized two slim-section cantilever pillars, which grew out the flat rear deck and extended forward through the roof section to gradually taper and join the windshield bar. The effect on the deck gave the appearance of blades separating

it from the quarter panels. A panoramic quarter glass on each side inthe rear, plus a panoramic windshield, provided virtually unobstructed viewing in all directions. Flip-up panels in the roof, about 6 inches deep, opened and closed automatically to facilitate entry and exit. Overall height was kept low with a measurement of 53 inches. A brochure described the look as "the most daring new design ever displayed."

Deeply extended wheel wells in front were painted vermillion, which contrasted well with the Dark Silver Metallic finish on the remainder of the exterior. Their shape was likely inspired by a Bertone-bodied Abarth designed four years earlier by Franco Scaglione who penned the famous Alfa Romeo B.A.T. 5. The elongated wheel openings exposed some of the front suspension components; hence they were chrome plated. Protruding headlight fairings that extended all the way back to the cowl had a wide air scoop atop them to funnel air into the interior. In front sat a simple latticework grille resembling the one on the new Chevrolet, and a divided gullwing bumper with pod-mounted parking lights hung beneath. Wheels for this experimental car were a deep-draw section of chrome with a brake cooling air intake, styled like a turbine impeller. The Strato-Star was reportedly powered by a 250-horsepower Strato-Streak 287. With the optional four-barrel carburetor, the 287 produced 200 horsepower in production form.

The six-passenger Strato-Star's red leather interior had bench seats. The dash strongly resembled that of the yet-to-be designed second generation Thunderbird. The door and rear side panels featured a concave projectile form with similarly shaped armrests. Overhead was a gray padded headliner with pleats running lengthwise.

A new and probably hand-built Safari (Pontiac's counterpart to Chevy's Nomad), also occupied a turntable at the Waldorf in 1955. The production version became available later during the spring.

Sales for Pontiac took a stratospheric leap for the 1955 model year. Output amounted to 554,090 units. The division's first overhead valve V-8 (and only the second V-8 in the division's history), along with fresh styling gave Pontiac its greatly needed sales boost.

At the second city on the GM Motorama tour for 1956, a Special Star Chief Custom Catalina four-door hardtop was shown inside the Dinner Key Auditorium. (Dinner Key is in the Coconut Grove section of Miami adjacent to Biscayne Bay.) This car was displayed over a pool of water from which color-lighted jets of water were sprayed while the car revolved on a turntable. It was painted aquamarine

The interior of the Strato-Star featured dazzling vermillion leather, carpeting, and enamel blended with chrome trim to produce "the ultimate in modern styling" according to GM. Hinged panels automatically rose when the doors were opened to ease entry and exit from the 53-inch-high Strato-Star; when the doors were closed, the panels automatically closed by an electric circuit. *Author collection*

Pontiac offered its own luxurious version of the Nomad; they named it "Safari." *GM Media Archive*

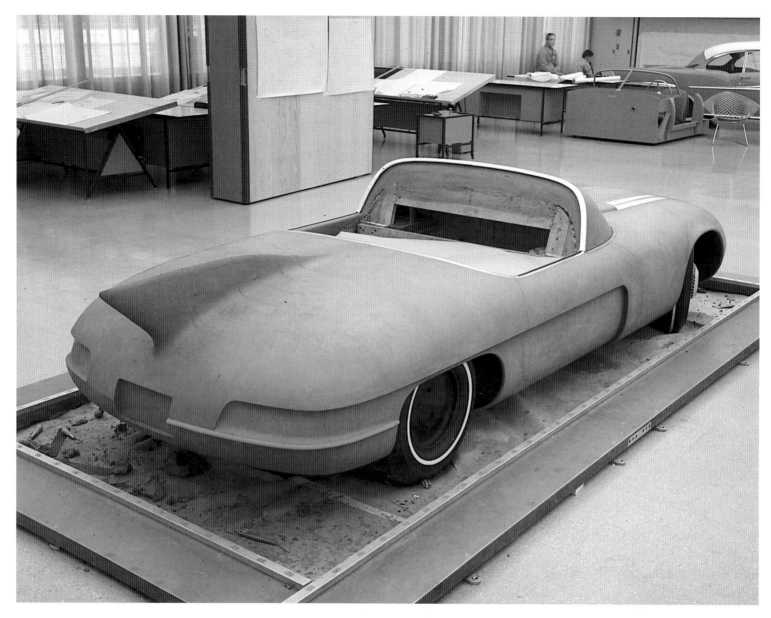

The Club de Mer was originally planned to have a one-piece wraparound windshield instead of the twin bubble windscreens used on the final version. *GM Media Archive*

blue and had exotic star sapphire trim, leather upholstery, and a roof covered in aqua-tinted opalescent Mylar fabric.

Pontiac's 1956 Club de Mer (XP-200, Shop Order 2488) was distinctive and exotic, to say the least; its French moniker translated "Beach Exclusive" and the car's namesake was Miami's fashionable Surf Club. Its unique design was credited once again to the very talented Paul Gillan, who had joined the Pontiac Studio in 1947 as a junior designer. Three years later he moved up to position of chief designer of that studio!

This sporty and compact two-seater was only little more than 38 inches high and barely more than 180 inches long. The wheelbase measured 104 inches and ground clearance was a scant 5 inches. (For comparison, the last generation Firebird stood 14 inches taller and had about 15 inches more length.) Unlike many Motorama cars, the Club de Mer was not built upon any existing platform, but had a custom-fabricated steel-tube chassis; the front suspension, however, was a modified stock system. Furthermore, the outer body panels were made of clear anodized brushed aluminum, which was painted translucent Cerulean blue. The lower body panels rolled under to seal the entire undercarriage; panels bolted over openings throughout the underside allowed access to the various systems. This feature kept the airflow relatively smooth underneath and was perhaps inspired by European race cars such as the Mercedes-Benz 300 SL, which had a bolt-on belly pan, but the design of the Club de Mer took the concept much further.

Other than its diminutive size, the Club de Mer's most apparent features were its twin-bubble windscreens and shark-like dorsal fin, which GM said "not only adds fleetness to the car's appearance but also functions as a stabilizing influence during operation." The nose did not have a conventional grille but rather an "air intake aperture for engine cooling." This opening was lined in chrome trim. Further engine compartment cooling was through outlets in the forward part of the doors, highlighted with a trio of chrome strips. The highway and parking lights were brought together in a dual arrangement with one placed directly over the other. Headlamp assemblies rotated into the Club de Mer's body when not in use to preserve its aerodynamic form. Familiar looking "silver streaks," somewhat like those of the production Pontiacs of 1956 and earlier years, adorned the hood, although Pontiac general manager Semon

The Club de Mer's outer body panels were made of clear, anodized, brushed aluminum and painted translucent Cerulean Blue. In the background is the Buick Centurion. *Charles D. Barnette collection*

Instrumentation was grouped in pods directly ahead of the driver; there was no panel for the passenger side. The steering wheel was a three-bar competition type. *Charles D. Barnette collection*

A beach setting was appropriate for the Club de Mer. Its namesake was the popular Miami Surf Club. *Author collection*

The vermillion red interior had a pair of chrome-trimmed bucket seats upholstered in soft-grain crushed leather separated by a chrome-plated console housing the controls for gear selection, remote deck release, ignition, and radio. *GM Media Archive*

"Bunkie" Knudsen was about to do away with the theme, which he viewed as out of touch with the growing youth market. The four exhaust tips exited through the lower rear panel, which had thin bumperettes attached. Finned wheel covers and U.S. Royal narrow-band whitewall tires, with a single white stripe on the tread, added even more visual interest to the sports car Dream Car.

The vermillion red interior had a pair of chrome-trimmed bucket seats upholstered in soft grain crush leather and separated by a chrome-plated console with the controls for gear selection, remote deck release, ignition, and radio. The console also served as the tube through which the driveshaft ran to connect the engine to the rear transaxle. Other controls were within easy reach of the driver; they were mounted at the forward end of the armrest set within the hollowed-out door panel on the driver's side. Brushed aluminum inserts decorated the door panels. Instrumentation was grouped in pods directly ahead of the driver and there was no dash panel for the passenger side. The steering wheel was a three bar competition type similar to that year's restyled Corvette. A small rearview mirror was mounted on the panel between the twin windscreens. For safety, competition lap and shoulder belts were installed and the entire rim of the interior was padded.

Underneath its distinctive and compact body were a de Dion rear suspension and the aforementioned transaxle. A Strato-Streak 317 V-8 with dual four-barrel carbs officially rated at 300 horsepower (305 horsepower, according to another source) was said to power the experimental sports car. The weight of the Club de Mer is not readily available, though it was perhaps around 2,700 to 2,800 pounds. Assuming that is accurate, then the weight per horsepower ratio would have been approximately 9:1. (A contemporary smaller, lighter Porsche Spyder 550 had a horsepower to weight ratio of about 11:1.)

One must wonder about the car's theoretical performance capabilities. A high-speed run probably never happened with the one-of-a-kind Club de Mer, which is in all probability a good thing since its titanium axle shaft was found to be sheared during the setup for the Miami show. The shaft may have been defective, though it could simply have been overstressed from the tie-down strap securing it inside the car hauler. The bad news was that the Club de Mer could not be rolled from its transport until it was repaired.

Bruce Berghoff (author of the book *The GM Motorama*) worked for the H. B. Stubbs Company at the time. Stubbs (which is still in operation and continues to do display work for GM) handled the complex on-site assembly for the GM Motorama. Berghoff said he never witnessed the Club de Mer move under its own power, never even heard it idling, and said the car was treated as a "pushmobile."

Though the Club de Mer was never considered for production, its styling does appear to have been the inspiration for the sculptured recess with three chrome-plated windsplits on the side of the Tempest, which came along in the early 1960s.

Pontiac's image was changing from a dull, yet dependable car to that of a performance car, thanks to the 1954 Bonneville Special, 1956 Club de Mer, fuel-injected 1957 Bonneville convertible, and the multicarb option for their V-8. In 1957, Pontiac won NASCAR's top award, the Harley J. Earl Daytona 500 Trophy, which enhanced its image all the more.

A motorized 1/4th-scale model of the Club de Mer was constructed and displayed at the GM Motorama. This model is now part of the Bortz Auto Collection. No record could be found on whether or not the child driver lost his driver's license for his parking violation. *Charles D. Barnette collection*

Chapter Four
Motorama Cars of Oldsmobile

The Starfire X-P Rocket convertible (Shop Order 1621) was Oldsmobile's Motorama Dream Car for 1953. Like the majority of these cars, the Starfire was bodied in fiberglass, although this one differed from many of the others in that it could seat six. Following Harley Earl's dictum, aviation and rocket themes were incorporated into GM's new models and this Oldsmobile's namesake was the U.S. Air Force's F-94 Starfire, designed and built by Lockheed. The styling of this aircraft-inspired experimental was the responsibility of Oldsmobile studio chief, Arthur "Art" Ross. While this particular design did not go into production, the Starfire name was applied to a specially trimmed production Olds convertible for 1954.

The Oldsmobile Division started the postwar horsepower race with its "Rocket" V-8. According to factory literature, the Starfire was powered by a 303 V-8 of 200 horsepower,

This rendering dated November 4, 1952, by the head of the Olds studio, Art Ross, shows a car nearly identical to the Starfire XP-Rocket show car. Professor Jim Perkins

which was 35 horsepower greater than the output of the engine in the 1953 Olds Ninety-Eight. Its increased output was achieved, at least in part, with a 9.0:1 compression ratio; the highest rated production Olds engine received an 8.3:1 compression. Not only did the Starfire have a "Rocket" under the hood, it also received a 12-volt electrical system, which Olds introduced for the 1953 model year, power steering, power brakes, and power twin aerials.

The Regal Turquoise Starfire was foretelling of future Oldsmobile styling and some features were adopted for the 1954 models. Others appeared on the limited production 1953 Fiesta convertible. The wraparound or panoramic windshields seen in 1953 became the norm on GM cars by 1955. This Dream Car's wide oval-shaped bumper/grille combination, side trim, and beltline dip was similar to that of production Oldsmobiles for 1955–1957. A unique feature of the Starfire was its door opening; the length at the bottom of it was much wider than at its top. The forward-leaning line formed by this shape paralleled the molding

The beautiful Regal Turquoise 1953 Starfire was Oldsmobile's Dream Car for that year's Motorama. Three were built and at least one was functional. *Author collection*

that began at the dip and angled downward before sweeping back to the rear of the car. This style of door-cut opening was intended as an aid to entry and exit for rear-seat passengers. Though the look of the Starfire was predictive of Oldsmobiles that came later, this particular feature was not adopted. The headlights of the '53 Starfire were covered with a conical bubble, but this attribute also failed to appear on production models.

A turquoise Orlon convertible top on the Dream Car slipped under a ribbed cover in a fashion like the Corvette, whereas production cars used a typical boot. The rear portion wore familiar-looking conical taillights, but the rear bumper was unlike other Olds cars in that the exhaust exited through it and beneath the back-up lights.

The brightly upholstered interior of the Starfire was as beautifully executed as its exterior. The turquoise and white ribbed leather seating, styled to give the appearance of four divided seats, was most prominent. Chrome moldings decorated the front seat, and the rear seat wrapped around. Interestingly, the latter feature would be found on the four-seat Ford

This angle on the Starfire (again inside the Waldorf) reveals the bucket-style bench seat in front as well as details of the virtually symmetrical dash. *GM Media Archive*

Thunderbird of 1958, which was a car not yet conceived by Ford at the time! The Starfire's two-toned interior was another concept pioneered with this experimental car. A total of three 1953 Starfires were built.

Oldsmobile also exhibited its Fiesta—a kind of "semi-custom" production car virtually hand-built in Lansing. It sported a unique, low wraparound windshield; notched beltline; two-tone paint; special deck lid molding; spinner wheel covers; special interior; two-way power seat; hydraulic window; 170-horsepower V-8, "Super Drive" Hydra-matic transmission; signal-seeking "Wonder Bar" radio 120-mile-per-hour speedometer; dual outside rearview mirrors; back-up lights; and "Autronic Eye" automatic headlight dimmer. The cowl, doors, and deck lid were special to the Fiesta; even the hood and front fenders, as well as the convertible top had to be altered to accommodate the panoramic windshield, which stood 3 inches shorter than a standard Olds windshield. Only the grille, bumpers, taillights, and some side trim were identical to its Olds Ninety-Eight counterpart.

The Starfire's two-tone interior foretold the near-term future of GM's production cars. Two-tone exterior and interior color schemes would be very popular in the 1950s. Note the "88" emblem on the quarter panel just behind the door opening. *Author collection*

A 200-horsepower "Rocket 8" was said to power the Starfire. *Author collection*

The Olds Fiesta, unlike the Buick Skylark, Cadillac Eldorado, and Corvette models that made their "Dream Car" debuts at the 1953 Motorama, would last only for one season, but to some degree would continue in the form of the 1954 Olds Ninety-Eight convertible. This one-year-only Fiesta retailed for $5,715 (roughly the price of a Cadillac Fleetwood and $2,752 above that year's Ninety-Eight convertible), which helps explain why only 458 were built. The price was even several hundred dollars higher than that for the limited production Buick Skylark, though the latter lacked the panoramic windshield, hence the costly labor of modifying the cowl was eliminated for that special model.

Oldsmobile's F-88 (XP-20, Shop Order 1939) represented that division's version of the Chevrolet Corvette. Its design is also credited to Art Ross. This sporty two-seater could easily have gone from Dream Car to production car in one year with assembly being done on the Corvette line. Unfortunately for Chevrolet, its Corvette was not selling well

and a divisional competitor made no sense by the time the F-88 arrived on the show circuit. Ironically, Oldsmobile was better suited to offering a sports car at the time as they already had a powerful V-8; Chevrolet would not offer a V-8 until the following model year.

Output for the 324 Rocket V-8, with a single four-barrel carburetor, was boosted to 250 horsepower for the F-88 and coupled to a Hydra-matic automatic transmission. A label on the fuel filler cap specified that 94 to 100 octane fuel be used. The compression ratio was pushed higher (to 10:1) than the stock 185 horsepower 324 that came with the Olds Eighty-Eight or Ninety-Eight. Writers for *Motor Life* magazine (April 1954) speculated that the top speed of the experimental car would be approximately 150 miles per hour. Regardless of the horsepower rating attributed to the F-88, it reportedly did not run during the time of the GM Motorama tour and only after the show circuit ended was its electrical system connected.

The fiberglass body was painted metallic gold with dark green wheelwells; the green paint even extended to the floor pans. A minimal of chrome trim—at least by 1950's standards—decorated the F-88. A simple chrome molding ran from the taillight pod to the dip in the beltline at the door, then turned back and down before circling rearward and terminating at the rear wheel opening. Large chrome "88" numerals cleverly disguised engine heat vents on the front fenders and an "around the world" emblem was affixed to the nose and deck lid. An oval-shaped honeycomb grille filled the opening of the combination bumper/ grille surround, and in back, a thin molding bordered the recessed license plate mounting. The oval exhaust openings at the rear of the quarters also got a chrome-plated surround. Furthermore, seven chromed

The limited-production Olds Fiesta was very nearly a Dream Car itself with its wraparound windshield, notched beltline, and two-tone color schemes. Modifications to the Olds Ninety-Eight body required plenty of hand labor, resulting in a high price tag for the model. Retailing for $5,715 (roughly the price of a Cadillac Fleetwood and $2,752 above that year's Ninety-Eight convertible), only 458 were built. *Dennis Adler*

bumper guards were mounted to the body-colored bumper. A long, conical taillight was mounted to the upper quarter panel extension; a similarly shaped taillight would later be used for the 1959 Cadillac. The wheel cover design for the 13-inch wheels resembled a turbine with a three-blade spinner or "flipper." During the Motorama tour, the wheels were fitted with black sidewall tires, though these were later changed to wide whites.

The F-88's convertible top folded into a well, which was covered with a hinged lid, just as on the Corvette. Its fuel filler was mounted just behind the top well and along the fore/aft center line of the car, with the deck lid opening cut around it. The trunk, as one would expect, was not spacious, but having the spare mounted under the trunk floor and accessed with a drop-down integral bumper guard did help maximize the usefulness of the volume provided. (The drop-down bumper section would show up on other GM Dream Cars before being adopted on a handful of production vehicles.)

Not surprisingly, the F-88 body sat on a Corvette frame, though provisions were made to adapt the "Rocket" V-8 in place of the Corvette's "Blue Flame" six cylinder. Wheelbase remained the same as the 'Vette's at 102 inches while the overall length of the car measured 167.25 inches. Overall height with the top down was just 45 inches.

Oldsmobile offered a special model dubbed "Fiesta" to entice potential buyers into dealer showrooms. *GM Media Archive*

The F-88 never stood a chance of going into production, as it would have been in direct competition with Chevy's Corvette. *GM Media Archive*

Ironically, the Olds F-88 might have been a more successful sports car than the first Corvette, which lacked so many of the features offered by the Olds, including power windows, external door locks, and a V-8 engine. *Dennis Adler*

The interior of the F-88 was quite different from the Corvette's. Though both featured bucket seats, the Oldsmobile's were of a different design. A bulkhead behind the seats had openings formed around the seats' backrests to provide recesses for their adjustment in the fore/aft direction. Between the seats and positioned on the bulkhead was a radio speaker grille. The seats and steering wheel were covered in pigskin; a set of competition-style instruments was arranged vertically in three round housings beginning at the top center of the dash. The upper housing contained an odometer along with a 150-mile-per-hour speedometer and a 6,000-rpm tachometer laid out concentrically; the center one was divided into the amp (above) and temperature gauges; the bottom housing did double duty, too, with the fuel gauge in the top half and the oil pressure gauge occupying the lower half. Fresh air vents sat atop the dash along the cowl edge and in the kick panels. The console, which was finished in chrome and textured metallic gold, carried a chronometer, shifter, radio, and radio controls. Initially, the dash, upper door panels, instrumentation stack, and carpeting were a golden color. At some point, the dash color was changed to dark green. Later the dark color was extended to the upper door panels, center instrument pods, forward console, and carpeting. The steering wheel was replaced with a production type as well.

Sometime after the 1954 GM Motorama ended, Harley Earl decided he wanted an F-88 for himself, so a second example, painted red with a white stripe across the hood was assembled for him. This car, as well as a third F-88, built for another member of GM's management (Sherrod Skinner), made this the most "prolific" of Oldsmobile Dream Cars. What is currently believed to be the only surviving example was sold for $3,000,000 (plus commission) at the 2005 Barrett-Jackson auction in Scottsdale, Arizona.

The metallic copper 1954 Cutlass (Shop Order 1981) was named to honor the U.S. Navy's F7-U Cutlass jet fighter plane. Oddly, the only place this name appeared was on the car's steering wheel hub. This two-seater Cutlass possessed a number of unusual features; the most noticeable was its roof with louvered backlight. This car (also of fiberglass) had no deck lid; luggage access was from inside via a body-colored, tonneau-like panel behind the seats.

An article in the February 1955 issue of *Auto Age* presented a comparison between the production Starfire and the experimental Cutlass. The report speculated on the contribution the Cutlass might make on future GM styling. "While the Cutlass in its present form is for the most part an entirely impractical vehicle, it does furnish us with the basis for an interesting comparison.

" . . . the Starfire [is] one of the largest [cars] on the road, a fact that is its very selling point to many people. But while the Starfire is long, powerful, and impressive, it is by some standards rather clumsy and even impractical when it comes to garage or parking space. . . . What is the alternative? Smaller—but not necessarily skimpier or less stylish—cars.

"This is where the Cutlass fits into the picture perfectly. It represents a trend toward the smaller, and presumably more maneuverable, automobile of the future. . . ." The Cutlass' combination bumper/grille surround carried split honeycomb grille inserts and a set of driving lamps. Its general appearance foretold the design worn by

The sleek Cutlass had, among many other features, an unusual headlight treatment— a vertical central "fin" was fitted over the upper half of each headlight. *GM Media Archive*

The engine in the Cutlass was reported to be a "Rocket" 324 that was modified to produce 250 horsepower. Note the chrome-plated air cleaner, valve covers, and radiator top. This car was functional. *Author collection*

The Cutlass and F-88 were the feature stars in this Motorama ad for the Chicago exhibit at the International Amphitheatre. *Author collection*

the 1956 Oldsmobiles. Instead of the chrome-plated fresh air vents, as found on the F-88 show car, twin hood-mounted scoops were employed to funnel air to the heater. The 13-inch wheels of the Cutlass were fitted with the same style wheel covers and black sidewall tires as those on the F-88 show car.

Other distinctive features of the car were its teardrop wheel openings with polished stainless-steel inner fenders with engine heat vents, aircraft canopy-like roofline, modest tail fins, and blade-like quarters decorated with small "88" numerals. Flattened dual-exhaust outlets were integral with the rear bumper. These outlets mounted at each end of the less-than-full-width rear bumper were each divided into fours, to simulate one exhaust per cylinder. A lidless rear deck sloped sharply, thus leaving the quarters with a bladelike form. The ends of each quarter panel were extended with chrome caps housing deeply recessed, semi-circular twin taillights. Lower quarters either detached or were hinged like those of the XP-300 to presumably allow the rear wheels to be removed. The low-cut, teardrop-shaped wheel openings would have made that procedure a bit more difficult otherwise. This design eliminated the more prominent seam created with a conventional fender skirt. The seam formed where the lower quarter joins the upper panel was almost fully hidden by the molded-in body side spear, which was capped by a narrow bright molding. A spare tire was stored in a compartment behind the fold-down rear bumper.

The Cutlass' many features included swivel bucket seats. *Author collection*

This photo shows the Cutlass with a Michigan license plate (with the tag number blacked out), which suggests it may have been driven on public streets. *Steve Wolken collection*

The instrumentation layout was identical to that of the F-88. The copper and white leather-covered seats swiveled to facilitate access. Rearward vision was provided with dual, wide-angle mirrors mounted on the central control panel. A body-color bulkhead behind the seats was designed like that of the F-88's, which was recessed. Unlike the F-88, however, the console between the seats held a radio-telephone.

The Cutlass was said to be powered with a 250-horsepower, 324 V-8, and Hydramatic—the same as the F-88. Because the car had so many characteristics in common with the F-88, the Cutlass was simply called "the long wheelbase F-88" before it was formally named. Its frame may have been a stretched Corvette platform; the wheelbase measured 110 inches. Overall length was 188.5 inches and overall height 51.5 inches.

Interestingly, post-Motorama photographs from July 1954 show the car with a Michigan State license plate instead of its decorative identification tag used during the GM Motorama tour. This suggests the car may have been driven on Detroit area streets for awhile, probably by some GM managers and stylists.

Another eye-catching exhibit from Olds was a Super Eighty-Eight Holliday two-door hardtop painted a highly iridescent blue metallic on its lower body, and white for the top. It was upholstered with dark blue nylon waffle-weave cloth and white leather.

Oldsmobile's XP-40 Dream Car (Shop Order 2251) project resulted in the two-toned blue Eighty-Eight Delta—a four-passenger, two-door hardtop that stood only 53 inches

In the February 1955 issue of *Auto Age*, the editors ran a story comparing the Olds Starfire with the 1954 Cutlass. *Author collection*

A modified 324 V-8 rated at 250 horsepower was said to power the F-88. *Author collection*

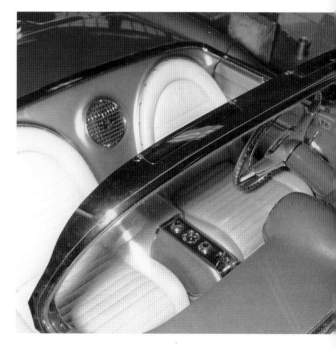

The F-88 show car had air scoops built into the windshield frame, which could be opened for ventilation when the top was up. *Steve Wolken collection*

The F-88 is posed near the new Starfire in this photo. *GM Media Archive*

The spare was carried inside a compartment accessed through the center section of the rear bumper. *Steve Wolken collection*

Stacked gauges were mounted centrally. Note the fresh air vents at the forward portion of the dash. Also note the color of the dash differs from its appearance as seen in earlier photos. *Don Baron collection*

high. The Eighty-Eight Delta's stylists set their imaginations on full throttle (as usual) when they went to the drawing boards to design this car. A factory-issued brochure described the Eighty-Eight Delta as having a "Supersonic Shape." The car certainly looked fast.

Up front were wide-set vertical ovals housing the head and parking lights as well as scoops for brake cooling. Between the wide ovals was the bumper/grille combination that carried a set of split, thin horizontal bars. The hood extended the entire distance between the fender crown lines; the hood cut lines were concealed with chrome strips. A jeweled around-the-world emblem let onlookers know this was an Oldsmobile.

All the glass was tinted light blue to harmonize with the highly metallic two-tone paint scheme and blue-tinted brushed aluminum roof; the backlight had a darker tint to give the impression that it was a continuation of the roof panel. The minimal A-pillars were set vertically and framed a wraparound windshield.

To impart a feeling of fleetness and elegance, the Eighty-Eight Delta was given a number of special styling cues. The car's profile featured a dropped beltline between the windshield and backlight. Its wheelwell openings were of a teardrop shape with the front ones getting polished stainless-steel inner fenders, while the rear wheelwells were cut low. Filling the dramatically styled openings were 7.60x15-inch-wide whitewall tires mounted on wheels with exposed brake drums. The brake drums had integral concentric cooling fins and exposed acorn-style lug nuts numbering six per wheel. Side trim on the Eighty-Eight Delta provided the two-tone line and gracefully mimicked the lines of the body panels. It followed the front wheelwell cutout then looped around and paralleled the fender line before dipping at the A-pillar and traveling straight back to wrap around the rear to form a bumper blade. The rear end had a wide, long, low deck, trimmed with a jeweled around-the-world logo that also served as the fuel filler door. Fifteen-gallon fuel tanks were built into each rear quarter panel. Wraparound taillights and individual letters spelling *O L D S M O B I L E* sat just above the rear blade-like bumper.

Note the many unusual features of this Cutlass—louvered backlight, canopy-like roof, rectangular exhaust outlets, etc. *GM Media Archive*

Oldsmobile's Starfire was a new model for 1954. *GM Media Archive*

The striking, multi-tone, blue leather interior with a rear floor that dropped between the frame rails featured four individual seats. An unusual instrument panel with a 130-mile-per-hour speedometer and 5,500-rpm tachometer were housed in a pair of separate oval pods on a detached, horizontal, leather-padded support. This support served as a structural tie bar and two-thirds of the lower portion could be pulled out to serve as a tray. The 17-inch steering wheel had exposed rivets like the 1954 Cutlass and the model identification on the hub.

A full-width grille with air and heater outlets, radio speaker, and drum clock were forward of—but detached from—the instrumentation panel. The emergency brake pedal and its associated linkage were installed at the left side kick panel; the kick panel concealed virtually all of the linkage. A map pocket was included on the right side kick panel. Carpeting for the Eighty-Eight Delta's interior appears to have been similar to the Daytona type used in luxury cars of the era. The tunnel between the front seats contained the radio dial and controls, ashtray, and a waste container with a disposable wax paper liner plus storage for refills; the lid on this container opened laterally from either side. A rear armrest dividing the seats provided storage space and contained the electric switches for the power rear windows, as well as an ashtray. The front seats swiveled for easy access and they also folded and pushed forward with one motion to allow passengers a more graceful entry and exit to and from the back seat.

The Eighty-Eight Delta's 324 V-8 was given upgrades (which included a 10.0:1 compression ratio and dual exhausts) to push the horsepower rating to 250 at 4,600 rpm and torque to a peak of 350 ft-lbs at 2,800 rpm. For comparison, the highest output stock engine—that installed in the Super Eighty-Eight and Ninety-Eight—had a rating of 202 horsepower at 4,000 rpm and a maximum torque of 332 ft-lbs at 2,400 rpm. The high-output "Rocket" engine was coupled to a Hydra-matic Super Drive automatic transmission.

The 88 Delta had wide-set vertical ovals housing the head- and parking lights, as well as scoops for brake cooling. Wheelwell openings were of a teardrop shape with the front ones getting polished stainless-steel inner fenders. *Author collection*

The 88 Delta had an unusual instrument panel with the 130-mile-per-hour speedometer and 5,500-rpm tachometer housed in a pair of separate oval pods on a detached, horizontal leather-padded support. *Author collection*

The Eighty-Eight Delta's wheelbase measured 120 inches, which was 2 inches shorter than that of the Eighty-Eight/Super Eighty-Eight series. Its fiberglass body sat on a modified Olds frame with a stock front suspension; brakes were production units as well. Ground clearance was stated to be 6.2 inches. Curb weight was a bit lighter than a Super Eighty-Eight—4,078 pounds versus 4,152 pounds for the production car.

For the 1955 model year, a total of 583,179 Oldsmobiles were sold the highest output in the division's history. Helping sales in that regard was new styling and a high number of two-tone paint selections. Oldsmobiles' general sales manager, G. R. Jones, explained to a reporter during one of the Motorama stops that "Bright, attractive colors are utilized in striking fashion to enhance Oldsmobile's low silhouette appearance."

A total of 89 two-tone color scheme combinations were offered for 1955; fourteen new paint colors were added as well. Emphasizing the point of two-tone color combinations at the 1955 GM Motorama were several Eighty-Eights and Ninety-Eights painted in such two-tones as Coral and Polar White, Twilight Blue and Frost Blue, Burlingame Red and Mist Gray, as well as Turquoise and Polar White.

Here is a view of the interior mockup of the 88 Delta. Its rear armrest dividing the seats provided storage space and contained the electric switches for the power rear windows as well as an ashtray. The model identification was embossed on the vertical bulkhead between the rear seats. *GM Media Archive*

Like many of the GM Motorama Dream Cars, the 88 Delta was equipped with swivel bucket seats in front. The wheels had exposed brake drums with integral concentric cooling fins and six acorn-style lug nuts. *Author collection*

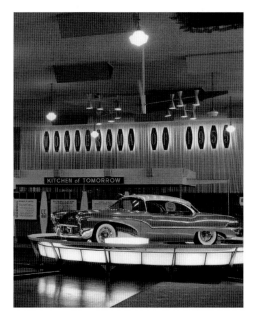

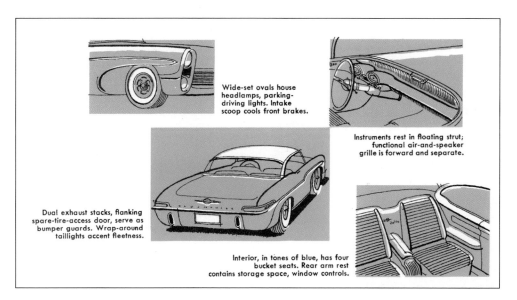

This view of the 88 Delta is from the GM Wonderama in Dayton, Ohio. *H. B. Stubbs Co.*

A small brochure about the 88 Delta was produced. *Author collection*

Oldsmobile's 1956 Golden Rocket (XP-400, Shop Order 2490) was certainly one of the most (if not the most) radically styled Dream Cars of the Motorama era; its design was the responsibility of Art Ross. In profile, it resembled a rocket laid on its side due to its twin-torpedo, pontoon-shaped fenders, and tapering quarters with small fins. General Motors described the car as having "a special look of grace and swiftness." That "special look" was almost certainly inspired by the styling of the experimental, turbine-powered 1954 Fiat 8001. The fact should be noted, however, that Earl's 1951 LeSabre also inspired many European designers in the 1950s. The Golden Rocket differed in very noticeable ways, but its general resemblance to this Fiat is a strong one.

The central nose of the Golden Rocket was projectile-shaped and it had a small, upside-down, U-shaped grille. The ends of the fenders wore chrome "Dagmar"-style bumpers with the headlights being mounted inboard of those. Cowl air inlets just below the windshield on either side of the hood allowed fresh air into the interior. Openings behind and below the backlight also let the fresh air flow out. Side running lights were located on the rear dorsal fins. Interestingly, the rear portion of the roof with its split, rear backlight is very similar to the appearance of the split-window Corvette seen in 1963. This was a favorite theme of Bill Mitchell, who would succeed his mentor Harley Earl as head of GM Design three years after the Golden Rocket made its national tour.

Upon opening the doors, flip-up roof panels were activated and the pair of front bucket seats swiveled and raised 3 inches. Tilt steering was another advanced feature of this experimental and would become optional equipment on some GM cars in the 1960s. Furthermore, the steering wheel folded away from the driver when two buttons were depressed simultaneously which allowed for increased ease of entry and exit.

The central nose of the Golden Rocket was projectile-shaped and it had a small upside-down U-shaped grille. The ends of the fenders wore chrome "Dagmar"-style bumpers with the headlights being mounted inboard of those. *Author collection*

In addition, the Golden Rocket's speedometer occupied the center part of its steering wheel! Upholstery was in dark blue leather, which contrasted sharply with the bright blue carpeting on the floor. One more unusual feature inside the Golden Rocket was the inside rearview mirror—rather than being mounted centrally on either the dash or windshield header, it was mounted on the lower windshield garnish molding beside the driver-side windshield post—an idea fortunately never adopted by anyone.

A 275-horsepower Olds 324 Rocket V-8 was said to power the metallic-gold fiberglass two-seater. If the advertised output was really true, then it produced 35 more horses than the standard Rocket V-8 used in the Oldsmobile Ninety-Eight. Hiding the fuel filler was among the latest design games, and Golden Rocket's was hidden behind the recessed license plate mounting, which itself was enclosed with a clear, contoured cover. One other bit of creativity was applied to the tires; white strobe stripes appeared on the side walls.

The Golden Rocket was never intended to go into production, but the name was put to use during the 1957 model year for Oldsmobile's Eighty-Eight series.

TELETALE ENGINE INSTRUMENTS
AMPERES OIL TEMPERATURES—HOT COLD

DEFROSTER GRILLES

FUEL GAUGE

CLOCK RADIO SPEAKER GRILLE

HEATER GRILLE

WINDSHIELD— WIPER & WASHER

REAR VIEW MIRROR

REAR VIEW MIRROR
STEERING WHEEL RELEASE CONTROL

LIGHT SWITCH (HIDDEN)

MAP POCKET

SPEEDOMETER

COURTESY LIGHT

HORN BUTTON BEHIND WHEEL

DOOR CONTROL

PARKING BRAKE

ARM REST

GLOVE COMPARTMENT

RADIO CONTROLS

COVER—CIGARETTE LIGHTER AND ASH TRAY

DEFROSTER & HEATER FAN CONTROLS

HEAT & VENTILATION CONTROLS

IGNITION SWITCH

TURN SIGNAL INDICATORS

JETAWAY HYDRA-MATIC SELECTORS

WINDOW LIFTS

TURN SIGNAL SWITCH

REAR VENT CONTROL

POWER BRAKE PEDAL

ACCELERATOR PEDAL

INSTRUMENT PANEL OLDSMOBILE "GOLDEN ROCKET"

This photo of an artist sketch of the dash provides a detailed look at the many features inside the Golden Rocket. *Author collection*

This color photo reveals the bright blue interior of the Golden Rocket as well as the split backlight. *Bruce Berghoff*

This bird's-eye view of the Golden Rocket is from its appearance at the Paris Salon in 1957. *GM Media Archive*

This view clearly shows the dramatic front-end design of the Golden Rocket, perhaps the most striking of all the Motorama cars built in the 1950s. *GM Media Archive*

Chapter Five
Motorama Cars of Buick

ROADMASTER V8 AND TWIN-TURBINE DYNAFLOW DRIVE
GIVE THE WILDCAT TERRIFIC POWER AND TAKE-OFF

In keeping with its jet-styled lines, the *Wildcat* is powered by the world's most advanced V8 engine, the same record high-compression Fireball V8 that gives the 1953 Roadmaster and Super such outstanding performance among America's finest cars.

Converting the *Wildcat's* magnificent power into whip-quick getaway with perfect smoothness at every pace, Twin-Turbine Dynaflow provides this experimental Buick with the finest automatic transmission ever built for an automobile.

FACTS AND FIGURES ABOUT THE BUICK WILDCAT

DIMENSIONS (IN INCHES)
Wheelbase 114.0
Over-all length.....................192.0
Over-all width.......................79.4
Over-all height (top up)..........54.0
Front tread...........................59.0
Rear tread............................59.0
Road clearance.......................6.0
ENGINE AND CHASSIS
Engine...........................90-degree
  Valve-in-Head V8

ENGINE AND CHASSIS CONT.
Horsepower........188 @ 4000 rpm
Bore and stroke...............4.0 x 3.2
Displacement..............322.0 cu. in.
Compression ratio...........8.5 to 1
Maximum torque..300 @ 2400 rpm
Electrical system...............12 volts
Carburetor.........................4-barrel
Transmission ....Twin-Turbine
  Dynaflow

ENGINE AND CHASSIS CONT.
Frame........................Double drop
  channel with center X-member
Springing.......4-wheel coil springs
Steering...............Hydraulic power
Brakes...................Vacuum power
Wheels..............15" with 6½" rims
Tires................................7.60-15
Radio.........................Selectronic
  with automatic antennas

LITHO IN U.S.A.

B uick celebrated its 50th anniversary in 1953 and garnered maximum publicity from the celebration, which coincided with the magnificent 1953 GM Motorama.

The fiberglass Wildcat (retroactively renamed Wildcat I once the 1954 Wildcat II was created) began simply as Shop Order 1714 and was the division's first Motorama Dream Car. The name was likely taken from the Buick Division's Wildcat tank built during World War II. The show car was created under the guidance of Buick's chief engineer, Ned Nickles, who was also responsible for the design of Buick's first hardtop—the 1949 Riviera.

At the Motorama, Buick offered a small booklet titled *Buick Wildcat—Trial Flight in Fiberglas and Steel* to those who were curious about the experimental car. (Fiberglas with one "s" is the trademarked name for fiberglass, which has become a generic term over the

A small booklet, *Buick Wildcat—Trial Flight in Fiberglas*, provided details of the Dream Car. At least two of these cars were built. *Author collection*

decades.) The car was described in this booklet as a "revolutionary sports convertible" with a "Fiberglas body." The eight-page booklet explained the reason it was built of Fiberglas, and the car's purpose:

"Adoption of easily-molded Fiberglas for the bodies of Buick experimental models shortens the time between new styling ideas and their incorporation in cars that can be tried and tested. And presentation of these futuristic models . . . affords an opportunity to 'pre-test' the motorists' reaction to various styling features incorporated in those cars."

The "trial flight in fiberglass" had interesting styling and mechanical features such as the concave vertical grille bars and "buffer bombs" integrated with a massive wraparound front bumper/oval grille frame, twin hood scoops for better carburetion, fender top "Ventiports" (three on each side), doors that opened from outside via a pushbutton, a slim sweep-spear line that traversed bumper to bumper, quarter panel louvers that served as cooling vents for the rear tires and brakes, and Roto-Static front hubs. The hub feature consisted of a stationary hub with a scoop on the leading side to aid in front brake cooling; the wheel revolved around the scooped hub. A power convertible top folded into a well that was completely covered by a hinged lid—a familiar theme among many of Harley Earl's creations. The rear had modest tailfins similar to those of a production Cadillac and the deck had parallel fin-like projections that began immediately behind the passenger compartment and ran to the rear center bumperettes, which surrounded the license plate housing. These projections bordered the center section of the grooved, recessed center section of the deck. "Roadmaster" was spelled out in

A black Wildcat appeared at the first stop on the 1953 GM Motorama tour—the Waldorf-Astoria in New York City. *GM Media Archive*

This perspective on the Wildcat reveals the dual fins on the deck as well as the ribbed surface between them. Note the twin trunk locks. *GM Media Archive*

The 1953 Wildcat was white in Miami, the second city of that year's Motorama. *GM Media Archive*

An experiment into the future
BUICK WILDCAT fiberglas-bodied sports convertible

See it at the
G.M. MOTORAMA
CIVIC AUDITORIUM
May 1 through May 7

You may well be looking at tomorrow when you come see this completely revolutionary automobile. For the Buick WILDCAT is an experimental model built with a body of molded, dent-resisting Fiberglas which permits far greater versatility in styling. This futuristic sports convertible has a 114-inch wheelbase, is powered by Buick's 188-hp vertical-valve V8 Fireball Engine with 8.5 to 1 compression. It has Twin-Turbine Dynaflow Drive—Power Steering —Power Brakes—hydraulic control of seat, dual radio masts and hide-away top—plus a host of other advances, including "rotostatic" front-wheel brake-cooling discs which remain stationary while the wheels revolve about them. Come see the WILDCAT, Buick's breath-taking experiment in tomorrow's motoring!

SEE THE GOLDEN ANNIVERSARY BUICKS AT YOUR BUICK DEALER'S

This newspaper ad appeared in the *San Francisco Chronicle. Author collection*

chrome block lettering set within the recess at the forward end of the rear deck. Just behind the lettering was a small vent to provide flow-through ventilation when driving with the top up.

A Buick Roadmaster powertrain consisting of the new 322 "Fireball" V-8 and Twin-Turbine Dynaflow automatic transmission was installed in this car. Upgrades were made to the Dynaflow in 1953 that included twin turbines in the torque converter to reduce the sluggishness of the previous version of the transmission. Other equipment included on the Wildcat was power steering with a 15:1 ratio, power brakes, hydraulically adjusted seat and windows, as well as a "Selectronic" radio with foot-control switch and twin rear-mounted automatic aerials.

The 188-horsepower engine was as beautifully finished as the rest of the car. It was coated in enamel paint and fitted with chrome-plated valve covers and power steering pump housing. Buick's 322 was a new oversquare V-8 with a bore and stroke of 4.00x3.20 inches. Torque was advertised as 300 ft-lbs at 2,400 rpm. The engine's valve arrangement was perhaps the most interesting mechanical feature; they were arranged vertically inline and required a specially shaped piston crown in order to obtain the compression ratio specification of 8.5:1. The 90-degree, valve-in-head V-8 was relatively compact (over 13 inches shorter than the straight eight it replaced) which made it possible to reduce the wheelbase of the Roadmaster this year. A modified Roadmaster frame (double-drop channel with a center X-member) cut down to a 114-inch wheelbase was underneath the Wildcat. The front suspension was an independent type with direct action shock absorbers. Other specifications given for the Wildcat were an overall height (top up) of 54.0 inches, overall length of 192.0 inches, overall width of 79.4 inches, and a ground clearance of 6.0 inches. For the first time Buick employed a 12-volt electrical system, which is what was installed on the Wildcat.

Black paint covered the body of the experimental car while it was on display at the Waldorf in January 1953; afterward, it appeared in white or a different car painted white was used for the Motorama tour. The total number built of the 1953 Wildcats is not clear, though it was at least two and perhaps as many as three.

Pleated bright green leather upholstery with white piping was used with both the black and the white exterior paint schemes. The double-roll dash design was somewhat like the one that appeared on the 1954 Buicks, though the steering wheel was from production stock (but with a special center medallion). The inside rearview mirror was mounted on the center top of the leather-covered dash. Finely grooved chrome inserts decorated the door panels.

The Wildcat I was predictive of Buick styling for the next several model years. Its combination bumper/grille and buffer bombs were similar to what appeared on the 1954 through 1957 models (though without the concave grille) and the sweep-spear would not only show

Green pleated leather with white piping covered the bench seat of the Wildcat. The rolled dash of the show car would appear in a similar form on the 1954 Buicks. Author collection

Production cars, including the limited-production Skylark, were shown on stage in a glamorous way at the 1953 GM Motorama. The Skylark, offered only as a convertible, featured a "chopped" windshield, a lower beltline, radiused wheel openings, and a deck lid with a faster slope. This photo was taken in Miami. Author collection

Dream Car collector Joe Bortz purchased the white 1953 Wildcat in the 1980s. The car required a full cosmetic restoration. Doug J. Mitchell

A pilot production Series 70 Roadmaster was used to build the Landau. *Steve Wolken collection*

The passenger portion of the Landau's interior was upholstered with tan leather and had the front and rear compartments separated by a glass partition. Note the cocktail set in the rear armrest. *Steve Wolken collection*

up on mid-1950s Buicks, but also on the full-sized 1967s. This feature would continue to be found on Buicks into the early 1970s. Furthermore, its modest fin design would be found on production Buicks the following year.

At least one of the 1953 Wildcats eventually left GM and became part of the collection of Dream Cars owned by Joe Bortz in the 1980s. Bortz found the car in Michigan in fair condition, having suffered only from time and neglect; usage certainly had no impact on its condition as it had traveled the grand sum of 50 miles. Today, it remains in pristine condition after its restoration (completed in 1988) and is sometimes shown at special events.

The Wildcat I was considered for production, according to *Motor Trend*. "Another one of the sports cars shown by GM this year is rumored to be ready for production on a limited scale. Chevrolet's Corvette will be first, but Buick's Wildcat is likely to be the next. Contracts for body engineering layout have been let to a Michigan supplier for a slightly modified version. Planned for 1954 introduction, the car will be powered by a 220-bhp Buick V-8. Steel will replace Fiberglas in the production version of the new two-seater."

Who actually considered the car for production is unclear. According to Homer LaGassey, who worked inside GM Design at the time, upper management was a little "scared" of the Wildcat because it was so different than production Buicks. Product identity was very important and the Wildcat was certainly a departure from the cars coming off the assembly line.

Buick celebrated its Golden Anniversary in part by putting into limited production what amounted to a custom-bodied convertible, dubbed Skylark. The new model was based on the Skylark prototype from the previous year to which the public response was considered sufficient enough to justify a production version. Charles Chayne had moved up to head General Motors engineering staff in 1951, but the team that had been under him at the

Buick Division, which included chief stylist Ned Nichols, was responsible for the design of the Skylark. The $5,000 price tag virtually guaranteed limited production of the special car; the Series 60 Special and all Series 62 Cadillacs were priced significantly less. Even so, there were 1,690 customers who preferred the Skylark over the less expensive Cadillac Series 62.

The body of the Skylark or Model 76X received a "chopped" windshield (though it was not a wraparound type as found on the Fiesta and Eldorado), a lower beltline, radiused wheel openings, and a deck lid with a faster slope. A "bombsight" hood ornament was recessed into the hood. Curiously, the traditional ventiports were deleted from the front fenders. The top of the front seat was lowered to align exactly with the beltline resulting in a car that appeared dramatically lower as compared to other 1953 Buick models, though in reality it was only about 3 inches lower. This lower look was sporty and Buick noted the Skylark's "sports car" qualities in advertising. Just as the Dream Cars were predictive of future styling characteristics, the Skylark was, too, since Buick's 1954 models would get radiused wheel openings and the sweep-spear trim. The 1953 Skylark's special body sat on a Roadmaster chassis with a wheelbase of 127 inches.

Enhancing the sporty look of the special model was a set of chrome-plated Kelsey-Hayes wire wheels. Its radiused wheel openings not only helped show off the glittering wheels, but

The unique Buick Landau featured a folding rear roof section reminiscent of luxury cars in the 1920s and 1930s. The rear of the car had a distinctive padded trunk with functional leather hold-down straps, again like cars of the classic era. *GM Media Archive*

also the wheelwells, which were painted a contrasting color. Sweeping over the wheel openings was a chrome "sweep-spear" unique to this model. Its shape helped to highlight the fenderline that flowed into the door and the hopped-up quarters.

Standard equipment for the Skylark, other than the wire wheels, included tinted glass, whitewall tires, two-tone leather upholstery, foot-controlled "Selectronic" radio, tinted glass, heater, power brakes, steering, seat, windows, antenna, and top (which was of synthetic Orlon) plus the 188-horsepower, 322 4-bbl. V-8 and Dynaflow transmission. Furthermore, the owner's signature was sealed into the Lucite steering wheel hub. With a price tag of $5,000, the special model was priced nearly $1,500 more than a Roadmaster convertible.

The 1953 model year left Buick in fourth place with a 7.9 percent market share. However, production increased by nearly 61 percent. Of the 488,755 Buicks built that year, well over half had the new V-8 engine

and eight out of ten were equipped with the Dynaflow transmission.

The second rendition of the Wildcat was much wilder than its predecessor. Just as the F-88 represented Oldsmobile's version of Chevy's Corvette, so did Buick's Wildcat II (Shop Order 1940). An objective of its design was to style the car completely free of any European influence; hence it was billed as an "American Adventure in Tomorrow's Design." The Wildcat II had little in common with the original Wildcat experimental, though it did have a panoramic windshield, as well as some similar styling in regard to the deck and rear quarters similar to that of the 1954 Skylark. Furthermore, it was a convertible with a top that retracted under a lid.

Regardless of the few similarities to other GM cars, the Wildcat II was the sportiest Buick built in the 1950s, period. Its design is credited to Buick's chief designer, Ned Nichols. The original specifications of the car were laid out in an experimental order submitted by the Technical Data Section of the Buick engineering department on May 19, 1953. Specifications were given as 100 inches for the wheelbase, a front tread of 59 inches, and a rear tread measurement of 57 inches. The seating arrangement was given as "similar to the 1953 Wildcat." That car had been fitted with a bench seat. Clearly this particular requirement got revised at some point. The general description also stated, "This is a special sport type car to be shown at the Waldorf show in January 1954."

The so-called "flying wing" front fenders resembling the appearance of a car of the 1930s, biplane bumpers reminiscent of a 1934 Cadillac, free-standing parking lamps, and chrome-spoke Skylark-type wheels gave a classic era look to the Wildcat II.

Bill Warner, founder of the Amelia Island Concours, performed a partial restoration on the well-preserved Buick Landau. It was shown at the 2005 Meadowbrook Concours. He has since sold the car. *Bill Warner*

This photo shows the Wildcat II in its original form with "Roto-Static" wheel covers similar to those of its predecessor. Skylark-type wire wheels replaced the originals. *GM Media Archive*

Interestingly, the wires were not fitted initially. Instead "Roto-Static" hubcaps like those of its predecessor were installed in front and smooth discs covered the rear wheels. The biplane bumpers were integrated with the wide oval grille surround and a set of Dagmar bumper guards sat over their intersection points. Chrome-plated front inner fender liners had vents to aid in engine compartment cooling. The open fenders left some suspension components exposed so these received chrome plating to add visual appeal. The hood and upper fenders were an integral unit that lifted conventionally from the front. To clear the sides and windshield wipers, the hood first moved slightly forward before swinging upward; the parking lamps lifted up with the hood. Ned Nichols' "ventiports" had become nearly traditional by 1954; these were located atop the Wildcat II's front fenders. Blending of 1930s speedster styling with the mid-1950s look certainly made for a unique Dream Car.

The Wildcat II's fiberglass body, painted Electric Blue, sat on a double-drop channel frame with a center "X" crossmember and box-type front crossmember. (Incidentally, Electric Blue would become a color offered on 1956 model Buicks.) Ground-to-cowl height measured only 35.3 inches, while overall height with the top up spanned a fraction of an inch more than 48 inches. Coil springs at all four points, direct acting shocks, and an 11/16-inch-diameter front stabilizer bar composed the suspension. The 322 V-8 that powered the car had four side-draft two-barrel carburetors to feed fuel and air to the cylinders. Its exhaust system was a dual type with a cross-over pipe, dynamic flow mufflers with 2-inch pipes going in and

The Electric Blue Wildcat II was powered by a 220-horsepower 322 V-8 equipped with four side-draft two-barrel carburetors. *GM Media Archive*

The Wildcat II and the Skylark made a spectacular pair at the GM Motorama. *GM Media Archive*

Here is a rare view of the Wildcat II with the top in the "up" position. *Steve Wolken collection*

1 ¾-inch pipes coming out. A twin-turbine Dynaflow transmitted the power to the 3.6:1 gearing and rear wheels.

The headlights of the Wildcat II are especially noteworthy; they swiveled (another tip of the hat to the 1930s) and were mounted similarly to spotlights through the lower windshield framing. This arrangement may not have actually been legal for production cars in some or any states.

In back, dual exhausts protruded directly from the body and in place of the bumper was a stylish version of nerfing bars. Left and right fuel filler caps were positioned directly beneath the taillights and were hidden behind the access doors within the wide chrome band that looped around the quarters.

The Wildcat's convertible top was electrically operated by a fully automatic system of pre-wound and prestretched aircraft cables, links, and gears. Pushing a single switch on the dash could activate the top mechanism. If the power windows were in the up position they automatically lowered with the raising or lowering of the top (not as a gimmick but rather because raised windows interfered with the path of the folding top).

The bucket seat interior was upholstered with white leather; the seats were shaped much like those of the Olds F-88, being rounded at the top of the backrest and recessed within the rear bulkhead. A radio speaker was also mounted between the seats on this bulkhead. The radio itself was a remotely controlled unit mounted in the trunk. Door panels received brushed aluminum and chrome trim. Carpeting for the Wildcat II matched the exterior color, as did the lower dash. The rolled dash appeared much like a production Buick's, but with additional gauges mounted in twin pods underneath and suspended on a pedestal atop the transmission tunnel. A short console between the bucket seats included additional instrumentation and the gear selector lever.

The Wildcat II did not lead to a production version and, in fact, there would be no two-seater Buicks until the Reatta of the 1980s. This magnificent show car was donated to the Alfred P. Sloan Museum in Flint, Michigan, in 1976 and can be seen there when it is not on tour. Sometime prior to its arrival at the museum that year, the Wildcat II was repainted in metallic tan and upholstered to match. It was recently restored to its original color scheme. Though doubtful, a second copy of the Wildcat II may have been built (see Chapter Eleven).

The Wildcat II was donated to the Alfred P. Sloan Museum in 1976. By that time it had been repainted in a rose-beige metallic and upholstered to match. It was recently restored to its original color scheme. *Rusty Thompson*

The interior of the Wildcat II looks like a cross between a Buick and a Corvette. *Rusty Thompson*

The Buick Skylark, like the Eldorado and Corvette, remained in production after the 1953 Motorama. This is a 1954 Skylark, which incorporates many of the styling cues seen on the one-year-only 1953 model. *Dennis Adler*

Some of the details of the actual Wildcat III differed from those seen on this clay model. *GM Media Archive*

Buick had another Dream Car entry in the 1954 Motorama—the four-door Landau (Shop Order 2308). This would be the only occasion Buick would field two Dream Cars for a Motorama. The dark blue (a Cadillac Series 75 color) Landau was based on the 127-inch wheelbase Series 70 Roadmaster that was built from a pilot production car assembled in Van Nuys, California. This model featured a folding rear roof section reminiscent of luxury cars in the 1920s and 1930s. The rear of the car had a distinctive padded trunk with functional leather hold-down straps, again like cars of the classic era. Material covering the trunk matched the tan fabric of the roof (with the forward fixed section being covered, as well).

The passenger portion of the interior was upholstered with tan leather, while the front section was upholstered in dark blue leather. The front and rear compartments were separated limousine style by a glass partition. A center armrest in the rear seat opened to reveal a bar with cocktail shaker and goblets. The Landau was also equipped with power windows and the spare tire was stored in a compartment accessed via a fold-down section of the rear bumper, in a manner similar to the Olds F-88 and other GM Motorama show cars.

After the show circuit ended, Buick kept the Landau and used it as an executive courtesy car in New York City. Its original turbine style wheel covers were stolen during this time. A log book was updated regularly which detailed the maintenance history and changes Buick made to the car over time. Harlow Curtice complained of the ride qualities of the car and Buick engineers made appropriate adjustments. Around 1959, a GM executive in Flint, Michigan, convinced GM to let him have use of the car, which they did with the proviso that it be returned to them. The executive believed that if he ever returned it, the Landau would be scrapped, so he kept it and later sold the car to a Clauson, Michigan resident. This owner kept the Buick for about a year and a half then sold it to American Motors engineer, Del DeRees. That was in 1965. DeRees sold it in 1982. Eventually the car became part of the Bortz Auto Collection for a while, but was sold to Bill Warner, who is the founder and chairman of the annual Amelia Island Concours d'Elegance. Between 2004 and 2006, the Landau was given a partial restoration and has been shown at Pebble Beach. A set of Skylark wire wheels replaced the long lost turbine wheel covers and steel wheels. The odometer

shows the Buick has logged only 26,000 miles. Warner sold the Landau to a collector in Texas during the spring of 2006.

Of the three "semi-custom" production cars from Cadillac, Buick, and Olds from 1953, only the Skylark emerged for 1954 without being almost completely changed from the original concept. The Eldorado was more like a Series 62 model, while the Fiesta was dropped entirely. This time, though, the Skylark was based on the revived Century, last offered in the abbreviated 1942 model year. Buick's Century combined the relatively light weight of the Buick Special body with the high-output engine of the senior Buicks. The Roadmaster grew larger and heavier for the 1954 model year, thus making the Century a more suitable platform for the sporty Skylark.

The heavily updated Skylark did not have the cut-down doors or windshield this time, but it did have quarters and deck styling unique to the car. It also had deeply scooped wheel openings to differentiate it from other Buicks; in some cases, the inner surfaces were painted a contrasting color. Furthermore, chrome-plated fins sat atop the special quarter panels. Like the rest of the Buick line, the Skylark had a wraparound windshield. A Roadmaster version of the V-8, Dynaflow, leather upholstery, power accessories, and the 40-spoke wire wheels remained part of the package. The Skylark and other models that year received an updated instrument panel patterned after that of the Wildcat I. The revisions included the "Redliner" speedometer, which was a red and black drum that turned up a red line across the panel instead of a needle as speed increased. At least two 1954 Skylarks were exhibited for the GM Motorama. One painted Lido Green (a color exclusive to this model), with a two-tone green interior,

occupied a turntable while another painted Condor Yellow, with a yellow and black interior, sat on the floor where people could see it close up. Only 836 Skylarks were built for 1954.

Also making appearances (in Miami at least) were a few Buicks with special features. One was a pearlescent green (lower body) and pearl white (top) Super Riviera, which featured gold-plated interior hardware and gold brocade tapestry upholstery accented with yellow pearlescent leather inserts. A Century sedan was specially painted in pearlescent yellow with a metallic green top. Its seats were covered in pearlescent yellow leather with green nylon inserts and the headliner was yellow leather. The instrument panel was in matching yellow with a dark green insert. Another Buick Century was painted in a stock two-tone combination—Titan Red with an Arctic

From this viewpoint, the Wildcat III almost appears to be a production Buick convertible. Steve Wolken collection

The dash of the Wildcat III received plenty of chrome housings for the instruments. Its steering wheel resembled that of the following year's Corvette. *GM Media Archive*

The interior almost looks like it was cast in one piece. As was often the case with Motorama Dream Cars, the Wildcat III had swiveling front bucket seats. Note the continuation of the ribbed pattern of the deck on the upper center section of the rear seat. *GM Media Archive*

White top, but inside it was reported to be an interior with dark green Swiss-dot nylon upholstery combined with light green metallic pleated bolsters! An error must have occurred in the *Miami Herald*'s paragraph describing the color combination of this car, or in the GM press release the *Herald*'s writer undoubtedly used as a reference. Perhaps these were two different cars—a red and white car with either a stock or special interior along with another car with the special green interior. If the article was correct, then there must have been a curious red, white, and green Buick available with a tremendous price discount after the show!

Thanks to new body designs the 1954 model year was a good one for Buick. During the year, Buick became the first automaker to build 500,000 hardtops.

For 1955 another incarnation of the Wildcat—this time as a four-passenger car—made its debut. The fiberglass Wildcat III (XP-35, Shop Order 2252) was described by Buick's general manager, Ivan Wiles, as "definitely a man's car . . . its bold, clean lines and its high-powered engine, suggests that this car was designed strictly for a man." That pitch line probably wouldn't fly today! Homer LaGassey was in charge of the Wildcat III's design; he had moved up from the Pontiac studio after his involvement with the Strato-Streak. The Wildcat III was more conservative than the Wildcat II, yet still very flashy in its monotone red color scheme. The official name for its paint was Kimberly Red; this label was chosen to honor race car driver and SCCA member Jim Kimberly who was well known at the time.

The frontal design was clearly that of a Buick, but close inspection by an onlooker would reveal some no production characteristics such as the roll pan with paired air

ducts for brake cooling on each side underneath the front bumper. The experimental car's hood was also recessed beneath the cowl to provide an improved air intake for the passenger compartment. The hood was sloped toward the front, which provided improved visibility immediately ahead of the car. The fine-screen grille was wide and low, the parking/directional lights mounted in the bumper "bombs," and conventional headlamps were embossed with the Buick emblem. Intakes near the front bumpers provided cooling air for the brakes.

The Wildcat III's profile appeared somewhat similar to that of production Buicks of that year, thanks largely to its sweep-spear molding, though it was clearly lower (only 51.75 inches high) than any production model built by the division. The beltline gently dipped, then kicked up just behind the door. When seen in profile, the cowl could clearly be seen sloping upward and merging into the dramatically raked-back wraparound windshield. As the cowl followed the base of the windshield's contour it met the upper forward edge of each door, where the line continued almost the entire length of the doors. Unlike many of the Motorama Dream Cars, this one did not have pushbutton outside door releases, but instead had a pull-out type. A cooling slot on each side for the rear brakes sat angled just above the dip in the sweep-spear molding.

Rather than having a small lid to cover the retracted convertible top as had the preceding Wildcats, the entire trunk lid opened from the front so that the red convertible top could be stored underneath when lowered. The deck lid also incorporated the top of the quarter panels, thus improving access to the trunk. At first glance, the gap that had been created by integrating the upper quarters with the deck lid made the car appear to be a four door. In reality, the Wildcat III probably never actually had a top installed—at least not during the Motorama tour. The seats were not adjustable, so there was no way to get the headroom needed with the top up, according to LaGassey. He said Harley Earl (who stood 6 feet, 4 inches) " . . . once sat in the car and his head and shoulders were positioned above the top of the windshield. We all laughed," though he quickly added, "but not for long!" Incidentally, the central section of the deck lid shared one feature with the original Wildcat— a ribbed section running the entire length of the lid from its leading edge all the way to the top of the license plate mounting.

Exhausts exited through rectangular outlets in the rear roll panel. There was no bumper except for a Dagmar-like cap at the bottom end of each quarter panel. Back-up lamps were housed in round openings above the exhausts outlets.

This is one of Chuck Jordan's original sketches of the Centurion. *Chuck Jordan collection*

The Sovereign Red interior had bucket seats in front and a bucket-styled bench seat in back, all covered in leather and trimmed in chrome. A padded vinyl covering, with a fine checkerboard pattern, was used in place of typical carpeting. The selector lever for the Dynaflow transmission was positioned between the front seats on the flattened transmission tunnel. Adding another sporty touch was a new steering wheel design similar to what Chevrolet would use on the all-new 1956 Corvette. A full array of instrumentation was mounted on an otherwise generally stock-looking dash.

A Buick 322 V-8 modified with four, two-barrel carburetors and special intake was said to power the Wildcat III; horsepower was claimed to be 280, which was a 44-horsepower increase over the stock engine with its single, four-barrel carb. Ironically, this high-performance 322 was in a car that apparently did not run. A photo of it, which appeared in a book by GM Styling staff, *Styling—The Look of Things*, shows it being pushed onto its turntable during preparations for a Motorama. Underneath all the glitz and glamour of the Wildcat III was a 110-inch wheelbase chassis.

While the Centurion was and still is a spectacular sight, it is especially so from above. *Steve Wolken collection*

The third edition of the experimental Wildcat series did not lead to a production version. This name, however, was picked up for 1962 when Buick first offered a sporty, Invicta-based, two-door hardtop with bucket seats and a console.

The Wildcat III of 1955 was shown at least into 1956. GM officially lists it as scrapped. This car may have been destroyed in the late 1950s at a Detroit area wrecking yard, which had a car crusher—a device relatively new at the time. According to Eldorado Brougham enthusiast and Michigan resident, Larry Muckey, he became acquainted with the owner of the first Detroit area salvage yard to get a car crusher.

Muckey remembers a story he heard from the salvage yard owner. Allegedly, GM officials wanted first-hand knowledge of how effectively the new car crusher did its job. As a test, a "Motorama Buick" was hauled to this salvage yard, placed in the crusher and destroyed. The yard owner was not happy about crushing the car. The process of elimination strongly suggests a Wildcat I or Wildcat III must have been the car destroyed in the crusher. A slightly different version of the fate of the Wildcat III, according to Don Keefe, author and former editor of *Pontiac Enthusiast*, said that GM bought a car crusher and first used it to crush the Wildcat III. Based upon the two stories from separate sources, most likely the Wildcat III met its end in this iniquitous fashion.

For 1956, Buick offered the XP-301 (Shop Order 2489), formally named Centurion, to rouse the spirit of Motorama attendees. This two-door, four-passenger hardtop was built of fiberglass and painted "Electron Red" on the upper portion of the body and bright white on the lower body (though a couple of early press releases

This view, possibly taken in San Francisco, shows the Centurion next to the Impala. *GM Media Archive*

about the car incorrectly gave the lower body color; one said it was bright silver and the other stated it had a "brushed metallic finish"). The two finishes were separated with a Roadmaster style sweep-spear. This sweep-spear and fully exposed wheels were the only outward features showing any resemblance to a production Buick. The Dream Car stood 53.7 inches high, stretched 213.1 inches from stem to stern, and had a width of 73.5 inches; its wheelbase measured 118 inches. A Buick 322 V-8 rated at 325 horsepower and coupled to a variable pitch Dynaflow transmission was said to power the Centurion. The engine, which glistened with chrome-plated hardware, was upgraded with four, two-barrel side-draft carburetors, and other modifications may have been made, too.

The recessed grille and hood of the Centurion were built as an integral unit and hinged in front, so as to lift from the rear. The headlights were deeply recessed

REFLECTION—Headlight well of Centurion, on display at GM Motorama, is used as mirror by Betty Bridges, one of New York models traveling with show.

This photo appeared in a Los Angeles newspaper. A model was using the Centurion as a vanity mirror—a feature its designers probably had not recognized! *Author collection*

The 1956 Buick Centurion was spared the destruct order. It can be viewed at the Alfred P. Sloan Museum when it's not at a special event. *Rusty Thompson*

within the ends of the fenders and were surrounded with turbine-style housings. Fresh air scoops for the air conditioner were located atop the front fenders and the wheel discs incorporated air scoops for cooling the finned brake drums. Styling of the rear of the Centurion was especially interesting. Stop and back-up lights were grouped behind a chrome-plated "Dagmar" at the end of the tail cone. Parking and directional lights were integrated on each side and mounted just above the exhaust outlets. A license plate mount was also installed to the left of the tail cone. The remainder of the rear deck area resembled that which appeared on the full-sized 1959 Chevrolets and Buicks. The Centurion's roof panel was transparent and combined with the wraparound windshield and backlight; only the essential framing interrupted a full panoramic view of the world from inside.

Just as spectacular as the exterior was the Centurion's interior design. Four bright red leather-covered bucket seats—each with seatbelts—were topped with adjustable

headrests. To ease entry/exit to the back seats, the front seat automatically moved forward when the upright portion was pushed forward, thus activating an electrical switch. Entry to and exit from the front seats was aided with the opening of the door, which activated another electrical switch that moved these seats back on their rails. There was no rearview mirror inside or outside; eliminating them provided a cleaner look. In their place was a patented, functional, rear-mounted TV camera with a wide-angle lens that transmitted the rear view to a 4x6-inch view screen on the instrument panel; the view was clearly visible even at night. The camera, weighing just six pounds, was made by University Broadcasting System, Inc. and mounted just above the tail cone. It was designed to be shock resistant, so that bumps in the road would not interfere with transmitting a clear image to the view screen. The conventional steering column was eliminated, too. Instead the aircraft-type steering wheel was connected to a cantilever arm attached at the centerline of the car. (Today, a conventional steering column is in place, though the cantilever arm still remains. When, as well as why, the column was added is unclear.) Other advanced gadgetry of the Centurion included a digital clock and a freestanding speedometer with a stationary indicator and revolving dial.

Chuck Jordan (later to become vice president of design at GM) was placed in charge of the XP-301 project. He explained that seeing Harley Earl's LeSabre really explained what was expected from the designers and that being in the work environment established at GM Styling allowed the freedom to be imaginative. Earl frequently walked through the studio to view

The wing-like rear deck styling appeared on the 1959 Buicks and Chevrolets. A functional rear-facing TV camera replaced the rearview mirror. *Rusty Thompson*

The engine compartment is dressed up with chrome-plated items and what was reported to be a 325-horsepower version of the 322 V-8. *Rusty Thompson*

The Electron Red interior is striking even today. *Rusty Thompson*

Bucket seats with headrests and retractable seatbelts were in back as well as the front. *Rusty Thompson*

the work of the stylists, made suggestions, and indicated his approval or disapproval of the various ideas presented. Jordan explained that these Dream Cars were meant to put forward new ideas and in the case of the Centurion he and his team decided fairly quickly that the cantilever steering arm and rear-facing camera would be part of the package. As he said, they "wanted an interior that went with the exterior." As for the experimental car's formal name, Jordan did not know who was responsible for it; that was done after his work on the project was completed. He did note that the most probable reason the name was chosen was because of its similarity with the name of Buick's highly popular performance model called Century. The Centurion nameplate would resurface at Buick for the 1971 model year when it replaced the Wildcat series.

The 1956 Centurion has been preserved and was displayed at the Petersen Automotive Museum in Los Angeles during Buick's 100th Anniversary Heritage Tour. It can be seen at the Alfred P. Sloan Museum in Flint, Michigan, when it is not on tour.

Also in 1956, Buick dressed up a 1956 Roadmaster convertible with a nonproduction paint scheme and posed it tilted sideways behind a railing and a wall with an arch opening cut into it to give a jewel box effect. The car was said to be pearlescent peach and cream in one reference and two-toned blue in another. Two mannequins stood, one at each end of the car, wearing evening gowns and a reported $2 million worth of jewelry. The mannequin to the right of the car was wearing the "Hope Diamond" valued then at $1 million alone. Two armed guards and additional law enforcement personnel in civilian attire were constantly stationed nearby.

Chapter Six
Motorama Cars of Cadillac

One of Cadillac's design proposals for the 1953 Motorama was a Dream Car called the Orleans (Shop Order 1619), a pillarless four-door hardtop with "suicide" rear doors. The gun-metal gray (called Damascus Steel Gray in an official press release) Cadillac also had a champagne RM-grain Naugahyde-covered top. The Orleans looked essentially like a six-passenger production car and, in fact, was the first production 1953 Cadillac built (which incidentally used a 1952 Coupe de Ville body shell). Its engine number was 5362 00001.

The car was sent to GM Styling for numerous modifications such as the installation of a "Panoramic" windshield and its suicide doors. Locks for the rear doors were designed

Trunk straps and the panel for the hide-a-way convertible top dominate this bird's-eye view of the Le Mans. *GM Heritage Center*

to release only when the Hydra-matic shift lever was in neutral. To make the body rigid, the rear of the front seat served as a structural brace. Another unusual feature of the Orleans was the inclusion of a standard household electrical outlet! A converter changed the generator's DC into AC to permit the operation of radios and other electrical appliances. Perhaps this was done as a reminder to the public that GM owned Frigidaire, which built household appliances. Other accessories installed included power windows and air conditioning. A compartment in the back of the front seat even contained an electric shaver and a vanity case.

The gray and champagne interior adornments of the Orleans were especially appealing. Its seat cushions and backrest inserts were champagne-colored nylon surrounded with gray leather. The headliner was champagne, perforated Naugahyde decorated with chrome-plated roof bows and scalp moldings contrasted by gun-metal-gray roof rail moldings. The upper door panels were covered in gray leather while the lower portion of each was gun-metal gray. Carpeting was gray and champagne Craftex fiber with gray leather binding.

A copy of the original build sheet in the files of GM's Heritage Center says nothing about engine modifications; therefore, it was most likely a completely stock 331 V-8.

The Orleans had great appeal to those who bought Cadillacs, preferred hardtops, but wanted four doors. Reportedly, Harley Earl got the idea for the four-door hardtop with no center pillar during a visit to Italy, where he saw a production Lancia sedan built in this fashion. Cadillac placed

The true color of the Le Mans is revealed in this photo taken at the 1953 Chicago Auto Show. Upholstery matched the car's metallic blue body color. This Le Mans could be any one of the original three show cars. The second and third show cars later received unique color schemes. *Author collection*

a four-door hardtop into production for 1956 called Sedan de Ville, sans the suicide doors, and with a short B-pillar. The exclusive Eldorado Brougham with suicide doors and no B-pillar went into limited production for 1957, becoming the most expensive American car for sale at that time. Buick offered a four-door hardtop beginning in 1955, ahead of Cadillac's Sedan de Ville, and Chevrolet brought their version for the 1956 model year.

The Orleans was not the only entry Cadillac had to show off at the 1953 Motorama. The "Standard of the World" Division also displayed an uncharacteristically sporty Metallic Blue (silver-blue) Cadillac, dubbed Le Mans (Shop Order 1709), after the 24-hour race held near Paris, France, in which the two Cadillac entries finished 10th and 11th in 1950. To emphasize the connection between the

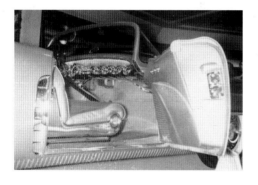

This photo taken by the author's father, Bill Temple, at the GM Motorama in San Francisco shows the instrument panel of the Le Mans; it had a matching series of chrome-housed dials extending the width of the passenger compartment. The cap on the side of the seat cushion covers a storage space for an umbrella. *Author collection*

This view from the Kansas City Motorama in June 1953 shows the Le Mans (background near center), an early production Eldorado on the "cloverleaf" (right), and a pair of Cadillacs with nonproduction paint and trim (at left and just behind the Eldorado). The latter two cars are wearing a vinyl top; a vinyl top was not a regular production item until 1956, when it became standard equipment on the Eldorado Seville. *H. B. Stubbs Co.*

Dream Car and its namesake, the Le Mans was displayed against a large painting depicting a scene from the *Vingt-Quatre Heures du Mans* road race. This Dream Car was powered by a modified 331 V-8 said to produce 250 horsepower (or 40 more than a stock version) at 4,500 rpm. Some upgrades contributing to the boost in power were dual four-barrel carburetors and a high-lift camshaft. Up front, Cadillac styling touches included hooded headlights and Dagmar bumper guards. The grille and parking light arrangement was predictive of the look scheduled for the 1954 model year. The Le Mans also had the wraparound windshield (which was offered only on the Eldorado at the time) and, of course, it received the obligatory tail fins resembling those of production Cadillacs. Its fiberglass body sat on a modified Cadillac frame on a shortened wheelbase measuring 115 inches.

A Le Mans (possibly the fourth one) was test-driven at the GM Proving Grounds by Detroit area newsmen according to the October 1953 issue of *Motor Trend*. "Floorboarding the engine with the reworked Hydra-matic unit immediately sends the tach over past 4,000 and the car gets 0–60 in slightly under 9 seconds, drops into fourth at about 87 miles per hour. This performance is the more surprising since the car weighs only 400 pounds less than a standard Cadillac convertible. Though the steering ratio is standard, the shortened wheelbase of 115 inches makes the steering moderately sensitive and the low center of gravity contributes to good roadholding." They also noted the car was "definitely too heavy and spongy for competition," and added that though the experimental car would not go into production, the 1954 Eldorado would "look much like the Le Mans but with a rear seat."

Although the Le Mans was not a sports car, Cadillac highlighted its sporty attributes and other features in an official press release. " . . . the Le Mans represents an ideal of motor car enthusiasts—combining elegance with power. . . . This three-passenger sports convertible has speed, power and roadability. . . . A view of the interior from the driver's seat provides a thrilling taste of sports car emphasis in a setting of sheer luxury."

The interior featured a hidden glove box underneath the passenger-side dash, which could be dropped down and pulled out for access. The silver-blue leather upholstery was embossed with the Cadillac "V" and crest, and the hood emblem was hand-engraved by a jeweler. An electrically adjustable seat was of the new "memory" type and when the door was opened, it automatically moved back; when the door was closed, the seat moved back to its previous position.

The silver-blue Orlon top was operated either with a switch or it could automatically raise itself when moisture hit a rain sensor (just like in the LeSabre). An umbrella was stored inside a tube within the forward edge of the seat bolster; this tube had a chrome cap with the Le Mans insignia. Removing the cap released a spring to eject the umbrella!

The Le Mans may well have been inspired by a one-off Cadillac that Harley Earl had built for a friend and co-worker named Harold R. Boyer. During the Korean War, Boyer was the plant manager of Cadillac Motor Car Division's Cleveland tank plant.

One day while Boyer was assigned to managing Cadillac's Cleveland Tank Plant, he had a conversation with Earl regarding automobiles. Boyer mentioned his Dream Car would be part Cadillac and part sports car. Evidently, Harley Earl became intrigued with the idea of a Cadillac sports car and began designing one with Boyer's input. A regular production Series 62 convertible was sent to GM Styling for conversion into a three-passenger Cadillac sports car. Overall length was reduced 10 inches, and

overall height was dropped another 6 to achieve the sports car look. The car's power top retracted into a well, which was covered with a hinged lid, just as on Earl's first two Dream Cars, the Y-Job and the LeSabre. The instrument panel was modified to include manifold and oil temperature gauges, as well as a tachometer and an aircraft-type clock.

The *Cleveland Plain Dealer* stated the car was equipped with a 230-horsepower, dual-carb engine, and was capable of 130 miles per hour. According to the newspaper, GM was "so impressed by the vehicle" that they were considering placing it into production. Perhaps the Le Mans actually tested the market for such a car. According to *Motor Trend*, dealers at the time were sampled on the sales potential of the Le Mans. This sampling revealed there was a market for about 5,000 of these cars, but ultimately only four were built. The first three were built as show cars and the fourth, assembled later in 1953, was for Jack Goodman, the president of Fisher Body.

Whether or not the Le Mans show car was built to test the market for such a design, it did reveal the public's approval of the styling to be seen on the production 1954 Cadillac lineup. The 1954 Cadillacs—the first new ones since 1950—sold well despite a 25-day halt in

This one-off 1952 Cadillac custom convertible (6237 DX) built for Harold Boyer, a friend of Harley Earl's and manager of Cadillac's tank plant in Cleveland, may have been the inspiration for the Le Mans. A regular production Series 62 convertible was sent to GM Styling for conversion into this three-passenger Cadillac sports car. Overall length was reduced 10 inches, and overall height was dropped another 6 to achieve the sports car look. The car's power top retracted into a well, which was covered with a hinged lid, just as on Earl's first two Dream Cars, the Y-Job and the LeSabre. *Dennis Adler*

The instrument panel was modified to include manifold and oil temperature gauges, as well as a tachometer and an aircraft-type clock. *Dennis Adler*

The Le Mans used for the GM Motorama tour—body number one, serial number 5300 00002—was customized in late 1954 by George Barris for his customer, Harry Karl, who owned a chain of shoe stores. Unfortunately, this car was destroyed in a fire in 1985. *Author collection*

production to change over to new production specifications. Though the Le Mans grabbed the attention of many during the Motorama tour, Harley Earl observed that those who would actually "back up their approval with a check" showed a preference for the Orleans.

Le Mans number one, the GM Motorama show car, is the car that went to shoe store mogul Harry Karl. Paperwork in the GM Heritage Center archives says that Le Mans number one was shipped to the Los Angeles Branch for the account of Clarence Dixon Cadillac, Inc. in Hollywood, California on July 7, 1954. The paperwork noted, "For H. Earl" though whether or not this car had its title actually transferred to Harley Earl is not known. Probably, the car was sold to the owner of Clarence Dixon Cadillac and then Harry Karl bought it, or perhaps it was transferred to Karl via the dealership. Either way it became his sometime in the latter half of 1954.

Karl had customizer George Barris do a restyle of the car before giving it to his wife, actress Marie McDonald, sometime in 1954

or early 1955. The lower fender panels were altered with custom-formed, blue-white chrome-plated steel. The trim between the lower chromed panels and the fiberglass body was ½-inch steel bar plated with 24-karat gold. Thirty coats of "platinum dust" sprayed over a polychromatic base sealer were applied to the body. A multi-piece custom top was formed in plexiglass and framed with chrome-plated steel; it could be lifted off entirely or the forward portion removed and the rear section (which was composed of the rear window with a chrome tiara) left in place. The quarter panels got stainless-steel fins and a continental kit was integrated into the deck lid. The 30-spoke wheel covers were plated in gold and chrome with the spokes receiving the gold plating.

The interior was reupholstered in red leather and had a number of gadgets installed. These included a television, tape recorder, radio-telephone, and a cocktail bar in the rear windowsill, which had a red leather cover to keep it out of sight. A current inverter was fitted to convert the 12-volt electrical system to the proper voltage to operate the TV and other devices.

The engine was repainted metallic green and dressed up with chrome-plated accessories, though some, if not all of these, were probably on the car when first built. It was reported to provide 300 horsepower—50 more than the figure quoted for the engine during the GM Motorama and 30 more than the official rating of a stock 1955 Eldorado engine. What, if any, modifications were done to obtain another 50 horsepower is not known. Perhaps the report of 300 horsepower was erroneous.

The customized Dream Car was pictured on the cover of the December 1955 issue of *Motor Trend*. Eventually, the Barris-built Le Mans changed ownership and made its way to Centerville, Ohio. The Le Mans was seen traveling the streets of nearby Dayton from time to time by Cadillac-LaSalle Club (CLC) member Bernie De Winter IV, during the 1964–1965 timeframe. Its owner at that time is rumored to have "squandered his fortune" and was later sued by a business partner; the partner won the suit, and as a result, the car changed ownership around mid-1984. De Winter recalled the Le Mans as being painted metallic green (but with parts of the body being in primer) and having a green interior. The once great show car was in somewhat deteriorated condition and many of the Barris add-ons had been removed. It then seemingly disappeared until it was offered for sale in late 1984. As it happened, the car had been placed in storage in 1966 and partially dismantled. Fred Miller acted as an agent for the owner of the Le Mans. Miller, who still lives in Ohio, recalled many details about the car. He stated that a classic car dealer bought the Le Mans in California and brought it to Ohio. It was eventually purchased by a son from a wealthy family.

Another Ohio resident and CLC member, Wayne Turner, spotted an ad placed in *Hemmings Motor News* and responded, as did many others. Turner made an appointment to view the car in Centerville, but it was sold (still in partially dismantled condition) to California resident John Crowell. Turner never got to see the car and Crowell had little time to enjoy his new acquisition. The car was destroyed in a fire, along with five other exotic cars, during the early morning hours of May 14, 1985—nearly 32 years after its last Motorama appearance. It had been driven a mere 7,945 miles.

Only the engine, wheel covers, and other miscellaneous parts still exist. Crowell's insurance company settled with him and took possession of the remains. Surprisingly, Crowell still has the bill of sale, which clearly identifies the car with its serial number (5300 00002) proving it was the first Le Mans. (Throughout the years, both Miller and Crowell had believed the serial number meant the car was number two of four until their respective telephone interviews for this book.) California resident Bill Pozzi bought remains of the Le Mans in 1991; some of the customizing pieces were included. According to him, the metallic green engine block is stamped "5300 00002X."

Beyond the LeMans, Cadillac also presented its new Eldorado at the 1953 Motorama. This car was part of the production "Dream Car trio" that included the Buick Skylark and Oldsmobile Fiesta. Oddly enough, the fourth Dream Car, the

The first production Eldorado, painted Artisan Ochre (pale yellow, as shown on this early production model) was seen at the Waldorf show in January, while the fifth and sixth production Eldorados, both painted Azure Blue (as well as possibly the fourth, painted Alpine White), were used as Motorama display cars, too. An early production Eldorado was also used as the Inaugural Parade Car for President-elect Dwight D. Eisenhower in 1953. *Dennis Adler*

Here is how the gun-metal gray Orleans appeared inside the Waldorf-Astoria for the opening of the GM Motorama tour. *GM Media Archive*

The nearly pillarless four-door hardtop Orleans was a forerunner of the limited-production Eldorado Brougham first offered in 1957. Spots are the result of water damage to the negative. *GM Media Archive*

This photo offers a rare look at the interior of the Orleans. Note the sliding-handle door release. *GM Media Archive*

Chevrolet Corvette, was not regarded as part of the Dream Car group as it was the only sports car.

The first production Eldorado, painted Artisan Ochre (pale yellow) was seen at the Waldorf show in January, while the fifth and sixth production Eldorados, both painted Azure Blue (as well as possibly the fourth, painted Alpine White), were used as Motorama display cars, too. An Eldorado was also used as the Inaugural Parade Car for President-elect Dwight D. Eisenhower in 1953.

The virtually hand-built model featured wraparound windshield, deep downward curves along the top of the doors to create a beltline dip, chrome-plated wire wheels, padded dash, special leather upholstery, white or black Orlon convertible top that, when down, was completely concealed with a metal boot, and under the hood a 210-horsepower V-8 (which was the same engine that powered the other Cadillacs for 1953). Only the front fenders, quarter panels, deck lid, and floorpan were shared with the other Cadillacs in the lineup; even the dashboard was different so as to fit the dogleg created as a result of the wraparound windshield. The windshield did not interchange with the Olds Fiesta, thus making it another unique component of the Eldorado. The special-bodied cars were lower than the regular Series 62 convertible; road clearance and overall height was 1 inch and 3 inches less, respectively. Extensive use of lead was required in building these cars and no two were exactly alike.

Additional standard equipment for the limited-production Eldorado included power windows and seat, power steering, heater, wide whitewall tires, fog lights, signal-seeking pre-selector radio, windshield washer, oil filter, license plate frame, and outside rearview mirror. Two factory-installed options were offered—E-Z-Eye tinted glass, and "Autronic Eye" automatic headlight dimmer. A power brake installation kit became available for the 1953 Eldorado the following model year. List price for the 1953 Eldorado is often quoted at $7,750.

At least three specially painted and trimmed Cadillacs were displayed during the Motorama tour in 1953. One was shown at the Waldorf-Astoria if not elsewhere; this one was a Coupe de Ville painted orange with a white Naugahyde-covered top. Another Coupe de Ville of an unknown color combination also was given a Naugahyde-covered top. (A vinyl top was not a factory option for Cadillacs until 1963, though it was standard equipment for the 1956–1960 Eldorado Sevilles and the 1960 Fleetwood.) A Fleetwood Sixty Special with a dark blue paint color and a matching Naugahyde top was exhibited, as well, during the 1953 tour.

Cadillac fielded even more attention getters for the 1954 shows. These were the Park Avenue (Shop Order 1930), La Espada (Shop Order 1928), and the El Camino (Shop Order 1929). All three were built of fiberglass, but the Park Avenue was a four-passenger luxury car, while the other two were akin to the previous year's Le Mans. The Park Avenue was described in this way by a GM press release: "Seizing the imagination of even the most conservative, Cadillac presents the fiberglass body Park Avenue four-door sedan at the General Motors Motorama for 1954. . . . Enhanced by a dark

The El Camino made its debut at the Waldorf-Astoria. *GM Heritage Center*

Antoinette Blue exterior trimmed with bright chrome, the Park Avenue is topped with a hand-brushed aluminum roof. Having an exciting quality of beauty gained from a restrained yet dynamically futuristic styling, this sedan is 230.1 inches over-all in length, 58.3 inches in over-all height and 80 inches in over-all width." The body sat on a stock Series Sixty Special frame.

The press release further stated, "Below the rear deck lid is a special compartment housing the spare tire, removed by lowering a bright chrome-trimmed door.

Much of the exterior styling of the El Camino (as well as its near-twin La Espada) —quad headlights, gullwing bumpers, wheels, etc.—was carried forward in the design of the production 1955 and 1956 Cadillacs. This glamour photo of the La Espada was taken in Miami. *Author collection*

The El Camino (Spanish for "the royal highway") was painted in a distinctive pearlescent silver-gray color and the bubble-type aircraft canopy–styled roof was of brushed aluminum coated with clear lacquer. *Author collection*

The interior of the El Camino was virtually the same as that of the La Espada. The El Camino, however, had a gray interior. Note the chrome-plated steering column. *Keven McConnell*

A structural part of the car, this door also serves as a bumperette and a license-plate mounting. Adding weight and balance to the rear fenders are twin exhaust ports trailing from their lower end in massive bright chromed steel housings.

"Aluminum alloy turbine blade, whitewall-tired wheels complete the exterior design.

"Single-tone gray leathers, including imported English calf with an unusual grain and suede-like nap texture are employed on the interior together with brushed and bright chrome trim. Seat inserts use the imported English calf, which is grained and napped by a special hot stamp process. . . ."

Some of the styling of the Park Avenue was clearly derived from another experimental car; the tail fins, quarters, and taillights looked very much like those of the LeSabre. The Park Avenue was one of three prototypes that would lead to the limited production 1957–1958 Eldorado Brougham. Incidentally, the name Park Avenue would be applied to a short-deck version Cadillac four-door hardtop in 1962 and 1963, and then later was adopted by Buick as a model name in the mid-1970s.

Cadillac's two other Dream Cars, the La Espada and the El Camino, were a convertible and a closed coupe, respectively. These fiberglass-bodied Dream Cars were virtually identical otherwise. Both were two-seaters, had a wheelbase measuring 115 inches, an overall length of 200.6 inches, and both were said to be powered by a 1954 Cadillac 230-horsepower, 331 V-8. Like the Park Avenue, these sporty Cadillacs had a compartment housing the spare tire concealed by a chrome-trimmed door and had aluminum-alloy turbine-blade wheels. Much of these cars' exterior styling—quad headlights, gullwing bumpers, wheels, etc.—was carried forward in the design of the production 1955 and

1956 Cadillacs. The quad headlights would take a little longer to adopt, as state laws had to be changed to make the setup legal in all states.

The interior of the La Espada was well equipped. Instrumentation: fuel, temperature, oil, and ammeter gauges, as well as a clock, were "scientifically engineered for perfect visual control," according to a press release. These circular shaped instruments were separated with a pair of inverted "V" right and left turn indicator lights, as well as a small circular generator light in the center above the Hydra-matic gear indicator, which was electrically operated. The actual gear selector was an aircraft-style joystick mounted on a machine-ground, stainless-steel-trimmed tunnel running through the centerline of the interior. This tunnel console also included air conditioning/heater controls and outlets, radio controls, cigarette lighter, armrest, and glove box. The air conditioner and heater system were operated through spectrum-lighted rheostatic controls—a first for automotive use, according to a press release. With this system, warmer temperatures were denoted with shades of red while cooler settings were in shades of blue. The side surfaces of the tunnel and glove box door were covered in black leather, while the steering column was chrome plated. A tachometer was mounted on the right of the column and speedometer on the left along with two toggle switches to control the interior and road lights. The dash was covered in padded black leather with the passenger side having a padded assist grip to ease entry into the low, sleek car. An automatic headlight dimmer dubbed "Autronic Eye" was mounted just below the top center of the panoramic windshield. A convertible top with ribbed elements, which allowed the top fabric to form a perfectly curved surface when raised, was stored under a hinged lid when not in use.

This view inside the Waldorf-Astoria shows the Apollo Gold La Espada with two other Cadillacs, one of which is a Series 62 Coupe de Ville with the Eldorado-type wire wheels. *GM Media Archive*

The aircraft-inspired cockpit of the La Espada was two-toned. *GM Heritage Center*

Both the La Espada and El Camino had a double-humped rear deck just behind the driver and passenger positions that flared into the bucket seats. *GM Heritage Center*

The La Espada is often stated to have been finished in Apollo Gold (metallic gold-tinted light cream). It was seen painted this color for at least the first two Motorama shows (New York City and Miami). It was also Apollo Gold when seen at the Chicago Auto Show in March of that year. Assuming only one was built (there is little to suggest differently), the show car was later repainted "Sword Silver." Its Spanish name translates into "the sword" hence the name of the paint color. As originally shown, the twin seats had black bolsters with "Apollo Gold" hot-stamped inserts. When seen in the Sword Silver paint color, the seats were solid black with hot-stamped Sword Silver inserts.

The only hint of the possibility that two cars were built is that the dates for the GM Motorama in Los Angeles (March 6–14) and those for the Chicago Auto Show (March 13–21) overlap by one day. Obviously, one car could not have been in two places at the same time. An absolute certainty is that a show car would not have been taken out of one location early to be sent to another; that is confirmed by Bruce Berghoff who worked for H. B. Stubbs Company and was involved in the 1956, 1959, and 1961 Motoramas (and is the author of the 1995 book, The *GM Motorama*).

Berghoff said the La Espada could have been sent to the Chicago Auto Show immediately *after* the Motorama in LA to join it already in progress. He brought cars into the International Amphitheatre for the annual Chicago Auto Show days after it began. Probably, only one La Espada was built and was simply given a fresh look for the GM Motorama in Chicago.

The El Camino (Spanish for "the royal highway") was painted in a distinctive pearlescent silver-gray color and the bubble-type aircraft canopy–styled roof was of brushed aluminum coated with clear lacquer. The windshield was a tinted panoramic type. The interior was upholstered in gray leather including the seats, door panels, and upper instrument panel. An insert behind the instrument dials was brushed aluminum. This medium was used in abundance elsewhere in the interior just as it was on the La Espada. Designer Dave Holls was assigned to the El Camino project under the direction of Ed Glowacke.

This photo taken in Miami shows the La Espada sitting a bit higher than when parked on its display base. It probably still had its spacers installed in the springs to prevent the car from being damaged in transit as a result of bouncing inside its transport trailer. *GM Media Archive*

Both the La Espada and El Camino had a double-humped rear deck just behind the driver and passenger positions that flared into the bucket seats. Both cars also featured a prominent insignia on each quarter panel. The left one actually served as the fuel filler door. This red, white, and blue insignia was the same as GM's Air Transport Division and served to underscore the aircraft-inspired styling of these two Dream Cars. The La Espada and El Camino also had a ribbed aluminum panel on each side; these panels were slotted to admit air to the air conditioning system. Door panel inserts on these cars were fluted aluminum. As explained in the aforementioned press release, the front of each featured "a recessed cellular grille guarded by massive sweeping front bumpers with resilient white vinyl to cushion shocks and prevent scuffing of the chrome."

The El Camino was shown in the United States and Canada into 1956 and perhaps longer. Reportedly, this masterpiece of the 1954 GM Motorama was destroyed. The name lived on when Chevrolet applied it to its car-based truck.

These two sporty Cadillacs drew a lot of attention, but just as was the case with the Le Mans, people who were serious about buying a Cadillac were more interested in owning a car similar to the Park Avenue.

Here is the La Espada as it appeared at the GM Motorama in Chicago during April 1954. By then it had been repainted "Sword Silver." Note the change to white-wall tires. *GM Media Archive*

Though the Park Avenue appears to be black in this color photo, it was actually painted a very dark color named Antoinette Blue. The roof was hand-brushed aluminum. *GM Media Archive*

A trio of stainless-steel tumblers and a stainless-steel thermos were stored in the center armrest in back. Note the three built-in cup holders. *GM Heritage Center*

Three other special Cadillacs were shown with these three experimental Dream Cars. A Fleetwood 60 Special was painted pearlescent gold and had a long-grain leather landau top. White leather and gold fabric covered this car's interior. A Series 62 Coupe de Ville had pearlescent Peacock Green paint applied to its lower body and a lighter shade of green for the top. Its interior received Peacock Green leather and light green nylon silver-threaded fabric employing a block "V" and Cadillac crest pattern for the seat inserts. The other member of this trio was another Fleetwood 60 Special, painted Caprice Blue iridescent on its roof and Jordan Gray (a Buick color) for the lower body. Upholstery on the bolsters was dark blue broadcloth combined with light blue nylon inserts. The block "V" and Cadillac crest pattern was also used on this car's seat inserts.

Shifting gears, work on the steel-bodied 1955 Eldorado Brougham prototype (XP-38, Shop Order 2253) began in May 1954 when the preliminary specifications were set and approval was given to create a seating buck plus a full-scale clay model. The earlier Cadillac Orleans and Park Avenue provided a number of characteristics that were carried forward in the design of this car such as a brushed aluminum roof, suicide doors, and the lack of a B-pillar and vent windows. Including an integral air conditioner with heater as standard equipment meant vent windows were no longer considered absolutely necessary. A departure from the past (with the exceptions of the La Espada and El Camino) was the presence of quad headlamp assemblies.

Ed Glowacke, who headed the Cadillac Studio from 1952–1957, had his team get the clay model ready to present to Harley Earl and the other managers within three months after the go-ahead decision. The eventual review of this design resulted in the rear overhang being reduced several inches to achieve "more compact proportions and improve handling and parking," commented Harley Earl. Furthermore, aircraft style air scoops were applied to the upper front fenders for pressurized ventilating. Once GM Styling's top management reviewed the revised mockup, it was moved to the Cadillac Studio for additional refinement.

Final assembly of the Eldorado Brougham began on November 6, 1954. It was not painted until days before it was to go on display at the opening of the 1955 GM Motorama at the Waldorf. Upon completion, the car was sent on to New York, arriving about a day before the grand opening of the show. Then disaster struck. The prototype fell from its transport dolly causing damage to its front and rear. With only hours available to work, personnel hurriedly repaired the damage so well that the admiring crowds could not see any hint of the accident.

A GM press release about the Eldorado Brougham said that it was "Completely functional in every detail . . . the grace and sleekness of the car is augmented by its extremely low over-all height of 54.4 inches. . . ." The press statement also noted that a highly iridescent exterior color called Chameleon Green was developed solely for the Brougham. A specially prepared brochure about the car stated, "Cadillac's Eldorado Brougham represents an exciting look into the future of automotive design and engineering . . . and offers still further evidence of Cadillac's leadership in automotive styling. . . ." This brochure highlighted the "special high-powered" engine, the specially designed lounge seats for four passengers, vanity case, and unique instrument panel. Other equipment included an "Autronic Eye" automatic headlight dimmer mounted at the top of the windshield, leather and silk interior, pivoting driver's seat, map light, and storage compartments in the dash and between the front seats.

The Eldorado Brougham's steel body was mounted on a modified Cadillac frame with a wheelbase of 124 inches; a stock Series 62 frame had a wheelbase of 129 inches. A 331 V-8 coupled to a Hydra-matic

The fins of the Park Avenue resemble those of the 1951 LeSabre. *GM Media Archive*

The front of the 1954 Park Avenue predicted the basic appearance of the 1955 Cadillacs. *GM Heritage Center*

A highly iridescent color called Chameleon Green was created especially for the 1955 Eldorado Brougham. *GM Media Archive*

The rear end styling of the 1955 Eldorado Brougham appears to have evolved from that of the Park Avenue. *GM Media Archive*

transmission composed its driveline. The engine may have been the Eldorado version complete with twin carbs, which produced an advertised 270 horsepower, though the one installed in the Brougham was said to produce 280 horsepower.

Also on display along with the Eldorado Brougham were three specially trimmed Cadillacs dubbed Celebrity, Eldorado St. Moritz, and Westchester. The Celebrity was a modified Coupe de Ville and the forerunner of the Eldorado Seville two-door hardtop that became available the following year. This one received spectacularly bright red paint with a matching red long-grain leather-covered top. The interior was upholstered in bright red; the bolsters were covered in leather and decorated with chrome buttons and silver welt, while the inserts were of silver thread V-pattern red cloth. Eldorado sabre-spoke wheels added even more pizzazz to the exterior.

The Eldorado St. Moritz was a modified Eldorado convertible painted pearlescent white with an elegant interior finish of white ermine trimmed in pearlescent white English grain leather and floor carpeting of white mouton fur. A built-in vanity was also included. Its namesake was the popular ski resort in Switzerland.

A modified Series 60 Special served as the starting point for the Westchester. It received special Korina gold paint and a padded black leather roof covering. The driver and passenger compartments were separated with a glass partition. Black leather covered the front seat while the rear seating was stated to be upholstered in black cloth interwoven with gold thread (though, as shown in photos, the cloth was surrounded by leather matching the exterior color). Carpeting was black mouton fur. A 14-inch television was mounted in the back of the front seat for viewing by rear seat passengers. Also included were air conditioning, a telephone, tape recorder, and Korina gold wood paneling.

The next year, 1956, Cadillac displayed another Eldorado Brougham (XP-41). This example was a near final form prototype of the production version of the model that went on sale the following year.

Photos of the engine compartment show that an engine was installed, but the car lacked a wiring harness and spark plug wires, thus it was not a running vehicle; the car served for publicity shots and further refinement even as the first production vehicles began leaving the assembly line. It was originally built with dual headlamps, but this feature was soon changed to the quad arrangement that made it onto the production cars. This car was first shown at the Los Angeles Auto Show before going to Paris in late 1955. It returned in time for the opening of the 1956 GM Motorama in New York City. After the 1956 Motorama ended, the car was displayed that fall at "America on the Move," held at the newly built New York Coliseum. By then the prototype was wearing the rocker panel molding and front fender nameplate that would be used on the production Eldorado Broughams, which became available for purchase within a few months of this show.

The Eldorado Brougham Town Car (XP-48, Shop Order 2491) was also displayed with the prototype Eldorado Brougham at the 1956 GM Motorama. Its design is credited to Ed Glowacke, who was still in charge of the Cadillac studio. Beyond the chauffer-driven characteristics and its being 4 inches longer than the Brougham prototype, it was very much like the latter car, which in turn was much like the production version offered the following year.

This Dream Car was somewhat more elaborate. Microswitches on the door handles at the forefinger position activated a relay for locking and unlocking all the doors at once after a key was inserted; the locking process also raised any lowered windows. The switches were designed so they would not engage when the car was in motion.

The front compartment had two individual bucket-type seats covered in black Morocco leather. Chrome plating was in abundance on the dash. The passenger section offered privacy with a dual pane, horizontally sliding glass divider and a partition bulkhead. Inside this compartment were many amenities that are not commonly found on luxury cars even today. A Cadillac press release regarding this portion of the car stated, "Gold-coloured hardware is used throughout the rear compartment. Mounted in the partition behind the front seat are the so-called 'comfort and

The doors of the four-door, pillarless Eldorado prototype locked into the rocker panel. *GM Media Archive*

The 1955 Cadillac Celebrity was a modified Coupe de Ville and the forerunner of the Eldorado Seville two-door hardtop that became available the following year. It received eye-catching bright red paint with a matching red, long-grain, leather-covered top. *Author collection*

Cadillac's Westchester featured a television and a tape recorder for rear seat passengers. *Author collection*

convenience' items. These include the radio-telephone unit to communicate with the chauffeur, air-conditioning, a vanity compartment, a cigar humidor, a thermos bottle and accompanying gold-plated tumblers. The compartment is luxuriously trimmed in black and beige." The "radio-telephone unit" referred to in Cadillac's statement was not actually functional, but it looked convincing; the chauffeur's unit was trimmed in chrome while the passenger set was trimmed in gold. Of course the air conditioning setup was non-functional, too. Other simulated systems include the gauges and lighting. Subtle visual details were not overlooked—the phony quad headlights actually had the "T-3" logo in place.

A General Motors' press release regarding the Town Car said this of the exterior styling: "Combining contemporary design with the outstanding characteristics of the classic town car, the fiberglass experimental model personifies the modern trend in luxury motoring. Its perfectly proportioned exterior presents a low graceful silhouette of shining black ebony, set off by slim chrome window frames, roof headers, and pillar facings. The car's low overall height is accented by the smoothness of the fender lines and characteristic Cadillac tail fins . . . . The clean front end lines of the special car are exemplified by the smooth contour of the exceptionally low hood line design. A forward sloping cellular grille is nestled between projectile shaped 'gull' bumpers beneath which are recessed rectangular fog lamps. . . . New methods of construction, including an all-new frame design, make it possible to reduce all the outer dimensions of the Town Car without sacrificing passenger (or driver) comfort."

The Town Car made its debut at the Waldorf-Astoria in New York City in January then went on to Miami (February), Los Angeles (March), San Francisco (late March), and Boston (April). It was also seen at other auto shows across the country and then, in October 1956, was shown at the Paris Salon.

Cadillac officials gave little, if any, serious consideration to placing the Eldorado Brougham Town Car into production, though there was much speculation that it would be. The Town Car would have had an even more limited market than the Brougham, which was the most expensive American car on the road, more costly even than a Rolls-Royce, in 1957.

Unlike some GM Motorama Dream Cars, the Eldorado Brougham Town Car has a history that goes well beyond the time it was supposed to have been destroyed. In 1989, Marc Bortz, the son of Dream Car collector Joe Bortz, checked into the persistent story of Motorama cars sitting in Warhoops Used Auto and Truck Parts and learned that the wood-reinforced, fiberglass-bodied 1956 Eldorado Brougham Town Car and three other Motorama Dream Cars were present in the yard. Shortly thereafter, an agreement was reached to purchase all of the cars. Bortz later sold the Town Car to J. C. Whitney & Co. owner, the late Roy Warshawsky. He planned not only to restore the elegant Cadillac, but also install a drivetrain and everything else needed to make the one-of-a-kind car drivable. Between 1991 and 1994, the wood framing was replaced, rear bumperettes were constructed from steel to replace the originals that had rusted, and a 1956 Eldorado Seville engine was rebuilt, but was not installed.

The rebuilt engine leads to an interesting story. For some years now enthusiasts have believed the show car never had an engine in it. A plausible explanation for the lack of a drivetrain was that the GM staff ran short on time to get the car ready and never placed a drivetrain in it, though it was intended. Anchors of some type were thought to have been installed to compress the front springs to make the Town Car sit level. The theory was

The chauffeur-driven Eldorado Brougham Town Car was never seriously considered for production. *Author collection*

RM Auctions sold the Eldorado Brougham Town Car on February 11, 2006. *Ken Wallace, RM Auctions*

supported by a few facts—when the car was recovered it had no drivetrain, it had a tow hook attached to the front of the frame, and the dash was a solid piece of wood carved into the appropriate shape with no provision for wiring. Chuck Jordan has confirmed that the car did have a regular, production Cadillac Series 62 V-8 and Hydra-matic as intended. Just before the car was to be scrapped, Jordan removed the drivetrain and donated it to a local high school. Even though an engine was present, there was no wiring harness to the engine compartment. Furthermore, a simulated fiberglass fuel tank was attached to the underside of the car and the braking was via the emergency type. Warshawsky's health deteriorated before the restoration could be completed. His subsequent death lead to the family decision of placing the Town Car (together with the rebuilt engine) on the auction block, however, it proved to be impractical to get the largely dismantled car to the 1996 Auburn Kruse

In 1989 the Eldorado Brougham Town Car was recovered from Warhoops Used Auto & Truck Parts by Dream Car collector Joe Bortz. The car was sold twice before it was finally restored. *Dick Baruk*

The cover for the Eldorado Brougham Town Car chauffeur's compartment is shown in place in this view. It is no longer with the car. *Author collection*

The original telephone system (between front seats) installed in the Eldorado Brougham Town Car was never functional. *Charles D. Barnette*

Auction. Later, arrangements were made for accepting bids by telephone and Livonia, Michigan, resident and Eldorado Brougham collector Dick Baruk had the high bid.

Prior to bidding on the car, Baruk asked his good friend and Brougham Owner Association member Larry Muckey to carefully inspect the unique automobile to learn if it was practical to perform a restoration on it. Muckey knew of the car's existence as far back as 1975, and came close to owning it in 1978, but decided the $7,500 asking price was a bit too steep. He literally went through every piece to be certain that no major items were absent. Obviously, missing pieces would have added greatly to the restoration effort. He found the Town Car to be 99 percent complete; the missing parts were not of the type to make restoration prohibitive. During the restoration, missing parts were cast, or existing stock Eldorado Brougham parts were used or modified as needed. The most unusual aspect of the restoration involved the sabre spoke wheels and center caps. In a strange twist of fate, Baruk obtained ownership of the wheels several years before acquiring the Town Car. As an Eldorado Brougham collector and restorer, Baruk is often in need of parts. While searching the ads in a hobbyist publication, he found a set of sabre spoke wheels for sale in Florida, which he bought. When he received them, he discovered the two center caps that came with the set (the other two were gone and had to be made) were unlike any he had ever seen on a production Cadillac. The mystery remained unsolved until he obtained factory photos of the car. Perhaps the wheels on the Town Car were sold at some point by Warhoops or the car was delivered to the yard without them; ordinary steel discs were

The 1956 Eldorado Brougham prototype underwent a variety of alterations. *GM Media Archive*

This view of the rear passenger compartment reveals the gold-plated amenities. *Charles D. Barnette*

on the car when Joe Bortz purchased it from the salvage yard. Another possibility is that the wheels came from one of the other Cadillac Dream Cars that had these type wheels—the Park Avenue, El Camino, and La Espada of 1954. The wheels may have even been spares for any of these cars. The original use of these particular wheels will probably never be known, but fortunately they were available for the restoration of the one-of-a-kind Eldorado Brougham Town Car.

The Town Car was remarkably well preserved considering its exposure to the elements for 30 years, but much of the interior (including the solid wooden dash) was heavily damaged and the plating inside and out was in poor condition. The plating on the fiberglass front bumper is an interesting topic in itself. Heavy copper cables and electrodes were woven into the fiberglass for the plating process, though the car probably was not unique in this respect. (Surprisingly, Cadillac's press release—the same one quoted earlier—said that the "front bumper assembly . . . was hand-formed sheet metal. . . .") The rear bumper is of steel with a cast-aluminum license plate housing. Amazingly, the unique windshield was like new, although the side glass and divider window were both broken. The rotted dash was replaced with a steel one from a Brougham parts car.

Baruk secured the services of several professionals to get the elegant Dream Car in top form as well as receiving assistance from GM Tech Center representative Steve Wolken who performed valuable research that included providing original photos of the various details of the interior.

When its restoration was finished, the Eldorado Brougham Town Car was mounted on a turntable inside Baruk's shop with his collection of 1957–1958 Eldorado Broughams. In 2002, this Dream Car went "home" to Cadillac; it was displayed there during the celebration of the Cadillac Centennial. On February 11, 2006, this unique show car was sold by RM Auctions in Boca Raton, Florida, which, fittingly enough, is not far from where it was proudly displayed

The interior of the 1956 Cadillac Castilian (a modified Eldorado Seville) was upholstered in black and white calfskin with silver nylon. *GM Media Archive*

The Maharani had everything, including a kitchen sink. *GM Heritage Center*

50 years earlier during the Motorama in Miami. The bid of $730,000 (plus commission) was enough to change ownership to a collector in Texas. By then, the Eldorado Brougham Town Car had an engine once again and was made drivable for the first time.

Finally, in addition to the models mentioned, four other special Cadillacs were displayed: modified production cars labeled Castilian, Gala, Maharani, and Palomino. An Eldorado Seville was selected to create the Castilian. This car received a repaint in Starlight Silver; the interior was reupholstered in black and white calfskin with silver nylon.

The Gala was a pearlescent white Sedan de Ville with pearl-white leather, satin, and nylon interior; carpeting was white mouton. Armrests in the front doors housed small umbrellas with silver and rhinestone covered handles.

The metallic maroon Maharani was created from a Series 60 Special and had everything *including* the kitchen sink! The interior included a recessed toaster, hot-plate, cutlery tray, folding dining table, cooling unit, coffee and water dispensers, as well as a lady's vanity, safe, and safety deposit box! The dispensers were supplied with tanks located under the hood and the cooling unit was mounted in the trunk. All the kitchen accessories were contained within a roll-top cabinet mounted in the right front portion of the interior.

The Western-themed Palomino was created from a Series 62 convertible and featured a metallic beige exterior along with a tan leather and calfskin hide interior. GM dubbed all four of these special Cadillacs as "mood cars."

The 1955 St. Moritz was a modified Eldorado convertible painted pearlescent white. The elegant interior was white ermine trimmed in pearlescent white, English-grain leather with floor carpeting of white mouton fur. Its namesake was the popular ski resort in Switzerland. *GM Media Archive*

The limited-edition 1957 Cadillac Eldorado Brougham became the most expensive American automobile for sale in the United States. The window sticker was a staggering $13,074. The stylish, pillarless four-door sedan featured a stainless-steel roof, which was to become an Eldorado hallmark for decades. The first generation Eldorado Brougham was discontinued after 1958. *Author collection*

Chapter Seven
GMC's Sole Motorama Dream Vehicle

At the 1954 GM Motorama, GMC proudly displayed its new pickup—the first ever to receive passenger car styling. For the next year, GMC built its only Motorama dream vehicle, which was very much ahead of its time; it was dubbed L'Universelle (GM Styling project XP-39, Shop Order 2280). This prototype was a panel delivery vehicle with front-wheel drive, two-way radio, torsion bar front suspension, fold-up cargo doors, and a midmounted Pontiac V-8 rated at 180 horsepower.

At the time the XP-39 project was conceived, there were only a few small and underpowered import models remotely similar; Volkswagen's was the only one to gain any significant popularity. The closest vehicles to a van that GM had to offer were the Chevrolet Carryall and the GMC Suburban and neither was very comfortable or easy to load.

The L'Universelle would serve as a prototype for a vehicle that was as comfortable as a car and that would be easy to load. This Motorama dream truck would eventually—though

To achieve the proper weight distribution the 180-horsepower Pontiac 288 V-8 was placed transversely behind the driver and connected to a Hydra-matic transaxle mounted ahead of it. To place the steering wheel at the desired angle—like that of a passenger car—an L-shaped steering shaft turning bevel gears was employed. *Author collection*

indirectly—lead to the Chevrolet Greenbrier/Corvan. The idea for the dream truck is credited to Phillip Monaghan who at the time was GMC general manager. He believed truck design had not caught up to the level of the car and presented his viewpoint to Harley Earl. Earl was very receptive to the idea of creating a dream truck for the 1955 Motorama; in fact, he had actually sketched some van-like trucks in the 1930s. Earl's ideas featured fold-up doors similar to those that would appear on the L'Universelle.

In April 1954, Chuck Jordan was put in charge of the "Experimental Styling Group" as an extension to his job as assistant chief designer in Luther Stier's Chevrolet Truck Studio, where he had developed the stylish Chevrolet Cameo and its companion GMC Suburban Carrier, both of which would go into production for the 1955 model year. Jordan, along with Bill Lange of the GMC Truck and Coach studio and the rest of his team, were given the assignment to design the new panel delivery truck, which meant creating a prototype vehicle that featured loading ease, full access to load, roadability, passenger car comfort, and side panels adaptable to glass inserts so station wagon, taxi, and "sportsman" versions could be made at low cost. Charles Chayne, then the VP in charge of the engineering staff, would supervise the engineering team. This dream truck would have engineering that was much more complete than most GM Motorama vehicles.

The design team began its early research on the project by driving a Chevy Carryall and a Volkswagen Microbus.

Jackknife doors would not have been on the production variant due to high cost of manufacture. *Author collection*

The L'Universelle was intended to go into production, but costs proved too high for GM to be able to sell them at a reasonable price. *Author collection*

The team started work at the rear, since the panel van was to be built around the ease of loading criteria. Ease of loading meant the need for a low floor height; to achieve this, a drop axle was used. This criterion meant a front-wheel drive system would be necessary. To get the proper weight distribution the 180-horsepower Pontiac 288 V-8 (GMCs used Pontiac engines) was placed transversely behind the driver and connected to a Hydra-matic transaxle mounted ahead of it. The positioning of the radiator and a way to get cooling air to it then became a problem. One solution was to place the radiator alongside the engine and duct air to it through a hollow pillar and door; however that would have meant the pillar post would need to be too thick. Ultimately, the solution was to place the radiator behind the driver's position angled upward, install a grille in the roof, and have fans pull air through the grille to the radiator.

Another problem the team solved would not have worked in an actual vehicle. The engine cover would not clear the distributor so a hole was drilled into the water pump housing and the distributor shaft placed there. With the transaxle being just an empty shell, the distributor placement made no difference; the L'Universelle was a push-mobile.

The layout at which the team arrived placed the driver directly over the front wheels; in order to meet the requirement of a comfortable ride, torsion bars were adopted for the front suspension. Furthermore, the steering wheel needed to be set at an angle like that of a passenger car rather than like the awkward angle of a bus. To accomplish this, an L-shaped steering shaft turning bevel gears was employed. The final layout provided a 13-inch floor height, a 1,000-pound load capacity, and 173 cubic feet of cargo space in a van with a compact 107-inch wheelbase, 71-inch overall height, 78-inch overall width, a 188-inch overall length, and a 60/40 unloaded weight distribution (54/46 fully loaded). This prototype was more compact than the Carryall/Suburban yet could carry more cargo and do so with passenger-car comfort.

The relatively compact arrangement of the L'Universelle also included unique styling. To escape the boxy look, a sharp crease wrapped around the front to the sides and curved downward to the rear wheels. The front end thus received a forward-leaning edge; the look was enhanced by forward-leaning roof pillars much like those of the new Nomad.

The "jackknife" style loading doors on the sides and at the rear were especially eye-catching. L'Universelle's side doors rose to provide a 46-inch-high, 48-inch-wide opening, while the rear-loading door was slightly smaller—38 ¼ inches high and 44 inches wide. The fold-up doors each lifted on a four-bar hinge and extended no more than 20 inches away from the body as they swung upward.

The public's reaction to the new prototype was so favorable that at the GM Motorama in San Francisco, GM president Harlow Curtice announced the vehicle would go into production as soon as possible. The project got as far as two test "mules" dubbed T-1443 and T-1478 and the purchase of a press to stamp out the roof panel. (The production version would have been built with steel.) Ultimately, the cost of the production van terminated the project. The vehicle would have to sell for more than the price of a Cadillac—an amount few people would be willing to spend.

General Motors went a different direction with the panel van idea. Within one year of the termination of the L'Universelle program, the first sketches were done of the Corvair Greenbrier/

Corvan. This project would be one of the last Harley Earl would oversee for GM. This completely different design proved much more practical and went into production for the 1961 model year. The futuristic design of the L'Universelle at least indirectly influenced the design of the first compact passenger van from Chevrolet and provided experience on how to build such a vehicle. Vans became all the rage during the 1970s, followed by the popularity of the minivan in the 1980s and 1990s. Furthermore, front-wheel drive emerged in the 1960s and eventually came into almost universal use by the late twentieth century. While the GM Motorama Dream Cars were in many cases predictive of near-term styling features, the L'Universelle was far ahead of its time—so far ahead that it required three divisions of GM to create it.

A radio-telephone was included in the L'Universelle. *Author collection*

Ground-to-cargo floor height was kept as low as possible. *Author collection*

LaSalle IIs and Firebirds—GM's V-6 and Turbine Power Projects

A particularly unusual part of the history of Motorama show cars can be found in a pair dubbed LaSalle II. Named after Cadillac's companion marque, last produced in 1940, these cars were created at the time V-8s were extremely popular with the motoring public. Increasingly greater horsepower was being achieved with growing cubic inches, higher compression ratios, multiple carburetion, etc., and this did not seem to be the time to test public reaction to a V-6 engine, but that is exactly what happened with the LaSalle II project.

At the other extreme were the Firebirds I, II, and III of 1954, 1956, and 1958. These turbine-powered cars seem more logical for the time as the 1950s was the golden age of aviation; jet- and rocket-powered aircraft were reaching higher Mach numbers. (Mach I represents the speed of sound.) Applying jet engine technology to automobiles was tested by the big-three automakers in the 1950s and 1960s (and even into the 1980s by Chrysler

According to GM's booklet, *Flight of the Firebirds*, Harley Earl "envisioned an entirely different type of car 'which a person may drive to the launching site of a rocket to the moon'" when he considered the styling for the Firebird III. *GM Media Archive*

The LaSalle II roadster is shown here undergoing construction. *GM Media Archive*

Corporation). In fact, the August 1954 issue of *Motor Trend* had a cover story about the subject titled "Detroit's Hottest Topic—Turbines Are Coming, But When?"

The pair of fiberglass LaSalle IIs show cars were not divisional specific. One was a six-passenger, four-door pillarless hardtop (XP-32, Shop Order 2217) and the other a diminutive two-passenger roadster (XP-34, Shop Order 2220). The pair was named after the first car Harley Earl designed for GM—the 1927 LaSalle. The four-door (with the rear doors being the suicide type) had a wheelbase of 108 inches and an overall length of 180.2 inches—just about the same length as some alternative sports cars of the day, like the Muntz. A more modern comparison is a mid-1960s Falcon. The roadster was even smaller with a wheelbase of only 99.9 inches and an overall length of 151.7 inches. Ground clearance for both cars measured 5.1 inches. In an era when longer, lower, wider ruled the shape of the automobile, the LaSalle IIs flew in the face of established principles, though they were certainly low. The hardtop stood 49.5 inches high, while its companion roadster peaked at a mere 42.8 inches. Each fiberglass body sat on a custom-built steel frame with an independent suspension utilizing torsion bars in front. The windshield for the LaSalle II sedan was an "astra-dome" type much like that of the Biscayne. Its exhaust pipes, mufflers, and ports were housed in the rocker sills on the roadster, while the exhaust exited through a port in each lower quarter panel for the sedan.

Frontal styling for both LaSalle IIs had vertical grille openings based on the proposed 1941 LaSalle. The side coves of the pearlescent white cars were painted a contrasting blue (Bahama Blue on the roadster and LeSabre Blue on the sedan) thus dominating the profile view of each car; they foretold the look of the Corvette for the following year. Carl Renner performed much of the design work on these cars and also worked on the restyled Corvette for 1956. He even went so far as to propose a 1957 Corvette based chiefly on the LaSalle II

The diminutive size of the LaSalle II roadster is clearly evident in this view taken in Miami. *GM Media Archive*

This version of the 1955 LaSalle II Sedan was a six-passenger, four-door, pillarless hardtop that stood only 49.5 inches high. Like its companion roadster, it was "powered" by an experimental aluminum V-6. In reality, the V-6 in both cars lacked internal parts. *GM Media Archive*

The LaSalle II Sedan is seen here with the Pontiac Strato-Star inside the Waldorf-Astoria prior to the opening of the 1955 GM Motorama. *GM Media Archive*

roadster's styling, but that is as close as this show car got to production.

The LaSalle IIs featured V-6 engines, although the ones in the actual Dream Cars were aluminum castings without internal components. Even though these particular V-6 prototypes were nonfunctional, GM had a V-6 research program in the works over the preceding seven years. The incomplete engines mounted within the LaSalle IIs represented aluminum (heads and block), fuel-injected, double-overhead cam (DOHC), power plants that would produce 150 horsepower. Today such engines are commonplace, but in 1955 they were quite radical. If they had gone into production, the history of the American automobile might have been very different—at least that is the opinion of Joe Bortz as quoted in an article by Charles D. Barnette for the Cadillac-LaSalle Club's *The Self Starter* publication. Bortz, who still owns both LaSalle IIs, said, "To me these cars are the turning point in American history. At this time in 1955, long before the European

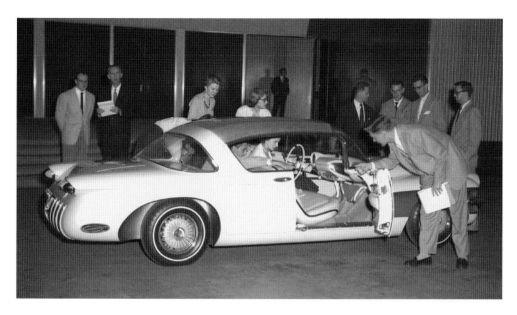

The LaSalle II Sedan is shown here being reviewed by GM personnel. *GM Media Archive*

Even on a display platform raised above the floor, the LaSalle II was a very low car as is evidenced by the people around it at this auto show, who have to bend down to see inside. *Author collection*

automotive invasion into the American market, General Motors had already thought of and physically produced these two cars which had aluminum block V-6, fuel-injection, double-overhead cam engines with independent rear suspension. As you know, during the 1960s, 1970s, and 1980s, these were the ideas that were brought forward from Europe, and eventually Japan, that set the American automotive market on its ear. As I always say, this was the turning point in American automotive history, where if they [GM] would have stepped up on [its] ideas with these two LaSalle automobiles, American automotive fortunes would have been greatly changed."

An additional feature of both cars was 13-inch turbine-style wheels with brake drums cast into their center sections. The wheel was bolted rigidly much further away from the center than a typical arrangement; tire removal meant lifting off only an assembly of the tire and rim, thus leaving the brake setup undisturbed. The bimetal brake drums bolted to the wheel hub to form a brake chamber that inhibited the entrance of moisture and dirt. These drums required only seconds to remove.

The LaSalle IIs were uncannily predictive of the future—a trait most Motorama experimental cars have in common. (Such prognostication was the result of advanced thinking within GM Styling, rather than through gifted insight into what would be in demand in the distant future.) The compact car would emerge in the 1960s, and Buick would offer a V-6 starting in 1962, an engine that would become very important to Buick in the 1980s.

The 1954 Firebird I (XP-21, Shop Order 1921) was certainly one of the more memorable Dream Cars. This experimental strongly resembled a jet-powered fighter plane and, in fact, its styling was based chiefly on the U.S. Navy's delta winged F4D Skyray interceptor. Harley Earl explained the car's styling origin in an article for the *Saturday Evening Post*, "I Dream Automobiles." He stated, "The Firebird tickles me because of its origin. In our 1953 Motorama

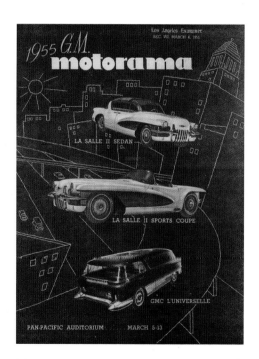

The front page of the Motorama section of the *LA Times* featured both LaSalle II Dream Cars. *Author collection*

The 1954 Firebird I is shown being prepared for testing; Indy 500 race driver Mauri Rose waits in the cockpit. Note the logo on the nose of the experimental car. Its basic design would resurface two decades later as the "screaming chicken" on the Trans Am. *GM Media Archive*

the spotlight model of the Dream Cars was the LeSabre, and just after it had been first shown to company officials, I was on an airplane trip. I picked up a magazine and noticed a picture of a new jet plane, the Douglas Skyray. It was a striking ship, and I liked it so well that I tore out the picture and put it into my inside coat pocket. Subsequently a traveling companion, also a GM officer, stopped at my seat to congratulate me on LeSabre. 'But,' he added, 'now what will you do for next year?' At that moment, I had absolutely nothing in mind. But I patted the pocket where the picture of the Skyray was tucked away. 'I have it right here,' I said. I was joking. I was merely answering his banter in kind. Then, bingo, I decided I had kidded myself into something. The result, as you may have seen, is that the Firebird is an earth-bound replica of the Skyray airplane."

Its purpose, as explained by Harlow Curtice, was to test whether or not the gas turbine engine could be used "to give efficient and economical performance in the low and normal automotive driving ranges."

With practical jet engines emerging at the end of World War II, the thoughts of adapting the technology for automotive use soon began. The British built and tested the world's first turbine-powered car, dubbed the Rover J.E.T. Interestingly, one of the turbine engineers for that project, as reported in *The Autocar* in late 1952, believed Americans would put the first turbine car into production and also predicted the expensive engine would go first into high-performance, luxury-class cars.

The idea of the Firebird I (originally called simply the Firebird) is credited to Harley Earl; he decided in early 1953 that such a car should be built and tested. This experimental car's GT-302 Whirlfire Turbo-Power engine and chassis were developed under the direction of GM vice president and general manager of GM Research Laboratories Division, Charles McCuen, along with William Turunen, who had done extensive research on the subject. Turbine engine research had been underway at the GM Research Laboratories Division for several years before the Firebird I got the go-ahead. The engine was originally conceived for testing in heavy-duty trucks and buses. The XP-21 Firebird project was a collaborative effort between this division and GM Styling, with Bob McLean in charge of the Firebird's design; the project built upon the knowledge gained from testing the GT-300.

The April 1954 issue of *Motor Life* reported that the GT-302 was "the essence of simplicity and compactness." In the XP-21's nose was a 35-gallon fiberglass fuel tank, while just behind the cockpit sat the two-part gas turbine engine consisting of the gasifier and power sections connected by a flexible shaft. The gasifier section replaced the engine and torque converter pump of a conventional automobile and the power section replaced the torque converter turbine, transmission, and rear axle gears. The Whirlfire gasifier section resembled a complete small jet engine.

A jet engine propels an aircraft through the expulsion of the exhaust, but in the case of the turbine engine that powered the Firebird, the exhaust gas had to be funneled through a power turbine connected directly to the car's rear wheels via a transmission. The Whirlfire's gasifier section was composed of the compressor rotor and a gasifier turbine wheel—both attached to the same shaft. Air entering

Speed brakes were included to help slow the turbine-powered 1954 Firebird. *GM Media Archive*

the compressor was pressurized to 3 ½ times standard atmospheric pressure prior to entering the engine's two combustion chambers where the gas temperature reached about 1,500 degrees Fahrenheit. The resulting blast of hot gas from the gasifier turbine ran the second turbine—the power section turbine—that was connected to the car's rear wheels through a two-speed planetary transmission.

The GT-302 idled at 8,000 rpm. The horsepower rating of this engine was 370 at 26,000 revolutions per minute of the gasifier turbine and 13,000 rpm of the power turbine. Though the revolutions per minute may seem high, they were in fact low for a turbine engine. The lower rotational speed

The jet plane–inspired styling of the 1954 Firebird is obvious from this high-angle view. *GM Media Archive*

any more than it described its power source. In front, the Firebird I got a double wishbone suspension along with torsion bars; the rear received a de Dion type. Its axle was suspended with two single-leaf springs, and included in the assembly was a "walking beam" stabilizer unit. The wings carried split brake flaps on the trailing edges, which could be controlled with switches on the steering wheel that activated aircraft-type actuators. Brake drums 11 inches in diameter were outside the wheels rather than inside them—a design that facilitated faster cooling of the drums.

Styling for the XP-21 Firebird was not just meant to get attention and underscore the nature of the power plant. The high-speed expectation of the experimental car brought a chance to test the little-known area of aerodynamics for land vehicles. A close approximation of the final body in scale form was sent to the California Institute of Technology for extensive wind tunnel research. These tests revealed the optimal contours for the fiberglass body as well as proper brake flap angles and the amount of negative angle of attack for the wings. The styling was also intended to convey the fact that practical turbine engines in everyday automobiles were considered by GM engineers and managers to be years away.

Within a span of months the Firebird went from idea to reality. With the high-speed potential of the experimental car recognized immediately, three-time Indy 500 winner and engineer Mauri Rose was called upon to evaluate its performance. The Firebird's potential was to be assessed at GM's test track in Mesa, Arizona. Expectations were that the car would easily surpass the record set by the experimental Rover J.E.T.

put less stress on the moving parts, thus increasing reliability. As it was, the stresses applied were high enough; a gasifier turbine blade tip speed could be as high as 1,000 mph, thus creating a 3,000-pound pull on each lightweight blade. The GT-302's weight of 775 pounds represented thirty-one percent of the Firebird I's total weight of 2,500 pounds. Top speed was expected to be beyond 200 miles per hour!

Conventional did not describe the Firebird's suspension and braking systems

GM personnel, including Harley Earl at far right, pose with the Firebird I inside a Miami dealership. Note the Corvette in the background with wire wheels and black sidewall tires. *GM Media Archive*

Before Rose could put the Firebird through high-speed runs, Charles McCuen decided to perform some tests himself. His decision was almost a fatal one. McCuen fired up the turbine and then proceeded to accelerate. The turbine took a while to wind up, resulting in a relatively slow acceleration, but once it reached high rpm it really began to move. Unfortunately, high speed was reached near the far turn in the test track. Letting off the accelerator did nothing to slow the speeding car because the turbine engine did not provide engine braking as in a conventional automotive engine and there was little time for applying the brakes to slow the car significantly. Even the high bank of the turn could not stop the car from skidding sideways and leaving the track. Standing only 41 inches high, the Firebird easily slipped under the guard rail and ended its tumble badly smashed. Only the built-in headrest kept McCuen from being crushed. After months in the hospital, he recovered enough to go back to work, but not for long; he took early retirement in 1956.

GM's president, Harlow Curtice, is seen in this photo sitting in the cockpit of the Firebird I. *GM Media Archive*

This magazine ad proclaimed the 1956 GM Motorama to be the "greatest." In many ways it was. Though no one realized it at the time, this Motorama was the last of its kind. The Motoramas of 1959 and 1961 had only one Dream Car—the experimental Firebird III—to exhibit. For those events, less elaborate, modified production cars replaced the likes of the Club de Mer, Golden Rocket, and the Centurion. *Author collection*

Since the molds for the fiberglass-bodied Firebird still existed, a second car could be built in time for display at the opening of the 1954 GM Motorama at the Waldorf-Astoria. Though Mauri Rose did test-drive the Firebird I, high-speed trials would not be attempted again, which left the top speed to educated guesses. With a short-wave radio inside the cockpit, Rose could monitor and report the readings of sixteen gauges keeping tabs on the performance of the experimental car. Rose reported that it performed reasonably well—though sluggish below 18,000 rpm—and drove smoothly. According to his report published in the April 1954 *Motor Life*, " . . . the steering was absolutely true. The car wanted to behave. It wanted to keep going straight ahead. It was perfectly stable." He also said with a note of strong conviction that, "With absolute sincerity I can say that the car itself is an outstanding job from both styling and engineering standpoints."

On the negative side, the Firebird was somewhat noisy, very fuel thirsty, and the exhaust temperature very high (roughly 1,000 degrees Fahrenheit)—problems which the next Firebird would tackle.

Following Firebird I, General Motors said its 1956 Firebird II (XP-43, Shop Order 2683) was "the first American gas turbine passenger car *specifically* designed for family use on the highway." (The statement was correct. Chrysler Corporation tested a turbine engine in a nearly stock 1954 Plymouth Belvedere, but this car was not designed from the start for turbine power.) Turbine power was not the only area of research being performed with the four-passenger Firebird II. It was also built to test the concept of futuristic electronic highways. The "imagineering" (as GM called it in their booklet, *Flight of the Firebirds*) behind this technology was that cars of the future might be controlled electronically for direction, speed, and spacing interval, thus eliminating driver error from automobile operation. General Motors even produced a special presentation, *Design for Dreaming* that showed how these highways might function. The movie was shown to Motorama attendees on a large screen; when the short presentation ended, the screen lifted up to reveal the Firebird II.

GM's movie opened with a scene of a family enjoying a vacation on wheels during a 1956 setting. Much to their displeasure, they encounter a clogged highway and begin dreaming of what might be 20 years later in the year 1976. The family is then whisked away in a Firebird II on the radar-controlled highway of the future where there are no traffic jams. Presented was the idea that with a flip of a switch one could activate automatic control that allowed electronic-impulse-emitting metal strips embedded in the road surface to communicate with electronic pick-up coils placed inside the pair of cone-like projections on the front of the Firebird II. These signals controlled steering, speed, and braking via the car's onboard computer. An automatic control setting freed the occupants to talk, play games, watch TV, or just watch the scenery going by. One could communicate with control towers along the route to obtain information on how to get to a location, find motel vacancies, make reservations, or get other information. The control tower operator could communicate by flashing messages on the two TV screens in the car or through voice communication. At the time the driver entered the "Auto-Way," the control tower operator would be able to check the fuel level and engine operation of the car as well as synchronize speed and direction while the driver manually positioned the car over the metal strips. If anything was discovered to be wrong with the vehicle at any point, the car could be guided automatically to a place out of traffic. Once this fanciful film finished and the screen lifted, not only was the Firebird II revealed but also the actor and actress seen in the film.

The automatic systems for the "highway of tomorrow" were tested and demonstrated to the press by GM engineers, but the original systems on the Firebird II did not function; instead they were only simulated. About two years after the 1956 Motorama ended, the real systems were installed and tested.

The engine and chassis engineering for the Firebird II was headed by Dr. Lawrence Hafstad, the vice president of the GM Research Laboratories staff. The turbine for the Firebird II was an upgrade of that used in the XP-21, though it was not as powerful—about

This is the nonfunctional Firebird II built with titanium. *Author collection*

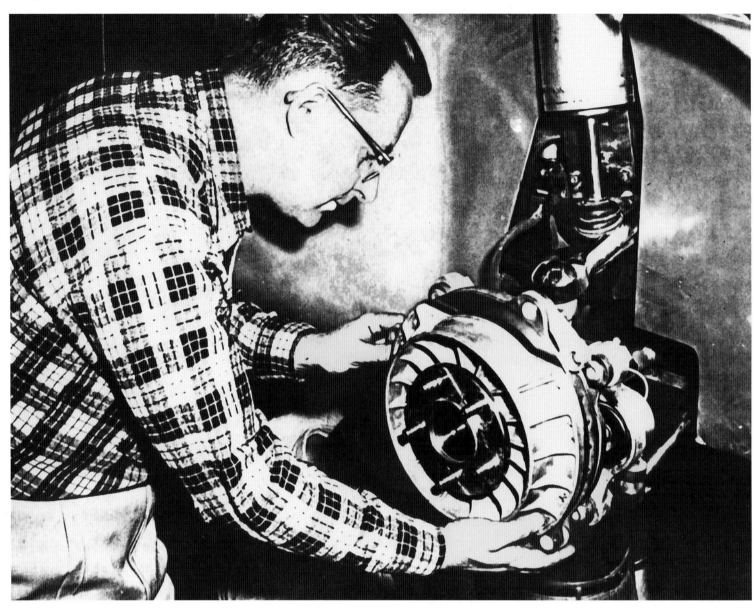

General Motors' Moraine Products Division developed the all-metal "Turbo-X" brakes used on the Firebird II. *Author collection*

half as much at 200 gross horsepower at 28,000 rpm—and it had to carry more than twice the weight. The GT-304 Whirlfire incorporated a newly developed regenerator which recycled 80 percent of the exhaust heat that was wasted in the GT-302. This improved regenerator was a metal mesh drum, which rotated first through the hot exhaust gas and then through the relatively cool compressor discharge air, carrying the heat of the exhaust to the incoming air. As a result of this more efficient regenerator, fuel economy improved significantly—almost to that of the average piston engine. Furthermore, the exhaust gases were about the same temperature as from a conventional automobile; the exhaust exited from stainless-steel pipes that ran through the rockers and terminated with ports atop the rear fenders. A silencer built into the nose of the car greatly reduced the noise level to near that of a conventional automobile. To start the Firebird II, a magnetic key was inserted and the starter button pressed. A Delco-Remy motor then brought the gasifier section up to 4,000 rpm, enough to make ignition automatic. The starter then continued to assist up to 15,000 rpm.

Two Firebird IIs were built, but they were not identical. The version that ran was built of fiberglass and used for the movie, while its companion had a body of titanium, but no engine. The latter example is the car shown on stage after the movie *Design for Dreaming* ended.

The titanium-bodied car represented another experiment of Earl's in studying the possibility of using something different for automobile construction. Titanium presented many challenges. As explained in the April 1956 issue of *Motor Trend* the metal works "about as easily as spring steel" and it can be vigorously filed with a coarse metal file "for half an hour before the surface is scratched." The metal had to be heated to 920 degrees Fahrenheit to stamp the appropriate shape into it. It also darkened when welded. The latter proved to be a considerable problem because Earl wanted the surface of the metal burnished rather than painted. The solution to this problem was simply to not weld it. Instead, General Motors Research Laboratories developed an epoxy resin that could bond the titanium skin to the body framing. The surface of the body was also to have a brushed satin finish. Hand finishing blocks with Pyrex glass particles bounded to them were used to get the desired appearance. Several coats of satin-finish lacquer clear-coat sealed the surface, not for the purpose of protecting the titanium from corrosion—the metal is extremely resistant to corrosion—but rather to keep it from being smudged with fingerprints. All this

Two Firebird IIs were built. This photo shows the interior of the fiberglass car, which was the running version. *GM Media Archive*

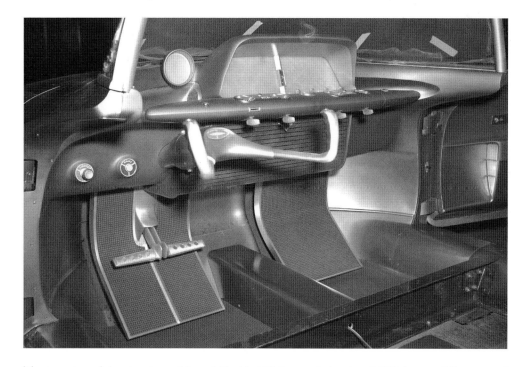

The interior of the titanium-skinned Firebird II featured simulated "Highway of Tomorrow" wizardry during its Motorama tour. Later, the electronic systems of the concept were actually tested. *GM Media Archive*

The 1958 Firebird III is shown in this photo undergoing construction; its canopy is in the foreground. *Steve Wolken collection*

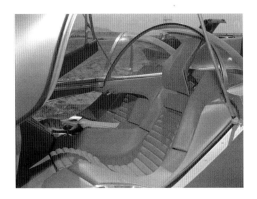

Access to the interior of the Firebird III was via an ultrasonic key. Just pointing the ultrasonic key at the door caused it to swing upward and forward; the side panel and bubble canopy were joined as one unit to form the door. As GM's booklet pointed out, one could step into the car without stooping and be seated in a comfortable lounge-chair seat. *GM Media Archive*

effort did result in a structure nearly as light as a comparable aluminum-bodied Firebird II would have been and nearly as strong as a steel-bodied version.

The design of the front of the car was distinctive, and there was function behind the look. Oil-cooling fins were immediately behind the electronic sensors in the projections; further back were what looked like turbine blades. These served to keep larger objects from getting into the engine air inlet. The small headlights retracted into the body when turned off, leaving only the turn signal/parking lamps exposed; when turned on, the head-lights extended outward several inches, and though diminutive, they emitted a strong beam of light. Just behind the Firebird logo near the front was a set of flaps that opened automatically to emit heat.

As on the original Firebird, the second-generation version had a dorsal fin in back said to aid directional stability by moving the center of air pressure from the front to the middle of the experimental car. Just as on some Motorama cars, this one had the red, white, and blue GM Air Transport Division insignia placed on the tail fin. Also in back were two "bombs"— one on each side—containing a combined total of 20 gallons of fuel. Another gadget tested on both Firebird IIs was a "freight elevator" in the rear deck. The entire trunk floor rose to fender height so no one would need to lean over for access to the trunk, which contained eight pieces of fitted luggage as well as twin 12-volt batteries. Taillights were housed in a large reflector that created a chromed effect in daylight and the appearance of a glowing jet exhaust pipe at night.

The interior of the nonrunning Firebird II received higher-grade trim with simulated "Auto-Way" instruments, a pair of cathode ray tubes for informative readouts, and a double-handled aircraft-style steering wheel, while that of the functional car had a full array of real instruments to provide data to the driver on the Whirlfire power plant. The running car was also equipped with an air conditioner and heater. Air conditioning was virtually mandatory due to the bubble canopy, which created a "greenhouse effect" capable of breaking a sweat on even the most composed passenger. Also available to cool the interior was a trio of flaps in the section between the lift-up plastic canopy panels.

The frame of the running car had to be built rigidly to prevent the canopy from cracking. The flip-up panels on the canopy opened when the magnetic key was inserted into a slot on the car's body side panels. Both cars had reclining aircraft-style seats with adjustable headrests. The rear seats wrapped around; this feature would be used by Ford on its four-passenger Thunderbird two years later. (Ironically, GM originally intended to use the name Thunderbird for its XP-21 gas turbine car. However, Ford trademarked it first, thus another name had to be chosen.) The seats and door panels were molded in resilient plastic foam and covered with plastic upholstery fabrics, having both the texture and color molded into them. The nonrunner received a luminescent headliner and red glowing courtesy lamps on the door panels; the latter feature would later be used for production cars as a way to warn motorists of open doors on parallel-parked

cars. It also had a rear-facing camera system similar to that installed on the Buick Centurion.

The functional Firebird II received yet another experimental system—an air-oil suspension. At each wheel, Delco-Matic air-oil suspension units replaced the conventional shock absorbers and springs. The air-oil unit used a cushion of air to provide a soft springing and a hydraulic leveling system to compensate for light or heavy loads to keep the car level. (GM said this was the first American car to have leveling in both the front and rear.) When in motion, the leveling system switched off and provided a smooth ride with air cushioning on the 120-inch wheelbase experimental car.

The brakes of the Firebird II were research tools as well. The Moraine Products

Technicians installed the Firebird III's turbine engine from underneath the experimental car. *GM Media Archive*

The Firebird III was *spared* the scrap order and was displayed for some time at the Henry Ford Museum. It is now a part of the collection of the GM Heritage Center. *Charles D. Barnette*

Division developed the all-metal "Turbo-X" brakes. The cast-iron discs rotated with the car's wheels. When the hydraulic brakes were activated, the discs were squeezed between movable pads of metal lining material on the inboard side and by fixed pads on the outboard side. The stopping power was directly proportional to the hydraulic pressure applied to ensure straight-ahead stops.

Both Firebird IIs still exist. The running car received a refurbishment (including a reproduction set of the original equipment U.S. Rubber Polyglas tires) several years ago and GM shows this car occasionally at special events.

Incidentally, GM built another car dubbed simply XP-500 that strongly resembled the Firebird IIs. Its nose was a flattened oval shape without the pair of cone-like projections and it lacked the shark-like dorsal fin on the rear deck. This experimental was used to test a free-piston engine.

Turbine research continued with the 1958 Firebird III (XP-73, Shop Order 90238). The last in the series of Firebird experimental turbine engine research cars is probably the most memorable, thanks to its dramatic styling. The tapered nose, twin bubble canopies, and seven tail fins must have made a strong impression on GM Motorama attendees. According to GM's booklet, *Flight of the Firebirds*, Harley Earl "envisioned an entirely different type of car, 'which a person may drive to the launching site of a rocket to the moon,'" when he considered the styling for the next turbine car.

The Firebird III certainly looked the part it was intended to play, but there was much more to it than that, as explained in GM's booklet, *Imagination In Motion—Firebird III:* " . . . the Firebird I for high performance, then the Firebird II for futuristic family car design and now the Firebird III that refines the outstanding features of both. . . ."

Underneath its fiberglass skin was a regenerative gas turbine GT-305—as well as a separate two-cylinder, ten-horsepower aluminum engine to run the electrical and hydraulic accessories (steering, braking

Harley Earl posed with his Firebirds at GM's proving grounds in Arizona. *GM Media Archive*

pumps, brake flaps, air suspension, and air conditioning). Furthermore, GM had not forgotten about its "highway of tomorrow" research, thus this car received a functional system—called "Autoguide." It also received a functional "Cruisecontrol" to automatically maintain a constant speed as well as a "Unicontrol" system for driver control of steering, acceleration, and braking. In GM's booklet about their Firebird III, the concept of human engineering was explained: "Automotive engineers have long recognized an area of development known as human engineering. Never before has its real potential been exploited, however, as it has in the new General Motors laboratory on wheels, the Firebird III. In this car, the driver has been viewed as a challenge rather than as a limitation to automotive engineering possibilities. Here is an opportunity to use new simplified control devices, to provide improved air-conditioned comfort, and the armchair ride of an entirely new high pressure air-oil hydraulic suspension system." The Firebird III was the first completely electronically controlled car.

The improved Whirlfire engine represented a significant advancement over the GT-304 version. It was lighter by 25 percent, more compact, developed just over 10 percent more power (225 horsepower at 33,000 rpm gasifier speed), and provided a 25 percent improvement in fuel economy. The GT-305 turbine engine, transmission, and differential were coupled together and mounted as one unit behind the passenger compartment. The transaxle included a Hydra-matic type transmission mounted directly to the differential case. This de Dion rear axle arrangement had a short driveshaft with two universal joints between each wheel and the differential. The axle driveshafts were mounted to the differential carrier by means of ball and trunnion joints. This setup eliminated the usual propeller shaft and universal joints.

The "Unicontrol" operating controls of the Firebird III were combined in a single swivel stick with a palm-fitting handle mounted on top. The stick, which could be accessed from either seat, had to simply be pushed left or right to turn, forward to accelerate, and backward to brake. To engage "reverse" the handle needed to be rotated 20 degrees either left or right. Rotating the handle 80 degrees in either direction engaged "park." Moving the control stick engaged servos controlled by three analog computers, which monitored vehicle speed and the turn angle of the front wheels. The computers could compensate for too much driver input such as a sudden turn at high speed to keep the car from overturning.

Access to the interior was via an ultrasonic key. Just pointing the ultrasonic key at the door caused it to swing upward and forward; the side panel and bubble canopy were

Firebirds I, II, and III are part of the GM Heritage Center collection today. In this view, they are parked on the GM Air Transport logo designed by Harley Earl. He used the logo as a personal stamp on much of his modern work, including the three cars seen here. *GM Media Archive*

joined as one unit to form the door. As GM's booklet pointed out, one could step into the car without stooping and be seated in a comfortable lounge-chair seat.

The electronic systems filled the trunk; the "black boxes" sat on one side and a pair of 12-volt batteries sat on the other. Access was through two deck lids—one on each side of the central fin.

The GM experimental car also utilized an anti-lock braking system. The 11x4-inch "Turb-Al" brake drums were cast into the alloy wheels with cast-in cooling passages being located between the drum and wheel. Air to cool the brakes was brought in through the hub and spun out through these slots. At speeds above 30 miles per hour, the airbrake flaps, which operated at 1,000 psi, were deployed. Furthermore, a "grade retarder" also went into action above this speed. The system used oil-cooled friction discs on the rear axle shafts.

The front and rear suspensions employed solid axles anchored to the subframe with four control arms on each. This setup reduced the car's overall height and kept the wheels perpendicular to the road at all times, thus improving handling. With interconnecting air-oil springs on the front and rear, any vertical force acting on a front wheel was simultaneously applied to the rear wheel. The result was suppressed pitching motion and thus a smoother ride. The 3,000-psi air-oil unit had a variable spring constant that resulted in a strong spring action when the car was heavily loaded and a relatively weak spring when lightly loaded. Height control valves always maintained the same road clearance, regardless of the load carried.

The first "flight" of the Firebird III occurred in August 1958. A movie about

This is a La Salle show car proposal by stylist Jerry Brochstein from May 18, 1957. *Dan and Fred Kanter*

the car's development was made and shown to Motorama audiences during the two-city tour in the fall of 1958. It was actually tested on public roads and must have practically stopped traffic! This car was included in the final GM Motorama, which toured three cities two years later, giving this experimental the distinction of being the only such car to make a repeat appearance for a GM Motorama tour.

Turbine research at GM did not end with the Firebird III. Further testing was done on a series of trucks including the 1965 Chevrolet Titan III.

The only Firebird III to be built still exists and underwent a refurbishment not long ago. GM still displays the car at various Concours events around the country.

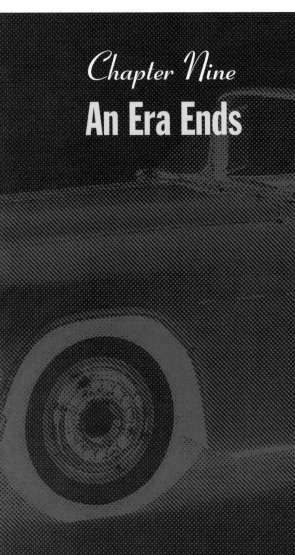

Chapter Nine
An Era Ends

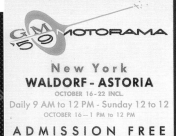

General Motors canceled the Motorama for 1957, but resumed with shows for the 1959 and 1961 model years, however, they were not quite the spectacle they once were due to a lack of Dream Cars. The Firebird III was the only Dream Car seen at the last two shows, even though this experimental was not the only flashy nonproduction car GM could have shown.

GM's 1959 Cadillac Cyclone (XP-74) could have been on hand for both the 1959 two-city tour, as well as the 1961 finale. It debuted instead at the first Daytona 500. Buick had the 1958 XP-75, a Pininfarina–built two-passenger version of its production 1959 models. Additionally, Pontiac had built the first of its X-400 series of cars. The X-400s were convertibles with supercharged engines and other custom features.

The 1959 GM Motorama began at the Waldorf-Astoria in October 1958. This illustration shows the art from a matchbook made for the event as well as the program guide. *Charles D. Barnette, Carla Tynes*

Bruce Berghoff explained in his book, *The GM Motorama*, that sales slipped during 1956 and they seriously fell during 1957 and 1958, although the decline in sales for the latter two years was due in part to a recession. This may have led to a decision to emphasize the production cars and keep the Dream Cars to a bare minimum. The 1956 GM Motorama did not put any of the production cars on stage, which Berghoff suspects may have had something to do with the slip in the sales that year. To put the spotlight on the production cars, one from each of the five divisions of GM was brought out on stage in a spectacular way for the 1959 shows held in New York City and Boston. As Berghoff described it, "The center of activity was the ninety-five-ton 'grasshopper' animated stage mechanism. Following a short fantasy film depicting 'Imagination in Vehicles,' the June Taylor Dancers introduced each car line in song and dance. With each introduction, the huge grasshopper arms delivered one production car up and over the audience for a brief spin, and then retracted behind a barrier to await the finale. The stage show ended with five cars spinning. With three cars high, two low, the orchestra blaring, and the dancers kicking, the audience roared with approval." These five cars wore identical Pearl-Mist White paint. According to Berghoff, this was DuPont's premier showing of their very fragile pearlescent finish, which was subject to rapid oxidation and yellowing. Consequently, three decades would pass before the paint industry perfected this pigment to the point that GM would offer a similar color as a production finish.

Changing tactics by emphasizing production vehicles evidently worked; GM experienced a 30 percent domestic sales improvement over the next three years.

At the 1959 Motorama, one of the more attention-getting displays other than the Firebird III was a Bonneville convertible mounted upside down. The purpose of the unusual position of the car was to allow visitors to see the new "Wide Track" chassis. Oldsmobile drew attention to its three-car turntable with an aviary housing fifty cockatiels imported from Holland.

The so-called grasshopper from the 1959 show was put into action again for 1961 to showcase the five GM car divisions. Again, the delivery of the cars was

The final GM Motorama show was held at the Pan Pacific Auditorium in Los Angeles from January 28 to February 5, 1961. *Charles D. Barnette, Carla Tynes*

For the 1961 GM Motorama, Chevrolet displayed this white Impala Special convertible with a customized gold and white interior. Miss Detroit seems to be getting more attention than the car, however! This photo was taken at the Civic Auditorium in San Francisco. *GM Media Archive*

CATALINA

BONNEV

Pontiac's Bonneville "Moda d'Oro" convertible was distinguished with a golden pearl exterior finish, gold-plated instrument panel, and an interior of gold cloth and ivory leather. Gold-plating was also applied to the moldings on the bucket seats, sill plates, etc. Mouton carpeting covered the floor and lower door panels of the car. *GM Media Archive*

choreographed to music. Initially, the 1961 GM Motorama tour was planned for five cities, but budget cuts reduced the tour to three—New York City, San Francisco, and Los Angeles.

The Firebird III was shown again along with production cars featuring nonproduction paint, interiors, and trim. These included the Buick Flamingo (based on the Electra 225), Pontiac Bonneville Moda d'Oro convertible, and the Chevrolet Impala Special.

Sitting near the Moda d'Oro was Pontiac's tilt-body Tempest. The first production Tempest was hinged at the rear to allow the body to be tilted upward so as to reveal the advanced transaxle and flexible driveshaft. All engine and chassis components received show-quality paint; the underside floorpans were fully painted and even the tires were dressed up with wide, white sidewalls on both the inner and outer sides. This car was

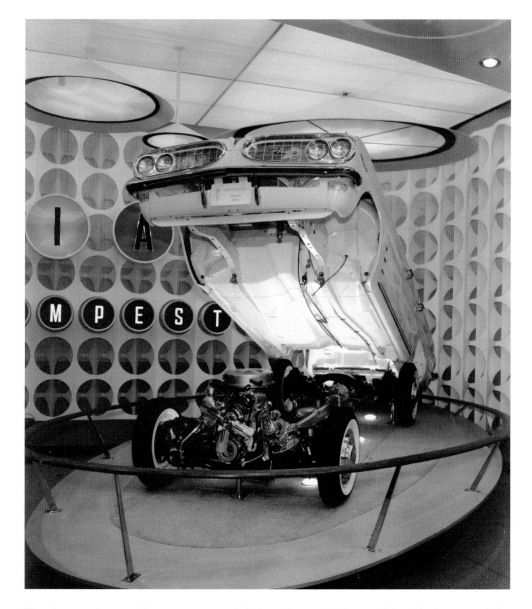

The first production Tempest was modified so that its body could be lifted to reveal the transaxle. *Bruce Berghoff collection*

The interior of the pearlescent orange Flamingo featured paisley upholstered bucket seats; the passenger-side bucket seat could be swiveled to face the rear seat. *GM Media Archive*

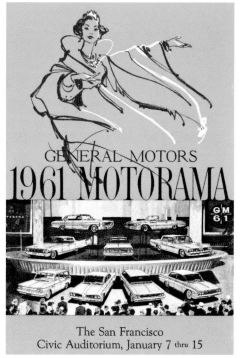

The GM Motorama was held for the last time in 1961. Here is the cover of the brochure for the next-to-last show, which was held at the Civic Auditorium in San Francisco from January 7 through 15, 1961. *Author collection*

probably scrapped after its show duties ended. However, the second production 1961 Tempest, which was displayed during the final GM Motorama, still exists and has been owned by the company since it was built.

The cost of producing the Motorama had grown to the point where there were now more economical ways to promote GM products. Special one-offs continued to be built and shown at various events around the country, but not on the large scale of the 1950s GM Motorama. As Chuck Jordan explained, "That period was the golden age of automotive design." All such periods eventually come to an end. They can never be repeated, and are seldom fully recognized for what they were until well afterward.

Chapter Ten
Twins, Triplets, and Quadruplets

In some cases during this era, duplicate or near duplicate Dream Cars were built. For example, three prototype Corvettes, a pair of Bonneville Specials, three F-88s, four copies of Cadillac's Le Mans, and two Firebird IIs were built. The original prototype Corvette (or "Waldorf Corvette" as it was often referenced inside GM Styling) was assigned a Chevrolet Engineering internal tracking number of "852." Four more prototypes were ordered, but only "853" and "856" were actually built; the two canceled orders were for a complete car and a complete chassis. Car 852 was assigned the formal identification of EX-52 and was assembled by GM Styling and Chevrolet Engineering, while the other two bodies were supplied by Fisher Body and assembled by the Chevrolet experimental department. Car 853 was the second show car and the other was a test car that received some heavy-duty test driving on GM's Proving Grounds. (No one really knew with certainty how well the fiberglass

Three Corvette prototypes were built. One was used for a variety of tests to study the limits of the chassis and fiberglass structure, thus it was not built to show-quality standards. *GM Media Archive*

154

Very little remains of two of the three Starfires built. John Perkins' father, an Oldsmobile chassis engineer, bought two sets of seats from two scrapped Starfires in the 1950s at an Olds salvage auction. *John Perkins*

body would withstand the stresses imposed by driving, so extensive testing had to be performed.) The second show car was the third one to be completed and it was displayed in Canada on two occasions and at various auto shows in the United States during 1953, including the Denver Auto Show (April 6–11) and the Michigan Motor Show (June 2–7). The two show prototypes were nearly identical, but the second car lacked the scoops on the front fenders and the Continental-type door release pushbuttons of the first car. Other minor details varied under the hood as well as in the interior.

Two prototype hardtop 'Vettes appear to have been built for 1954. Commonly seen photos taken in Miami show a pale yellow car with its top in place often posed with the Nomad, Corvair, and a regular production Corvette. Reportedly, the yellow car and a maroon car were shown simultaneously, meaning the yellow car could not have been given a new look, thus there had to have been two such prototypes. The 1953 Corvette with serial number E53F001260 is the second of the two cars and was displayed at Canadian shows and perhaps elsewhere. It was taken off the line and given the same, or virtually the same, modifications as the first car, but with a gold-tinted maroon exterior and interior.

According to an article written by Wayne Ellwood and Noland Adams for the Summer 1999 issue of *SHARK Quarterly* magazine, 'Vette number 260 was sold with its roll-up windows and other experimental parts by GM in August 1957 to an employee in the truck sales department in Oshawa, Ontario. This car still exists and has had numerous owners, though since 1973 it has had the same owner who lives in Vancouver, BC.

The second 1954 Bonneville Special was built to tour Pontiac dealerships across the country, though it reportedly made its debut in Los Angeles at the Pan Pacific Auditorium during the GM Motorama tour. This example was painted metallic green with a green and pewter interior. Other differences between it and the first car included the gauges

At least two 1953 Buick Wildcats were built. This one has the radiused rear wheel openings similar to those of the limited-production 1953 Skylark. It was driven by the Buick zone manager for several days in Oklahoma City around the time of the Oklahoma State Fair where the car was displayed from September 26 to October 3, 1953. He snapped this picture of his daughter seated inside the car. *Jim Jordan collection*

Le Mans number two led the motorcade of Dream Cars on the newly opened Turner Turnpike in Oklahoma for the Oklahoma Oil Progress celebration in mid-October of 1953. *GM Media Archive*

Four 1953 Cadillac Le Mans were built. This is the second example, making an appearance at the 1953 Glidden Tour in mid-September. The route went through Cleveland, Ohio, where these photographs were taken. Wilfred Leland, son of Cadillac founder Henry Leland, was in attendance. *GM Heritage Center*

(less elaborate than those of the original), four air vents in the leading edge of the hood (sans chrome trim), a chrome-plated radiator core support, and a cylinder head painted red instead of being chrome-plated like that of the original.

Bonneville Special number two was rumored to have been seriously damaged at the Pontiac dealership in Pontiac, Michigan, and subsequently scrapped. Perhaps there is some truth in the car receiving damage at the dealership, but it was definitely not scrapped, though its condition did deteriorate. Somehow the car became privately owned, and in 1992 Joe Bortz purchased it approximately two years after first hearing of its alleged existence. By that time, the second copy had been virtually forgotten, leaving most enthusiasts believing only one Bonneville Special was built. Bortz received a phone call from a gentleman during 1990 asking, "Why do you claim to own the Bonneville Special when I have it?!" Bortz justifiably doubted the caller's claim believing instead that the car must have been a customized Corvette someone made to resemble the Bonneville Special. Still he was curious and asked for pictures. The photocopied pictures he received a short while later were not the best quality, but the image shown on them did show a Bonneville Special. Bortz attempted to make contact again with the owner, but was unsuccessful after several attempts. Finally, two years later, he made another try and learned the man had passed away shortly after their first conversation. However, Bortz was able to purchase the second Bonneville Special from the estate. Even though the odometer read about 700 miles, the obscure show car needed a thorough restoration.

Bortz did not pursue the restoration, but instead sold the car several years later. Well-known Denver, Colorado, collector Roger Willbanks took on this ambitious task and finished in time to proudly display it at the 2000 Meadow Brook Concours d'Elegance.

Bonneville Special number two sold on January 21, 2006, at Barrett-Jackson in Scottsdale for $2.8 million plus commission, while one of its designers, Homer LaGassey, watched the event from the stage. When invited to make a few comments about the metallic green show car, he noted that the Bonneville Special was one of the cars that set the stage for Pontiac's entrance into the youth market in the 1950s and 1960s. This car is presently in the collection of Ron Pratte in Arizona.

Sometime after the 1954 GM Motorama ended, Harley Earl decided he wanted an F-88 (XP-20, Shop Order 2292) for himself, so a second example, this one painted red, was assembled for Earl. GM vice president (and the former head of the Olds Division) Sherrod Skinner had another F-88 (XP-20, Shop Order 2264) built, but it was not absolutely identical to the first F-88 (i.e., no quarter panel molding, wider pleats in the upholstery, etc.). Toward the end of 1955, Earl had his F-88 restyled. Less than a year later, the car was updated with a new body; it became the F-88 Mk. II. For Earl's retirement an all-new F-88 Mk. III (XP-88, Shop Order 90388) was built that featured a number of experimental systems and a retractable top similar to the Ford Skyliner.

On the Buick side, the number of first-model Wildcats built is uncertain, though it may have been two or even three. Photos exist showing a Wildcat I with radiused rear wheel openings like those of a 1953 Skylark.

Le Mans number three was displayed in the showroom of Pemberton Cadillac Company in Toledo, Ohio, during May 1953. *Charles D. Barnette and Toledo Library*

In the Cadillac Division, four examples of the Le Mans were built, and each has an interesting and varied history. Le Mans one through three were assigned engine numbers of 5300 00002 through 5300 00004 and built at the same time. The last one, with engine number 5300 91300, was built much later—near the end of 1953 production, in fact. For clarification, the "53" in the engine number is the year of the car; next would normally follow the series number such as "62," but in this case there is not a series number since the Le Mans was not a production model nor was the design built from a production model, hence it simply had "00" as a series number. The Orleans was assigned engine number 5362 00001, so for the next three cars the Le Mans were sequentially numbered.

Thanks to Matt Larson, who is the coauthor of *LaSalle—Cadillac's Companion*

These photos of the Le Mans were likely taken at a Toronto area Cadillac-Oldsmobile dealership in late July 1953 and this is possibly the car that was shown at the Canadian National Exhibition between August 28 and September 2. If correct, then this Le Mans is probably the third example built. *Charles D. Barnette Collection*

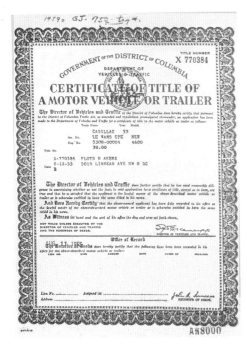

Surprisingly, still in existence is a photocopy of the original title issued by Washington, D.C., to Floyd Akers for the third Le Mans sold to him by GM in 1955. *Charles D. Barnette*

Car, a longtime member of the Cadillac-LaSalle Club, and the Cadillac archivist for the GM Heritage Center, the records on these cars in the files of the GM Heritage Center can be reported.

The record of the first Le Mans was detailed in Chapter Six. The second Le Mans has an unusual history. This car's build sheet in the files at the GM Heritage Center says, "Cars in Company use, for use of Harley J. Earl." The car was transferred to Earl on August 21, 1953, so he owned it for awhile. Internal correspondence at the center makes reference to a Le Mans, which was titled to Earl, sitting in a warehouse. The correspondence authorized the car to be transferred back to the company and gave its net asset value as one dollar. The engine number is not given, but unless Earl owned two Le Mans, then number two must be the subject of the memorandum. Notes also indicate Earl's car was repainted black sometime in 1953. (All four Le Mans were originally painted Metallic Blue with paint code F-272-X-75276.) Le Mans number two (5300 00003) was definitely repainted black by the time it appeared in Cleveland, Ohio, for that year's Glidden Tour in September. A few photos still exist showing it with cars from the early 1900s, including a shot of it posed with a 1909 Cadillac. Afterwards, the car was sent to Oklahoma at the request of the state's governor, Johnston Murray, to participate in the Oil Progress Exposition held in mid-October. This car, along with two other 1953 Motorama cars—Starfire and Wildcat I—as well as a Corvette, was on display at the Oklahoma City Municipal Auditorium for two days before being driven in the Oil Progress Motorcade and on the newly completed Turner Turnpike. The Le Mans and the other cars went on to Tulsa to be exhibited there. Le Mans number two went back to Oklahoma City to be displayed in the showroom of Greenlease-Moore Cadillac-Chevrolet during the first week of November. No information was uncovered to determine where the

Le Mans number three was sold to Floyd Akers, who owned Capitol Cadillac in Washington, D.C. Later the car became the property of Coleman Cadillac and is shown in this photo inside the showroom of this dealership. The photo was taken in the mid-1980s. *Richard Sisson*

Le Mans number three was modified with an aftermarket air conditioner. Numerous other modifications were made to the car to make it roadworthy. *Richard Sisson*

car went afterwards or even if it still exists, though incorrect stories have appeared in print stating the second Le Mans was sold to the owner of Capitol Cadillac in Washington, D.C., Floyd Akers.

On the third LeMans, little information exists. GM records list it as a "Car in Company use" that was shipped by flatbed truck to Pemberton Cadillac Company in Toledo, Ohio, for display in the dealership's showroom May 14–16, 1953. This is the car sold to Floyd Akers who had a Cadillac distributorship. No documentation apparently exists in GM records to confirm that fact, but a photocopy of the certificate of title issued by Washington, D.C., to Akers in 1955 does exist. The serial number appearing on that document—5300 00004—confirms the car's identity as the third one built.

Former mechanic Buddy Abell, who worked at Capitol Cadillac when the Le Mans was delivered there in June of 1955, recalled the mechanic staff there had to make the car roadworthy from its nonrunning condition.

The last Le Mans built was assembled for the president of Fisher Body, James Goodman. It was given a detachable hardtop, though it was evidently discarded long ago. *GM Heritage Center*

James Goodman's Le Mans was updated with new styling and a 1959 powertrain just prior to Harley Earl's retirement from GM. *Author collection*

Le Mans number four still exists and was displayed at the 1999 North American International Automobile Show in Detroit. It is now part of the collection of the GM Heritage Center. *Rusty Thompson*

Seen in profile with the canopy doors raised, the Bonneville Special looks part aircraft and part European sports car. The reproduction wheel covers were not yet complete (lacking blades) when this photo was taken at the 2000 Meadow Brook Concours d'Elegance. *Dennis Adler*

Not only did a modified 1955 wiring harness need to be installed, but also functional instruments had to be built. Furthermore, the laws of Washington, D.C., specified a minimum road clearance, which the Le Mans as built did not meet; installing taller springs and spindles got the car street legal. Some work on the car was performed by Derham in Rosemont, Pennsylvania, though exactly what is unknown. Most likely the company is responsible for the Le Mans script mounted on the deck lid; no other period photo of the rear of a Le Mans found during research for this book revealed such a script.

The Motorama cars were not really intended to be driven, but evidently the Le Mans was reasonably well built. It did have one design flaw that required a fix. A weather seal had to be made to stop rain water from pouring into the interior

through the base of the convertible top; it was not very effective, though.

In the early 1960s, and after the car had been driven about 6,100 miles, it was put into storage at Floyd Aker's other dealership, Suburban Cadillac. Then in 1977, the car was inadvertently sold with this dealership, which then became Coleman Cadillac. Somehow no one thought to exclude the car from the dealership's inventory when the contract was prepared. Somewhere along the way, the car was repainted; the color was changed from a pale yellow (perhaps Apollo Gold or Cape Ivory) to a shade of white. In the 1980s, the car was displayed in the showroom of Coleman Cadillac in Bethesda, Maryland. Around 1989, this Le Mans was sold to its current owner who prefers to remain anonymous, though the car's whereabouts can be stated to be in the Washington, D.C. area.

Le Mans number four was built specifically for J. E. "Bud" Goodman, the CEO of Fisher Body and a close friend of Harley Earl; the car bore Goodman's initials in the center of its steering wheel. This Le Mans was assembled late in the model year (probably the fall of 1953) judging by its engine number, 5300 91300. (Cadillac built its 100,000th car of the year on December 1 before switching over to the 1954 model year on the 10th.) This one lacked the rain sensor, cornering lamp, and corrugations on the rocker panels that the other three Le Mans had. Of the four Le Mans built, this car and the second example are the only ones known to have been made operable by GM. Le Mans number four is probably the car used in the Rose Bowl Parade on January 1, 1954.

This car received multiple engine transplants and other modifications including having a detachable hardtop before being

Bonneville Special number two had a 268 straight eight, but with a painted cylinder head instead of a chrome-plated one as on the original example. There were other minor differences between these cars, too. *Dennis Adler*

The second Bonneville Special was not a carbon copy of its predecessor. It was painted metallic green, had a green and pewter interior and its instrumentation was not as elaborate. *Dennis Adler*

restyled and updated to 1959 specs for Goodman shortly before Earl left GM. Changes in the styling included quad headlamps, flatter hood, simulated air scoops on the quarters, revised tail fins and tail lamps, and removal of the simulated trunk straps. The car was repainted and reupholstered in matching Silver-Gray. (A previous exterior color was reportedly Sea Mist Green.) Under the hood went a 1959 Eldorado 390 V-8 and Hydra-matic as well as a low-profile Harrison radiator. In 1963, Bud Goodman gave the car to his son who had become the owner of Clarence Dixon Cadillac in Hollywood, California. The updated Le Mans was displayed in the showroom there and years later it was put on exhibit in the Petersen Automotive Museum. Le Mans number four also appeared in a scene in the 1978 movie, *The Buddy Holly Story*. In 1999, it was displayed at the International Auto Show in Detroit and shortly thereafter, the Cadillac Historical Collection purchased the car from Goodman. It is now part of the collection of the GM Heritage Center.

Incidentally, at least one custom car that resembles the early Le Mans models currently exists. And, undoubtedly, other vintage customs are out there, some of which could be mistaken for a Motorama show car.

This F-88 is believed to be the third in the series. In this photo, it is shown touring with GM's Parade of Progress. *GM Media Archive*

PART III

The Legacy—Motorama Car Mysteries and GM's Newest Concepts

This F-88 was assembled in the 1990s from components originally sent to E. L. Cord in 1955. When this photo was taken, the car was part of the Blackhawk Museum collection. *Dennis Adler*

Chapter Eleven

Fates of the Motorama Cars—
Mysteries Solved and Unsolved

Tales related to the disappearances of Motorama Dream Cars are not unlike stories of mysterious disappearances within the Bermuda Triangle or of crashed flying saucers stashed away at Area 51. Maybe if these cars were fictional and the subject of a mystery novel (perhaps titled The GM X-Files), then an excerpt from such a book might read something like this:

The night was moonless and still as two enigmatic figures met in deep shadows cast by the street lamps surrounding a nondescript warehouse known to be leased by the automotive giant, General Motors. Quickly they enter. Their secret encounter was brief and to the point.

"Hey, Pete."

"Hi, Dave. Thanks for meeting me. I suppose you know why I asked you to meet me here?"

Dave closes his eyes in mock disgust, and shaking his head replies, "I'm guessing it has something to do with the scrap order issued for the Nomad. You saw it, didn't you?"

Two 1954 Corvairs were probably built. If this is correct, the red Corvair seen at the Waldorf was not simply repainted light green after its appearance there as is commonly believed. This was the scene at the GM Motorama in Chicago. *Author collection*

"Oh, yeah . . . I saw it. The top brass wants it hauled to the scrap yard in a few days where it is to be crushed."

"That's a shame," Dave says, "but there's nothing we can really do about it, Pete." Then half-seriously, he adds, "Of course, we could go to the boss and try to persuade. . . ."

Pete quickly interrupts his friend's suggestion. "Tried it—was told to drop the matter." He pauses, takes a deep breath, and finally comes out with it. "The Nomad is not going to the crusher." Dave harrumphs and stares inquisitively as his friend continues. "We've put too much work into it. It's not just some useless hulk; it's a work of art. All of those cars inside this building are."

Sharing his associate's awe for its contents, Dave turns on his heels and scans the contents of the warehouse. "Boy, I agree, but you know the reasons for the order. I mean, what can you do? It's not like you can just walk in here, put the Nomad on a trailer, and tow it back to your house!"

Pete's momentary silence confirms the deed. "The Nomad is *already* in my garage."

"Pete! You can't be serious! You are serious!" Dave scans the contents of the warehouse a second time. The Nomad is gone.

Pete laughs, "What can I say? My wife has been bugging me for a while to get her a station wagon."

"Oh, that's funny, Pete. I always knew you're the type to take some risks, but this! That's your plan to save the Nomad, steal it?" Then Dave stops and reflects on what he has just said. Almost stuttering he starts to ask, "How did you . . . I mean . . ." and then exasperated at the thought he raises his hands and says, "Never mind . . . I don't even want to know. So how do I fit into your clever scheme?"

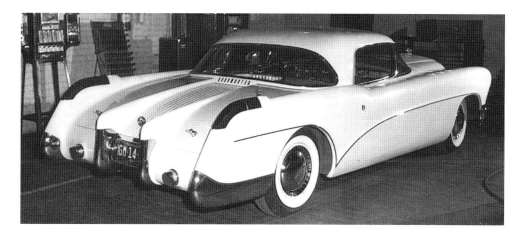

"Dave, all I need you to do is make the right adjustments to the paperwork. The big boys aren't going to be nosing around the scrap yard or here . . . they assume their orders will be carried out. Besides, they have the quarterly board meeting to prepare for. The guys at the scrap yard don't even know we are supposed to bring anything to their place."

Dave interrupts his calculating friend. "I'm way ahead of you now. I'll take care of the rest." Then Dave adds the following to make light of the obvious. "By the way, I suggest you keep the Nomad well hidden for the next couple of *decades* and if any of the bosses drop by your house for a visit, don't let 'em anywhere near the garage!"

Pete plays along with his new co-conspirator's humor. "Sound advice, Dave." Then his tone becomes serious. "Thanks for your help." Pete flips off the lights as they leave the warehouse and disappear into the night.

Could characters like Pete and Dave have actually carried out a covert action like this? Possibly, or even probably, if the story about the first Bonneville Special's escape from GM is true.

The point of this "pulp fiction" is to illustrate the web of intrigue surrounding the destiny of some Motorama Dream Cars.

This 1953 Buick Wildcat shown in this photo has a detachable hardtop. It is one of two or three built, but may have been unique in having Skylark-style rear wheel openings. The photo is dated January 12, 1954. *Author collection*

Curiously, the Wildcat was shown in black in this Motorama promotional ad, which appeared in a Miami newspaper. Though a black Wildcat appeared at the Waldorf-Astoria in January, a white one was exhibited in Miami and succeeding GM Motorama shows of 1953. *Author collection*

Shown here is one of the F-88s built after the Motorama show car; it is probably number two built for Harley Earl. If this is correct, then the scalloped wheel openings, appearing on Earl's car, were added to the car at a later date. Seated in the pictured F-88 are Dan Perkins ("driver") and his brother John. Their father, Ralph, was an Oldsmobile assistant chassis engineer and he drove the car to his house while en route to the GM Proving Grounds in Milford sometime in 1954. The car was painted black at this time. Note the side pipes. *John Perkins collection*

The rumor about the fate of the 1954 Nomad is an old one. Supposedly, the car was stolen from GM long ago and has been residing in a warehouse somewhere in California.

What is known is that some (at least four) of the Motorama cars and some experimental engines were hauled to Warhoops Used Auto & Truck Parts in Sterling Heights (just north of the GM Tech Center) where they were to be destroyed. Four cars were purchased from the yard in 1989. Several of these cars were stored in a GM-leased warehouse on Mound Road in Detroit, but roughly around the time Bill Mitchell took over from the retired Harley Earl, the lease was terminated, and something had to be done with its contents. Officially, that something was to destroy the cars. A few within the company may have risked their careers to save certain Dream Cars before scrap orders could be executed. If that is true, a small conspiracy may have been required to save them.

Dream Car collector Joe Bortz said some of the cars escaped the destruct order with the tacit approval of higher-ups; the stylists simply did not want their creations destroyed and some managers just took a "know nothing, see nothing" attitude in response to the stylists' pleas.

The whereabouts of many of the Motorama cars are documented, but several of these cars are still unaccounted for, which adds the captivating element of mystery to the subject. In a few instances, however, there was no need for a clandestine operation to save the Motorama cars; some of the early ones were simply sold and others were sent back to their respective divisions where they are maintained to this day. Most of the experimental cars, though, were assumed by many people to have been destroyed.

Why were any of these special cars destroyed? Retired GM Design staff executive Larry Faloon was quoted as saying Harley Earl was opposed to destroying any of the Motorama cars and is said to have given some of them away to people who wanted the cars.

According to the late Dave Holls, who worked under Harley Earl, some of the 1953s got into the hands of people outside GM and, "It was nothing but a disaster. They were thrown together for a show and not really roadable. (Some Motorama cars were built to high enough standards, however, that they could be made roadworthy.) People wanted the cars and GM didn't really think that much about it, so it sold them. Afterwards though, the cars were impossible to keep running or to repair. Even the paint was impossible to match. Everything was custom built, so no parts existed. (Some spare parts were made, just not in mass quantity.) After that, GM said that all of the Motorama cars were to be scrapped in '54 and '55. A lot of us lamented the loss of the cars that were scrapped, but the attitude at GM was that you shouldn't whine about it. Don't live in the past. So you kind of kept your mouth shut, went on, and did new cars." Holls' commentary originally appeared in Dennis Adler's article, "1954 Oldsmobile F-88," published in the January 1995 issue of *Car Collector* magazine.

Why all the mystery surrounding these special cars? The reasons are varied. For one, record keeping was poor by today's standards. Records were often written in pencil on 5x8 index cards. The files on the Motorama cars were active until GM was through showing the cars; at that point, the files were boxed and stored in any convenient place, which was typically any unoccupied corner of a basement—not the best place to preserve paperwork and photographs. Longterm preservation was not considered paramount either. Moreover, anyone involved in conspiracies to save the Dream Cars did not make their schemes public knowledge. The best we enthusiasts have heard, if anything, is something vague—a story almost totally lacking in specifics, like the old rumor associated with the Nomad. An additional complication is if any of the cars mentioned here do still exist, their respective owners are maintaining their silence on the matter. Conceivably, anyone in possession of one of these "lost" cars may fear legal action by GM if word got out about it. The law regarding such a matter is a bit complex and would depend on a multitude of factors.

What happened to the Motorama Corvette EX-52 (aka 852) and the other 1953 Corvette prototypes? Much research has been done on this subject by one of the founding members of the National Corvette Restorers Society (NCRS), John Amgwert. In an article he wrote in 1993 for the club's official publication, *The Corvette Restorer Magazine*, he detailed the history of the earliest Corvettes through work orders, which still exist and are in the possession of the NCRS. According to these memorandums, the number one Motorama 'Vette body was burned at the Milford Proving Grounds for a flammability test and its frame salvaged for the 1954 "Waldorf" Nomad. One of the work orders is dated November 6, 1953; it has a detailed description of the results of the flammability testing conducted. The final notation describes the body collapsing from the flames at 11 a.m. This test was performed to determine whether a flame retardant should be mixed into the fiberglass or not.

Harley Earl's F-88 was driven to Watkins Glen. At the time, the car was reportedly red with a white stripe. *GM Media Archive*

Adding the retardant would have added a few dollars to the cost of building each car. The tests revealed that a "reinforced plastic body is superior in resistance to fire than a conventional steel body."

Automotive historian Don Keefe also reached the same conclusions regarding the fate of EX-52 in an article he wrote for *Corvette Fever*. Some, however, argue the Corvette with serial number EX-122 is the original Motorama show car; EX-122 still exists. A number of writers including former GM officials such as Russell Sanders, of Chevrolet's engineering department and later director of engineering and sales at GM's Rochester Products Division, have referred to EX-122 as the Motorama car. Amgwert and Keefe both concluded from examination of the same stack of work orders that EX-122 actually began as the second production Corvette, E53F001002.

Whether or not EX-122 was a Motorama prototype, it was definitely rebuilt to serve as a test car for the experimental Chevrolet small block V-8. Russell Sanders bought EX-122 in 1956. The records used by Mr. Amgwert for his article also reveal information regarding 1953 Corvettes, which were assigned to GM's Proving Grounds in Milford, Michigan. These 'Vettes received reference numbers beginning with "3950" (serial number E53F001001). Corvette "3955" (serial number unknown) was delivered to Creative Industries, an outside contractor to GM, specializing in custom design work, on December 4, 1953. It was ordered the preceding month as a no-paint, no-primer car to be sent to GM Styling. Perhaps this Corvette became one of the "hardtop" Motorama show cars.

What was the fate of the second Motorama 'Vette show car? Presumably, it was scrapped. The aforementioned set of work orders in the custody of the NCRS show that the body of the prototype test car (#856) was ordered on December 31, 1953 to be replaced with the body from the second show car (#853). Body "856" and frame "853" were returned to Chevrolet Experimental for scrapping. Eventually, the hybrid 853/856 show car was probably destroyed, but its true fate is unknown.

The second 1954 F-88, the one built for Harley Earl, was given a new body for 1957. In this guise it is known as the F-88 Mk. II. This car and his later F-88 Mk. III were never shown at a GM Motorama. *GM Media Archive*

What made the prototypes significantly different from the production cars (beyond the few plainly visible trim differences) was their thicker fiberglass and one-piece body. The production 'Vettes had rocker panels joined to the body with glue and rivets. A lip formed where the body components came together and was hidden with the chrome spear that aligned with the front and rear bumpers. If anyone ever stumbles across a GM factory-made one-piece 1953 Corvette body, that person will have found a very special Corvette!

The Nomad is allegedly locked away in a warehouse in Newport Beach, California—at least that was the rumor in the 1960s and 1970s—but there is another version of its fate. Chapter Eleven of Noland Adam's book, *Corvette American Legend Vol. 2*, recites an interview conducted with a GM employee who began working for the company in 1955. His first assignment was to assist in scrapping some show cars, and one of them was the Nomad. The date given for its destruction was on or about July 11, 1955. However, the Nomad was later discovered to have been on display at a Washington State dealership six weeks *after* the show car was supposed to have been scrapped. If both stories are accurate, then there had to be more than one Nomad built. Did Fisher Body assemble a second Nomad as in the case of the second Corvette show car?

There is still another rumor regarding the Nomad. It was to be destroyed, but a GM executive managed to put it in his garage before that happened. When he died, the car was put up for sale, but no title existed. How that problem was overcome, or if the rumor even has a grain of truth to it is not known. Perhaps this rumor somehow ties into the car being in a warehouse in California.

GM's Floyd Joliet says the records he has seen indicate only one Nomad was built and that it was destroyed; Chuck Jordan agrees. Joliet also recalled that either Dave Holls or Bill Mitchell confirmed to him that the Nomad was destroyed. Reportedly, a work order calling for the Nomad's destruction was in GM's files, but without a completion order attached. Does a 1954 Nomad exist now? A new rumor about it surfaced while this book was being written; it ties into the next subject, the Corvair.

What happened to the 1954 Corvair and how many were built? According to two eyewitnesses interviewed for a 2003 story about the GM Motorama cars in *Car Collector* magazine, the car—described by both as a red 1953 to 1955–style Corvette fastback—was seen at Warhoops sitting atop one or two other cars.

One of the witnesses, Mark Auran, now living in East Texas, was a Michigan resident in the 1960s and 1970s. As a teenager, he frequented Warhoops in search of GTO parts and distinctly recalled seeing the Corvair as well as the Biscayne. The other witness interviewed was Larry Muckey—the same man who came close to buying the Eldorado Brougham Town Car in 1975 and later assisted with its restoration. He said the car disappeared from Warhoops around 1978.

When Joe Bortz was asked if he was aware the Corvair had been sighted in the Warhoops yard, he said he was not and added that Harry Warholak Sr. never mentioned the Corvair to him. (By the time Bortz purchased the four Motorama cars from him, about a decade had passed since the "red fastback Corvette" was last seen.) When Harry Warholak Jr. (who now runs his late

father's salvage yard) was asked about this matter, he was certain that only the Biscayne, LaSalle II Roadster, LaSalle II Sedan, and the Eldorado Brougham Town Car were brought to his father's salvage yard; he did not believe any additional Dream Cars of any type were ever there. With the death of Harry Sr. several years ago the controversy cannot be resolved—at least not until the red Corvair appears somewhere—which might happen in the not-too-distant future! Assuming the Corvair was at Warhoops until the late 1970s and then disappeared, the obvious conclusion is that someone acquired ownership of the car. Reinforcing that conclusion is a recent, but at this time unsubstantiated, rumor that the red Corvair still exists and that its current owner possesses a 1954 Nomad!

The presence of the red Corvair at Warhoops was the key to learning that two Corvairs had to have been built. The reason the sightings are the key element to the belief that two Corvairs were built is simply that the Corvair shown at the Waldorf was red; the Corvair shown at Chicago (the final stop on the 1954 GM Motorama tour) was light blue-green; the Corvair at Warhoops was red. The likelihood of the Corvair getting repainted light blue-green only to be returned to red after the Motorama seems extremely remote. Do both Corvairs still exist?

Whether or not the first Corvette "hardtop" still exists is unclear. Getting GM to part with the second example took a while. Finally, a legal waiver signed by the buyer satisfied GM officials enough to sell the car with its experimental parts. Maybe something similar happened with the first example though reportedly a scrap order does exist for this car.

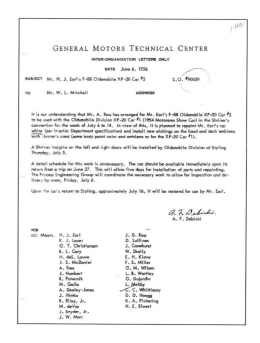

This letter to Bill Mitchell reveals that the original F-88 show car was still in the possession of Oldsmobile as late as the summer of 1956. The letter was in regard to using the original F-88 show car and Earl's for the Shriners Parade. The letter also says Earl's F-88 was to be repainted white for the event. *John Perkins collection*

This photography work order for GM Photographic indicates that the third XP-20 F-88 was built for Sherrod Skinner, who had served as Oldsmobile's general manager. The third car in the series differed somewhat from the original show car. Its interior (top right) had minor differences, including wider pleats in the seats. This F-88's quarter panels lacked the side molding and louvers. *Steve Wolken collection*

The 1956 Chevrolet Impala reportedly was scrapped. During the aforementioned interview in Noland Adams' second volume of his series of Corvette history books, the GM employee who gave his account of the demise of the Nomad stated he believed the Impala was scrapped not long after he began working for GM (mid-1955). The Impala did appear at the 1957 Chicago Auto Show in January and at the Oklahoma Semi-Centennial Exhibition in June of that year along with the Club de Mer, Golden Rocket, Centurion, and Eldorado Brougham prototypes. Perhaps the latter event was the final showing of the Impala before it was scrapped.

The 1954 Pontiac Strato-Streak was allegedly scrapped in the late-1950s or early-1960s, but Bill Warner, the founder and chairman of the annual Amelia Island Concours d'Elegance, suspects this one might still exist.

An Oldsmobile Engineering logbook shows three 1953 Starfires were built, but no information could be found on whether or not the extra Starfires were identical to the show car. They may have all had the same color scheme as the show car judging by the apparent lack of photos showing any Starfire in a differing color, thus it would be difficult or impossible to determine which car was which in a photo without accompanying documentation. Sometimes, duplicate Motorama cars were painted and upholstered in differing colors, making them easily distinguishable from one another, but not always.

What can be confirmed about two of the Starfires is this—they were scrapped in 1954 or 1955. This information comes from John Perkins, the owner of the referenced Olds engineering logbook as well as two front and rear sets of 1953 Starfire seats. His father, Ralph Perkins, who worked as a chassis engineer for Oldsmobile, purchased the two identical turquoise and white sets of seats in 1954 or 1955 through the Oldsmobile factory salvage department. The total price for the custom-fabricated seats is believed to have been around $40. A wood base and casters were added to the base of the seats. Except for these modifications, the seats remain as new. Perkins (now retired from Oldsmobile) attempted to locate the only 1953 Starfire known to him at the time for the purpose of restoring it. The second set of seats was presumed to have been a spare. His search in the mid-1970s led him to the man who said he destroyed *two* Starfires. This is when he learned of a second Starfire having been built. Only when the author contacted Mr. Perkins for information about the 1953 Starfire and the 1954 F-88s, did he dig out his father's Olds engineering logbook and discover three were listed as built.

At least one of the Starfires was fully operable. According to John Ross, the son of Art Ross (Oldsmobile's chief stylist), his father got to drive one of the Starfires for a while (as well as an F-88). Furthermore, one was driven during the Oklahoma Oil Progress celebration with the number two Le Mans in October 1953.

Clearly, one Starfire could still exist.

And what about the F-88? The history of the F-88 built for the 1954 GM Motorama show circuit and the ones that followed it is intriguing and confusing. Three are believed to have been built; that is what is shown in the previously mentioned Oldsmobile Engineering logbook. Those consulted about this subject also believe only three complete cars were built. Presumably, only one was planned at the time of the 1954 GM Motorama tour. As mentioned in Chapter Ten, a second example was built for Harley Earl's personal use around the time the 1954 GM Motorama tour ended. His car was reported to have been painted red with a white stripe across the hood centerline and possibly across the rear deck. Photos exist showing a 1954 F-88 painted black and having side pipes. A GM press release from March 8, 1955 made mention of a bright yellow car being displayed at the Parade of Progress. Still another photo in color was published in the letters section of the June 2004 issue (page 6) of *Collectible Automobile* showing a metallic blue 1954 F-88 at the GM Parade of Progress in Green Bay, Wisconsin, on September 2, 1955. There is another report of a white F-88. Further adding to the mystery of how many were built, are photos showing an F-88 with scalloped wheel openings somewhat like those seen on the limited production 1954 Buick Skylark. Various photographs from GM's archives show the car with differing grille and bumper treatments. There is a story of an F-88 burning while parked on an Olds engineer's driveway and of a spare body being built and given to E. L. Cord (of Cord Automobile fame).

Thanks to an article by automotive historian and award-winning author Michael Lamm, which was published in the October 2003 issue of *Collectible Automobile*, as well as assistance from former Olds engineer John Perkins, collector Joe Bortz, and Motorama car enthusiast Don Baron, along with examination of archival photos taken by GM Photographic Services of the F-88s, the author believes a somewhat clearer picture of the history of these cars can now be presented.

This page from an Oldsmobile Engineering logbook reveals three 1953 Starfires and three 1953 F-88s were built. *John Perkins collection*

As explained in Chapter Ten, the second F-88 was built for Harley Earl in 1954. The car went through a few color changes and restyles. The author has concluded, as a result of examining photos (many with dates), that Earl's car was originally built as a near duplicate of the F-88 show car displayed at the 1954 GM Motorama. Photos taken by GM Photographic Services in December 1955, show the car with modifications which included a grille with a central divider (it looked much like that of the 1954 Cutlass but it was not the same) and scalloped wheel openings. The group of photos also show the installation of what appears to be a supercharger and dual carbs mounted on a special intake that placed them on either side of the engine (much like the configuration of the cross-ram 413 used by Chrysler in the 1960s). Whether this was part of the late-1955 upgrade or was already present from the start is not currently known.

The body of Earl's F-88 was probably removed from its frame and replaced in 1957 with the Mk. II body, which featured quad headlights and short (both in length and height) tail fins. What happened to the original body of F-88 number two? Presumably, it was scrapped.

Harley Earl received another F-88 (XP-88, Shop Order 90388) built to his specifications in late 1958; it was a farewell gift to the retiring GM design chief. The 1959 F-88 Mk. III was the ultimate version of the series. Its many features included a fiberglass body, tubular frame combined with a 1959 Olds front suspension, stainless-steel retractable top, wraparound windshield, experimental fuel-injection setup by Rochester, and an experimental automatic transmission.

After Harley Earl died in 1969, the Mk. III was reportedly meant to go to a new NASCAR museum. (Earl and NASCAR founder, Bill France, were friends.) Unfortunately, the construction of the new museum was delayed. During the delay, Earl's successor, Bill Mitchell, asked NASCAR officials to return the Mk. III. Some time after it was sent back to Warren, Michigan, the car was ordered to be scrapped.

As mentioned in Chapter Four, a third XP-20 F-88 (Shop Order 2264) was built for Sherrod E. Skinner, who had moved to GM corporate headquarters after serving as Oldsmobile's general manager. This car was thoroughly photographed by GM Photographic Services on October 6, 1954. The work order numbered 2264 (the same as the car's shop order number) issued for the photography has "Skinner" and "#3" in parentheses next to the description of the car. This F-88 was nearly identical to the original show car and may have originally been painted the same color. (With only black-and-white photos available to view, there is no known way to confirm the original color.) The third F-88 lacked the cowl vents, louvers on the quarters, and the body side molding like those of the Motorama show car. Furthermore, the pleats in the upholstery of the third F-88 were of a different width. The interior was a monotone scheme that may have been the same color as the exterior. Heel pads sewn into both the driver- and passenger-side carpeting featured a grid pattern and were bordered in bright metal trim—a feature shared with the original F-88. The hood scoop is open on the number three car, while the scoop on the number one car had a mesh grille recessed within the opening.

Michael Lamm's article for *Collectible Automobile* ended with the conclusion that the only known F-88 to still exist probably is the Motorama display car, but

This F-88 has the same features as the original show car. *Dennis Adler*

carefully noted that we will likely never know with certainty unless some documentation exists and can be found at GM to confirm this. Supporting Lamm's conclusion in part is the fact that, prior to its restoration, the car had green paint in the wheelwells and floorpans, according to one of its past owners—just as the original show car did. The most important clue seems to be the presence of cowl vents; the original F-88 show car had that feature.

Joe Bortz saw the "Cord" F-88 prior to it being assembled. He saw a body that had not had the door openings cut out. Moreover, a copy of an interoffice memorandum sent to Bill Mitchell, now in the possession of former Olds engineer John Perkins, sheds light on the matter of whether or not this F-88 is the number one show car. The memo details the use of a pair of F-88s for an upcoming Shriners Parade. This memo dated June 6, 1956, begins with, "It is our understanding that Mr. A. Ross has arranged for Mr. Earl's F-88 Oldsmobile XP-20 Car #2 to be used with the Oldsmobile Division XP-20 Car #1 (1954 Motorama Show Car) in the Shriner's [sic] convention for the week of July 6 to 14." The date on the memo is nearly fifteen months after E. L. Cord received his F-88 in crates. This memorandum, as well as what Bortz described seeing, certainly appears to completely eliminate the possibility that the only currently known surviving F-88—the car auctioned in early 2005 at the Barrett-Jackson Auction—is not the GM Motorama show car. Lastly, this car was reported in Barrett-Jackson literature to have the S.O. number "2265." The original show car was Shop Order 1939. (To the author's knowledge, this F-88 has never been represented as the original show car, but there has simply been speculation in that regard.) Regardless of

The only F-88 known to exist was sold for $3 million plus commission at the 2005 Barrett-Jackson Auction in Scottsdale, Arizona. *Danny Page*

what components make up the only F-88 currently known to exist, it is a magnificent specimen and is a special piece of automotive history; it is a car given by one automotive legend to another.

After E. L. Cord received his F-88 components in March 1955, the unassembled car remained in its shipping crates at his residence for several years before being sold. (The car is now in the possession of its fourteenth owner.) An unanswered question lingers. Why was it sent to E. L. Cord? One explanation put forward is that Cord owned the Pan Pacific Auditorium in Los Angeles, which GM used for its Motorama shows. Most likely, E. L. Cord saw the F-88 at the Pan Pacific and expressed an interest in owning it or one like it. Without Cord or Harley Earl available to tell us, we may never have an absolute answer to this question.

What happened to S.O. 2264 built for Sherrod Skinner? After the sale of the F-88 at the 2005 Barrett-Jackson Auction, someone from the audience told one of the announcers broadcasting from the event that he owned two F-88s! Could the claim be true? It could if some combination of the original show car, the first body of the second XP-20 F-88, or the F-88 Mk. II replacement, or the third XP-20 F-88 still exist.

According to Joe Bortz, who over a span of many years has spoken to numerous people who were associated with the Motorama cars, one of the original three F-88s did burn, which may explain the used pieces shipped with the unassembled car sent to Cord, and perhaps discount the claim made by the auction attendee. The process of elimination points to the Sherrod car (number three) as the one that burned.

However, F-88 number three almost assuredly is the car in the aforementioned color photo from September 2, 1955. The car in that photo lacks the sweep molding and the vertical louvers on the rear quarters. (Unless body one was repainted metallic blue and the trim removed during the late summer of 1955, the car in the photo must be the third F-88. Home movie film taken in June or July of 1955 by Michigan resident Don Barron, shows the number one car still in its original color and trim configuration.) If this car burned and any salvaged parts from this car were sent to E. L. Cord, they could not have been sent in March of 1955, but rather afterwards. The author's opinion is that used parts shipped in the crates containing the F-88 sent to Cord came from F-88 number two—Earl's car—which appears to have been first restyled prior to March 1955. Parts such as the "88" numerals on the front fenders of the second car were removed during a restyle.

The other member of the Dream Cars of the 1954 GM Motorama that wore an Oldsmobile badge, the Cutlass, is rumored to have been sold and perhaps was, or still is, in New Jersey.

And, what of Buick's 1953 Wildcat? As explained in Chapter Five, one of the attractions at the 1953 GM Motorama was the Buick Wildcat I. Joe Bortz owns one used for the Motorama show circuit that year; he obtained and restored it approximately two decades ago. However, there is clear evidence to show at least two, if not three, of these cars were built. Photographs illustrating a white Wildcat I with radiused or 1953 Skylark-style rear wheel openings still exist. A seemingly plausible explanation for the situation is that only one car was built and that its wheel openings were altered, but that is not possible. Dated photographs prove both styles of Wildcats existed simultaneously.

Moreover, during the restoration of his Wildcat I, Bortz inspected the car for evidence of restyling; none was found. Neither was evidence found to suggest his car had ever been painted black. Furthermore, several years ago, someone approached him with a set of the special Roto-Static hubcaps, which were specific to the 1953 Wildcat I. These hubcaps appeared to Bortz to have been used with both showing virtually equal wear. His belief is that only two examples were built and one of them was restyled, repainted, and later scrapped.

This theory is likely valid, but three 1953 Wildcats could actually have been built—a black car (shown at the Waldorf), a white one (in the Bortz Auto Collection), and the white Wildcat with the radiused rear wheel openings. Furthermore, the radiused wheel openings may have been planned for the aborted production version. If photos dated October 1953 (the time of the Oil Progress Exposition when the "Skylark"-style Wildcat, second Le Mans, and other such cars were driven on the new Turner Turnpike) or afterwards are ever uncovered showing a black Wildcat I, then evidence will have been found to prove that more than two were built. Incidentally, a detachable hardtop was made for at least one Wildcat I—the one with the Skylark-type rear wheel openings.

A second copy of the 1954 Wildcat II may have been built, though this cannot be proven with the surviving records available through the Alfred P. Sloan Museum. The museum's records definitely do give cause for suspicion, however. If a second Wildcat II was actually built, it would have been for Harlow Curtice, who became president of GM in early 1953; previously he had been president of the Buick Division.

Recall the May 19, 1953, specifications mentioned in Chapter Five? At the end of the first page was the order to build the show car as "runable, so that Mr. Curtice and Mr. Wiles might decide whether or not a number two is to be built for their use." (Ivan Wiles was Buick's general manager and GM vice president at that time.)

Let us go back to the records at the Alfred P. Sloan Museum. An operating manual for the car is in the files of the museum. The manual was printed specifically for Curtice; his name is printed on the cover. Also, a Michigan Passenger Certificate of Registration, issued for a Wildcat II in 1959, is in the museum's files and shows in the blank provided for the vehicle or engine number, "2667332." The Wildcat II at the Alfred P. Sloan Museum has an

An Olds 324 V-8 "Rocket" is under the hood of this F-88. *Dennis Adler*

BUICK WILDCAT II

EXPERIMENTAL ORDER

H. H. CLARK   EXPERIMENTAL ASSEMBLY
R. C. COOK   SPECIFICATIONS DEPT (2)
P. E. MC GRATH   ROAD CAR OFFICE
                     PROVING GROUNDS
                     DYNAMOMETER DEPT.   Experiment No. ___15.53-21
                     DRAFTING ROOM
                     FILE   Date ___5-19-53

Subject: DEVELOPMENT OF A SPECIAL SPORT CAR DESIGNATED 4XC

Requested by: R.C.COOK   Approved by: V.P.MATHEWS

To be followed and reported by:

Description and Instructions:

          THE WHEEL BASE OF THIS CAR IS TO BE 100", FRONT
     TREAD 59" AND REAR TREAD 57".
          SEATING ARRANGEMENT WILL BE SIMILAR TO THE 1953
     WILDCAT.
          THIS IS A SPECIAL SPORT TYPE CAR TO BE SHOWN AT
     THE WALDORF SHOW IN JANUARY 1954.
          CAR IS TO BE MADE RUNABLE SO THAT MR. CURTICE AND
     MR. WILES MIGHT DECIDE WHETHER OR NOT A NUMBER TWO IS TO BE
     BUILT FOR THEIR USE.

     OBJECT:
          FOR PARTS LIST AND RECORD PURPOSES ONLY.

                                        F. C. GERLACH

This engineering order for the construction of the Wildcat II specifies that the car be made "runable" in case Harlow Curtice or Ivan Wiles decided to have one built for their use. *Andrew Clark, Alfred P. Sloan Museum*

odometer reading of 620 miles and has a VIN tag that reads "2667332."

Todd Lemmons, who is a technical advisor for www.Buicks.net gave meaning to this number. Decoding it provided some interesting information. The last digit of the engine number, "2," is probably a series identification. Buick had in 1953 (when the show car would have actually been assembled) Series 40, 50, and 70 in their lineup. Engine numbers for those cars would end with a 4, 5, or 7 depending on the model. Evidently, the Wildcat II was designated as a Series 20. The rest of the number, 266733, indicates a late production 1953 engine. Engine numbers for that model year ranged from between 2000 and 273956, which place the engine number in question as the 7,223rd from the end of 1953 production. This analysis simply indicates the car in the Alfred P. Sloan Museum is the show car used for the GM Motorama, but it does not prove a second example was or was not built. Perhaps the show car was upgraded and used (sparingly) by Curtice, and the proposed second Wildcat II was never built. If the second Wildcat II was built, it had to have been made for someone other than Curtice.

Incidentally, photos taken on July 2, 1954, now in the files of GM Media Archives, illustrate the Wildcat II with alterations from its original form. The work order issued for these particular photos of the car, which is numbered 1940 (the Shop Order number of the show car) has the notation "Curtice" in parentheses just as a similar work order regarding the third F-88 had "Skinner" noted on it. Another notation says "Showing canvas top and new lights." The reference to new lights must mean the headlights, which were relocated to the front bumper.

(As explained in Chapter Five, the Wildcat II show car had headlights mounted on the cowl like spotlights. At some point, this arrangement was modified with the headlights being relocated to the bumper outboard of the parking/directional lamps and spotlights being mounted where the original headlights were installed.) The S.O. number for a second Wildcat II would be different than the one assigned to the show car, so the photos must be of the original show car.

Beyond all of these models discussed, the fate of Cadillac's Orleans is not completely known, but it was not scrapped. Matt Larson, who has exhaustively researched 1953 Cadillacs, said he heard through a credible source that the car was in the San Diego area in the 1970s, although he never personally saw the car. In addition, he spoke with a former employee of the GM Styling facilities who had the chance to purchase the car in Louisville, Kentucky, in 1961 or 1962. Records within the GM Heritage Center show the car was transferred to Charles E. Wilson on March 31, 1953. (Wilson had been appointed secretary of defense in the Eisenhower administration two months earlier.) Moreover, a GM-issued press release from 1956 that included an index of experimental cars from the company referred to the car as "Cadillac Custom 4-door hardtop Coupe de Ville for C. E. Wilson." The Shop Order number given in the press release was the same as that issued for the Orleans—1619. Where is the car today?

Speaking of Cadillac, according to one record in the GM Heritage Center's files (a memorandum titled, "History of Cadillac's Motorama Dream Cars," and dated March 28, 1956), the La Espada was used for show

duty in Europe during 1956. It may have been shown into 1957 or even 1958. One could assume since the nearly identical El Camino was supposedly crushed that the La Espada was destroyed as well. But, was it? Perhaps someone reading this has a definitive answer.

The 1955 and 1956 Eldorado Broughams could still exist, but in the opinion of Joe Bortz these two were likely destroyed.

The destinies of one 1953 Olds Starfire, the second 1953 Cadillac Le Mans, 1954 Cadillac Park Avenue, 1955 Pontiac Strato-Star, 1955 Olds Eighty-Eight Delta, 1955 GMC L'Universelle, 1956 Pontiac Club de Mer, and the 1956 Olds Golden Rocket are un-known. In the case of the latter two, there are at least rumors of their existence. The Club de Mer is rumored to have been ob-tained by a GM executive before it could be destroyed. There is also a rumor that places the car in Salt Lake City, another that says the car is somewhere in California, and another that claims it is in Oklahoma. The one-quarter scale motorized model of it that GM built does exist and is owned by Mr. Bortz. It was restored and is quite spectacular.

The Olds Golden Rocket may be owned by a collector in or near Palisades Park, New Jersey, but so far it has eluded Dream Car hunters. Interestingly, this Dream Car was not always metallic gold. A seldom seen color photograph with Bill Mitchell and a guest standing beside the Golden Rocket shows the car's exterior was painted blue at some point and it had narrow-band white-wall tires rather than the strobe striped ones it wore during the Motorama circuit. The Golden Rocket was shown at the Paris Salon in 1957; perhaps it was repainted for that or some other post-Motorama show.

(At the time of this writing, the author has seen only one black-and-white photo of the car at the 1957 Paris Salon, so its color at that time could not be determined.) Seemingly, the only other possibility to explain the blue Golden Rocket is that an-other was built. However, a page from the Olds Engineering logbook lists only one example of the Golden Rocket, which would rule out that possibility. This photo is dated February 6, 1962, which is intriguing since it means this car stayed with GM a few years after other Motorama cars were sent away to their demise. What happened to the car after February 1962? Could it have been sent to a dealership for display and never sent back to GM, as in the case of the 1953 Pontiac Parisienne?

If Warhoops Used Auto & Truck Parts received only a few of the Motorama cars, where did the others go for scrapping? Warhoops may not have been the only yard selected for destroying some of GM's Dream Cars. Allegedly, another salvage yard in the River Rouge area received some of the Motorama cars (as well as Dream Cars and prototypes from other automakers).

GM design chief Bill Mitchell (right) and a guest identified simply as Mr. Payze from Australia, pose with the repainted 1956 Golden Rocket at the GM Tech Center on February 6, 1962. The fact the Golden Rocket was at the GM Tech Center at that time adds a trace of credibility to the rumor of this car's existence today. Most, if not all, of the Motorama show cars GM officials ordered destroyed were either smashed to bits, slipped out of the company's warehouse secretly, or in the case of at least four of the cars, sitting inside a salvage yard intact or partially dismantled by 1959. Did GM simply keep this car longer than the others, and then destroy it at a later date? *GM Media Archive*

The second Le Mans was sent to Greenlease-Moore Cadillac-Chevrolet in Oklahoma City for display in early November 1953. Greenlease-Moore was one of the largest distributors of Cadillacs at that time. Vice president and general manager of the dealership, Robert T. Moore, is shown standing beside the Le Mans; the Oklahoma State Capitol building is in the background. The fate of this car could not be determined. *GM Heritage Center*

However, that salvage yard no longer exists, so this story cannot be verified. Some cars were scrapped on-site at GM.

Notably, other Motorama cars besides the Dream Cars existed; these were the production cars with nonstandard paint and upholstery—cars such as the 1955 Cadillac Celebrity. What happened to them? The 1956 Cadillac Maharani survived and was in the Bortz Auto Collection for many years, but has changed ownership; at the time of this writing, the car was for sale. Its condition is excellent as it should be having been driven a mere 1,600 miles over the last half century.

What was the fate of the 1949 Cadillac Coupe de Ville prototype, El Rancho, Caribbean, and Embassy? The Coupe de Ville was driven for several years by GM president and later secretary of defense, Charles Wilson; in 1957, he gave it to his secretary. Presumably, the other three cars could have been used by or sold to other GM representatives or even outsiders. In fact, the prototype Coupe de Ville may still exist; it was advertised for sale in *Hemmings Motor News* sometime in the mid-to-late

1970s according to Tim Pawl, former president of the Cadillac-LaSalle Club Museum & Research Center, Inc.

Many more such cars were built. This type of car may have been ordered destroyed after 1953, as was the case with the Dream Cars. Presumably the degree of modification would be the determining factor in making the decision to destroy or sell them.

The 1950 Cadillac Debutante may still exist. As rumor has it, the car was last seen in a Detroit garage in rough condition, though still with its leopard skin interior; that sighting was in 1979.

What of the Buick Flamingo and a specially trimmed Impala convertible that were show cars? Floyd Joliet believes these cars were sold to General Motors' employees. However, the Flamingo's passenger front seat that could be rotated to face the back seat might have been enough of a modification to send it to its destruction, though seemingly it could have been replaced with a standard seat, and then sold. Any modification(s) that implied potential litigation risk or potential servicing problems would generally seal the fate of these cars.

There was one more type of GM Motorama car—the cut-away. Some production cars were displayed with their body cut lengthwise or with specific areas cut away to reveal the inner structure. Joe Bortz said that some of the cut-away cars still exist. These were clearly rendered useless, so the fact that some still exist is quite surprising. Perhaps those that survived were donated to area schools with an automotive curriculum.

The other cars of the GM Motorama were of course production cars. A relatively recent advertisement on the Internet and in at least one trade publication offered for sale what was said to be one of the actual 1955 Nomads displayed at the GM Motorama. The advertisement described the car as fully restored.

At least one of the Pontiacs exhibited still exists—a 1961 Tempest four-door sedan (as noted in Chapter Three). GM kept the car, but incredibly it was lost for a number of years while it was stored in a GM warehouse. Over the years it was eventually forgotten once it became hidden behind stacked crates. It was recently rediscovered, dusted off, and later photographed for an article about the 1961–1963 Tempests published in the December 2002 issue of *Collectible Automobile*.

The sixth 1953 Eldorado built served as a GM Motorama show car and is also believed to still exist; it was last reported to be in Brazil in the early 1990s. The fate of the first production 1953 Eldorado shown at the Waldorf-Astoria remains unknown.

This almost completes the summation of rumors and strange stories related to the GM Motorama cars. "Almost completes" is accurate, because many more years will likely need to pass before final resolutions are found regarding the Motorama cars' fates.

Even while these words are being written, a fresh though sketchy story from a reliable source has emerged. If verified, this will represent one of the more amazing stories in Motorama lore. Regardless of whether or not this claim is true, one or more of the lost examples from Motorama history will likely resurface within the next few years.

Joe Bortz expects more such cars are in garages waiting for their respective owners

"to decide it's time to sell." With the multi-million dollar bids for the F-88 and the Bonneville Special televised before car-collecting hobbyists, someone is likely to make the decision to sell soon.

What surprises lie ahead? Whatever they are, one can expect one or more "destroyed" cars to surface in at least a restorable state. Any paperwork that says a car was destroyed proves nothing. For example, a receipt on file at Buick headquarters says the sole prototype 1953 Buick Skylark hardtop built was destroyed. It was not. The car was finally tracked down by a collector who purchased the car in 1979. The four cars rescued from Warhoops give further evidence that paperwork attesting to the destruction of such cars is far from conclusive proof. With few exceptions, any of the GM Motorama cars still unaccounted for could exist.

Those who appreciate these cars should not miss seeing the surviving examples should the opportunity arise. Viewing these cars is a step back to a very different time—not just in terms of automotive history, but also in terms of the American way of life, which in retrospect appears as a much simpler and optimistic period. It was certainly a time when General Motors could produce the greatest automobile show in the world—the GM Motorama!

Like the LeSabre that came before it, the Le Mans inspired at least a few customs. This one was built in the 1960s and is at the time of publication of this book owned by Charles Marshall of California. *Charles Marshall*

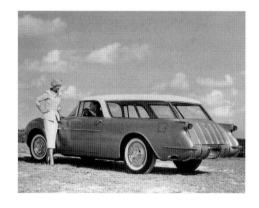

There has been a persistent rumor over the decades about the existence of the Nomad. The latest, but unconfimed, report is that it was recently sold to a collector who owns the red 1954 Corvair. *Wayne Ellwood collection*

Chapter Twelve
GM's Newest Concepts

The 2004 Nomad was designed in Britain and assembled by Pininfarina. *Charles D. Barnette*

The 2004 Chevrolet Nomad was said by the ad writers to represent "the taste of apple pie, the flair of cappuccino." The latest rendition of the Nomad was introduced at the 2004 North American International Auto Show in Detroit. This concept car was based on GM's new Kappa rear-wheel- drive platform, which serves as the foundation of the Pontiac Solstice and the Saturn Curve concept car.

Simon Cox, the design director for GM Advanced Design, United Kingdom, said "The Nomad is the type of vehicle that creates an instant bond with certain personalities."

The team who designed the latest Nomad not only created a modern vehicle, but also evoked the spirit of the original 1954 Nomad. The round headlights, gently curving front fenders, Corvette-like grille, forward leaning B-pillar, tailgate with recessed ribs (which mimic the look of chrome strips on the 1954 Nomad), and rolled panel under the tailgate are features of the car from 50 years ago yet the design is also clearly of twenty-first century thinking. The head and taillights are of LED technology, though the latter has a shape that deviates from the small, round style lamps of the first Nomad. They are housed within tall, narrow forms that fit flush with the surrounding fiberglass panels.

Lighting for the interior also has a modern touch. The instrument panel has a large semi-circular speedometer registering to 150 miles per hour encompassing a round 7,000-rpm tachometer. This cluster takes on a three-dimensional appearance with the anodized blue aluminum background and special lighting; all other gauges have an anodized blue aluminum face. Seating done in black leather and classic bow-tie insignias on a metal band that runs the length of the dashboard serve to increase the visual appeal of the interior. The upright portion of the seat is divided into three sections—the left and right passenger seat backs and a center armrest. Any one can be folded down individually or in any other combination for carrying various sizes and shapes of cargo.

The newest Nomad has a sports car–based platform with an independent front and rear suspension attached to a rigid chassis that uses a pair of full-length, hydroformed frame rails as its foundation. (Hydroforming is a low-cost method of forming metal into precise asymmetrical or irregular shapes for low-volume projects.) The 2+2 passenger configuration rides on a 107-inch wheelbase, 2 inches longer than the other Kappa-based designs. Powering the concept car is a 250-horsepower DOHC turbocharged Ecotec 2.2-liter four-cylinder

engine coupled to a five-speed Hydra-matic 5L40-E electronically controlled automatic transmission.

Will the Ice Blue Metallic concept car lead to a production version? The lead interior designer for the 2004 Nomad project said, "The idea for a compact vehicle like this is more relevant now than ever. As much as people crave a sporty, great-looking vehicle, modern lifestyle interests demand functionality. The Nomad has both—an unmistakable character, like the SSR. . . ." Perhaps the past and the future will soon meet in a production version.

At the 2006 North American International Auto Show, Chevrolet unveiled the spectacular Camaro concept. With the demise

With ever increasing worldwide demand for oil, technology is being looked to as a solution for the demand for energy. This experimental car, the GM AUTOnomy, tested a variety of concepts including fuel cell technology. *Rusty Thompson*

At the 2003 North American International Auto Show, Cadillac took the spotlight with its concept car dubbed simply and elegantly "Sixteen." The name emphasized the 830-cid V-16 of 1,000 horsepower and 1,000 ft-lbs of torque under the car's long hood. *GM Media Archive*

of the F-body at the end of 2002, many enthusiasts wondered if a new Camaro would ever again emerge from Chevrolet. One has, at least in concept form, and, judging by the public's reaction, Chevy may have a moneymaker in the Camaro, which borrowed a few styling characteristics from the 1969 model. A 400-horsepower, 6.0L LS2 V-8 coupled to a six-speed T56 manual transmission, power this rear-wheel-drive concept car. Plus, it gets up to 30 miles per gallon, thanks in part to a system called Active Fuel Management.

Underneath it is a sophisticated independent front and rear suspension featuring progressive-rate springs and gas-pressurized dampers. Four-wheel vented disc brakes with 14-inch rotors provide "confident stopping under all conditions" according to the official press kit about the model.

The Camaro's interior is designed with fighter-plane-inspired forms like the new Corvette. Its gauges and a splash of orange trim hint at classic first-generation Camaros, yet appear completely modern. That was the goal with the styling of this concept—modern with hints of the past, yet not retro. There is a chance this one could be in production around 2009. Even if it does not reach production, it represents some creative thinking on the part of GM's designers—something recognized through the "Concept Implementation Award" presented at the 2006 NAIAS by the organization, Eyes on Design.

One further note on Chevrolet: discussion of a new Chevy, based on the Kappa platform, is occurring. To be dubbed the Sting Ray, it would be powered by a high-output engine.

Beyond Chevy, Pontiac's Solstice concept commanded much attention. The Solstice is striking in its purity and simplicity, says Bob Lutz, GM vice chairman for product development and chairman of GM North America. "The exterior lines are strong, bold, and clearly Pontiac—but not over-the-top. . . ."

For the Solstice, a pair of concepts—a roadster and a coupe—was created using existing technologies from GM and its partners, such as its steering system derived from the Subaru WRX. According to reports, Lutz pushed these two concepts from idea to reality in only four months! The Solstice was voted Best in Show at the 2002 North American International Auto Show. The show circuit revealed the public loved the Solstice and now the two-seater roadster is in production as a 2006 model. *Road and Travel* magazine gave the Solstice their Sports Car of the Year award; it was also a runner-up for *Motor Trend* magazine's Car of the Year award.

The Solstice is powered by a 2.4-liter version of the twin-cam Ecotec four-cylinder engine, coupled to a five-speed close-ratio transmission. Horsepower measures 177 in this model, but a 260-horsepower 2.0-liter turbocharged engine powers the high-performance 2007 Solstice GXP.

Buick has kept busy producing concept cars, too. In 2000, they offered the retro-styled Blackhawk based on 1939 Buick styling, as well as the LaCrosse. The latter's name appeared on the replacement for the Regal in the 2005 model year.

In 2001, Buick brought out the Bengal—a sporty, two-passenger roadster. At the 2004 New York Auto Show, Buick unveiled another roadster—this time named Vélite. The Vélite received an all-aluminum V-6 engine rated at an impressive 400 horsepower. Behind it is a six-speed automatic transmission equipped with manual tap-shift gear selection. Styling cues such as signature portholes, a waterfall grille, oversize wheels, and long dash-to-axle proportions give a nod to Buick's design history while simultaneously appearing modern.

Meanwhile, Buick went a different direction for the 2006 North American International Auto Show; it introduced a luxury SUV, the Enclave. This one, which has unitized body construction, is said to combine the "athletic proportion of a modern crossover vehicle with the romantic forms characterized by Buick's rich design heritage." Signature Buick cues include a waterfall grille and portholes similar to the new Lucerne sedan. Inside the cocoa and light cashmere colored interior are six individual leather-covered seats with a large bronze-tinted skylight overhead. The passenger-side visor can function as a mirror or a DVD view-screen. Flip-up panels on the console between the third row of seats function as view-screens as well. An overhead vanity contains more screens for passengers in the second row of seats.

The Enclave has a 119-inch wheelbase and is powered by a DOHC 3.6-liter V-6 with variable valve timing said to produce 270 horsepower. This luxury SUV also has all-wheel-drive and four-wheel independent suspension.

And what about Cadillac? At the 2003 North American International Auto Show, Cadillac took the spotlight with its concept

For 2004, Buick displayed this two-seater concept car. *Charles D. Barnette*

car dubbed simply and elegantly "Sixteen." The name emphasized the V-16 of 1,000 horsepower and 1,000 ft-lbs of torque under the car's long hood. This experimental 830-ci, 32-valve V-16 (or XV-16 concept engine to be completely accurate) featured "Displacement on Demand" technology that allows cylinders—in this case, half of them—to shut down during normal driving and automatically and seamlessly reactivate the others for more demanding conditions.

Thomas Stephens, vice president of GM Powertrain, said, "The V-16 affirms Cadillac's leadership with a powerful statement."

Bob Lutz, GM chairman, said, "The Sixteen is a modern interpretation of everything that made Cadillac the standard of the world and can again." The XV-16 was coupled to an electronically controlled Hydra-matic 4L85-E four-speed automatic transmission.

The Sixteen was not just about an engine—it featured dramatic styling, too. The four-door pillarless hardtop with an all-glass roof exuded the look of grandeur seen in the original Cadillac V-16 models of the classic era. It also made the most of modern technology in the extensive use of aluminum, Baer six-piston caliper brakes, Bose sound system, rear-seat DVD information system, power-operated hood, LED head and taillights, and fifth-generation On-Star in-vehicle safety and security communication equipment.

The aluminum body sat on a 140-inch wheelbase, aluminum-steel chassis and rolled on 24x9-inch aluminum wheels. Its chassis employed high-arm SLA suspension up front and independent semi-trailing arm suspension in back. Four-wheel steering enhanced maneuverability.

The Sixteen's interior was equally well thought through. Its dash, door panels, and front and rear consoles were trimmed with walnut burl veneer inlays. The light cream upholstery was hand-stitched Tuscany leather with the right rear seat featuring power adjustable slope to recline like a chaise longue. Hand-woven silk carpeting covered the floor.

Oldsmobile, after more than 100 years of operation—nearly all of that time as a division of General Motors—was discontinued in mid-2003. The division's last concept car was given the simple moniker "04."

Beyond the venerable brands mentioned, a division that did not exist in the glory days of the GM Motorama is emerging as a leader in styling—Saturn.

On November 29, 2004, Saturn unveiled the all-new Sky roadster. This model is scheduled to go into production as a 2007 model. The Sky started as a concept vehicle in 2002. At the time, that design was not meant for production, but it certainly raised some eyebrows and showed Saturn was in a state of change. That change has placed it just above Pontiac in the GM hierarchy.

The Sky is a badge-engineered version of Pontiac's Solstice, and will be powered by the same Ecotec 2.4-liter four-cylinder, though it will have a more upscale interior. A number of features that are to be optional on the Solstice will be standard on the Sky; these include On-Star, power windows, remote locking, and air conditioning.

With ever increasing worldwide demand for oil, technology is being looked to as a solution for the energy mandate. General Motors has been at work developing an alternative to the gasoline-powered internal combustion engine. The GM AUTOnomy and its successor, the aptly named Sequel, are the first vehicles designed from the ground up around a fuel cell propulsion system. AUTOnomy, which tested a variety of concepts, was the first to combine fuel cells with "x-by-wire" technology, which allowed steering, braking,

With the success of the latest Mustang, GM has reconsidered the fate of its legendary Camaro, and has produced a concept car that has a few design cues reminiscent of the 1969 version, yet it still has a very modern appearance. GM Media Archive

185

Bob Lutz, whose remarkable career has taken him from Ford to Chrysler to GM over the past 30 years, is the man behind the latest styling innovations at General Motors, among which is the Pontiac Solstice, a GM concept car not long ago and now one of the division's hottest sellers. *GM Media Archive*

and other vehicle systems to be controlled electronically rather than mechanically.

According to Larry Burns, GM vice president of research and development and planning, the AUTOnomy "is an entirely new vehicle architecture that is far greater than the sum of its innovative parts. With AUTOnomy, an almost endless variety of affordable, all-wheel-drive vehicles could be built from a limited number of common chassis—possibly as few as two or three—emitting only water from the tailpipe and using renewable energy . . . AUTOnomy has the potential to reduce petroleum consumption, decreasing emissions and increasing our energy independence."

He added, " . . . Since a fuel cell propulsion system is about twice as efficient as an internal combustion engine, a fuel cell vehicle could provide twice the fuel efficiency of a comparably sized conventional vehicle, and an optimized fuel cell vehicle like AUTOnomy would be even more efficient."

There are other advantages offered with the concept. With all of its propulsion and control systems contained within a 6-inch-thick skateboard-like chassis, the vehicle body does not necessarily have to follow traditional design requirements.

"There's no engine to see over," explained Wayne Cherry, GM vice president of design. People could literally sit wherever they are comfortable. Drivers wouldn't have to sit in the traditional left-hand location. They could move to the center of the vehicle or they could move much closer to the front bumper or further back. It will take a little getting used to, but it's maximum freedom, maximum space for people and their stuff. There wouldn't be foot pedals or a steering column. The body shape could be literally anything you want it to be."

If such a fuel cell propelled car goes into production, this could lead to customized bodies and more individualized expression, Cherry said. "In fact, a customer could lease multiple bodies and swap them out throughout the week, depending on their needs. We've chosen this sleek, futuristic two-seater, but it doesn't have to be that way at all," Cherry said. "Next, we might do a mobility body that allows a wheelchair user to roll right into the driving position, or a 10-seat transit bus. We've even talked about a seating position that puts the driver right up front, like a helicopter pilot. . . . This new way to build and sell vehicles would dramatically affect the way vehicles are built, distributed, and even marketed. The unit is intended to last for years, much longer than a conventional vehicle."

One of the key features of the AUTOnomy is its universal "docking port," or connection, at the center of the so-called "skateboard" chassis. The docking port creates a simple way to connect all of the body systems to the chassis. That makes the vehicle body lightweight and uncomplicated.

Since computers control the x-by-wire systems, software upgrades can be downloaded to improve vehicle performance or tailor handling to suit a particular brand character, body style, or customer preference. General Motors has partnered with SKF, a Swedish-based global supplier, to develop the x-by-wire technology for AUTOnomy. Italian-based Bertone is another key supplier.

There are no pedals to operate in the AUTOnomy. Control is achieved through its x-by-wire system and the driver uses a steering guide called X-Drive to steer. This, in turn, frees up the seating to be more flexible and comfortable. There is no

driveline tunnel; the interior floor is completely flat, creating more interior space. With its stout 42-volt electrical system, the car is configured to run any number of devices in the passenger compartment.

General Motors pointed out that "more than 100 years after the automobile's invention, only 12 percent of the world's population currently enjoy its benefits. The AUTOnomy concept, we believe, could be the foundation for extending the benefits of personal transportation to the remaining 88 percent of the world's population."

As fascinating as the AUTOnomy is, it is still not production ready, so for 2005, GM showed the follow-up to the AUTOnomy—the Sequel. With each vehicle, GM comes a bit closer to a production car using fuel cell technology. The biggest difference between the AUTOnomy and the Sequel is that the latter is thought to actually be doable. The AUTOnomy was simply a concept that was not fully operable; some of the technology it showcased was not yet invented.

The Sequel has a completely functional powertrain, though it is still not economically feasible to mass produce. Still, it is the next step in the evolution of the fuel cell automobile. The Sequel is able to travel an impressive 300 miles on its hydrogen supply while accelerating from 0–60 in under 10 seconds, bettering the competition's concepts such as the VW Jetta TDI and Toyota Prius Hybrid.

The GMC Graphyte is a hybrid concept vehicle. It is a refined SUV with four-wheel-drive and 25-percent-improved fuel economy enabled by GM's latest two-model full hybrid propulsion system.

The mid-size Graphyte uses a two-mode full hybrid combined with a Vortec 5.3L V-8 with "Displacement on Demand" technology, to deliver strong, continuous power in all driving conditions. It is similar to the hybrid system that will be available on GMC Yukon and Chevy Tahoe full-size SUVs in 2007. Cadillac plans to follow with an Escalade powered by a two-mode full hybrid system for 2008.

The Solstice made the leap from concept to production in almost record time. Introduced in 2005 as a 2006 model, the Solstice will be joined by a second, higher performance 2007 GXP model. At the heart of the new GXP is a Ecotec 2.0-liter turbocharged engine, GM's first direct injection offering in North America. The new Solstice model will offer drivers a rousing 260 horsepower, making it GM's highest specific output engine ever, at 2.1 horsepower per cubic inch of displacement. *GM Media Archive*

The first mode provides fuel-saving capability in low-speed, stop-and-go driving—the kind of driving typical of urban commuting—with a combination of full electric propulsion and engine power. The second mode is used primarily at high speeds to optimize fuel economy, while providing full engine power when conditions demand it, such as trailer towing or climbing steep grades.

Two-mode full hybrid technology is at the center of GM's three-prong advanced propulsion strategy that aims to take automobiles out of the energy and environmental debate. The system fits within the space of a conventional automatic transmission, with a 300-volt NiMH cross-vehicle battery pack located beneath the rear passenger seat providing the electric power. Accessory systems under the hood support the electrically driven HVAC, power steering, and power brake systems. The drive system (which includes two compact electric motors and a series of gears that provide an infinite range of drive ratios) is contained within the case of a Hydra-matic 4L60-E automatic transmission.

The Graphyte's suspension ride height can be adjusted by the driver to a range of 4.7 inches, with the lowest height providing improved aerodynamics and the raised height providing more ground clearance when driving off road.

Jeweled xenon headlamps rotate left and right as well as move vertically to follow the attitude of the vehicle; LED illuminated lights are in back. The tailgate operates independently of the upper hatch to rotate and fold straight down, easing cargo loading.

Intuitive driver controls for the hybrid drive system are located in the center console and consist of an easy-to-operate drive-by-wire system. Gear selection is performed via a pushbutton rather than with a shift lever. A liquid crystal display screen in the console keeps the driver aware of the hybrid system's operational details, while a divided instrument panel with analog gauges in front of the driver provides read-outs for the speedometer, tachometer, and other instruments. The console screen also provides access to the vehicle's satellite navigation system and other "infotainment" options. Another screen folds down from an overhead console for rear seat passengers.

Also on board the 2006 Graphyte is an On-Star GPS system. All On-Star–equipped vehicles come with Automatic Crash Notification. If air bags are deployed, the system sends a signal to an On-Star Emergency Advisor, who contacts the vehicle occupant(s) to see if help is needed and can contact an emergency responder to send for help. In many cases the occupants are severely injured and cannot speak for themselves. On-Star's GPS unit allows Advisors to tell emergency responders the vehicle's location. The Graphyte's GM-exclusive Advanced Automatic Crash Notification (AACN) system

detects collisions, even rollovers, regardless of whether air bags deploy. AACN also transmits other crash data, such as the direction of impact force, the number of and which air bags deployed and the maximum change of impact velocity, so that emergency responders are more prepared with this critical information before they arrive at the accident scene.

Designers at GM are using the latest technology for added fuel efficiency, greater convenience, and increased safety and security. A half-century ago, the LeSabre, XP-300, and Firebird series represented the cutting edge of technology. Today the vehicles leading the way are Graphyte, Sequel, and AUTOnomy. What is next? Keep an eye on General Motors.

A two-mode hybrid engine was exhibited by GM at the 2006 North American International Auto Show. *Charles D. Barnette*

Appendix A: Number Built and Status of Motorama Show Cars

CAR	NUMBER BUILT	STATUS/COMMENTS
1951 LeSabre	1	Owned by GM
1951 XP-300	1	Displayed at Alfred P. Sloan Museum in Flint, Michigan
1953 Corvette prototypes	3	2 show cars and 1 test car, See Chapter 11
1953 Parisienne	1	Updated for 1954 auto shows, restored to 1953 configuration, in Bortz Auto Collection
1953 Starfire	3	2 Scrapped, 1 Unknown
1953 Wildcat I	2?	2 or 3 built, See Chapter 11
1953 Le Mans	4	3 accounted for, See Chapters 6 and 10
1953 Orleans	1	Not scrapped, Location unknown
1954 Corvair	2?	1 (red car) rumored to exist, See Chapter 11
1954 Nomad	2?	See Chapter 11
1954 Corvette w/Hardtop	2	1 known to exist
1954 Bonneville Special	2	Both exist, both pristine
1954 Strato-Streak	1	Unknown
1954 F-88	3 + 1 body	See Chapters 10 and 11
1954 Cutlass	1	Rumored to have been sold
1954 Landau	1	Restored, in private collection in Texas
1954 Wildcat II	1	Displayed at Alfred P. Sloan Museum in Flint, Michigan
1954 La Espada	1	Presumed to have been scrapped
1954 El Camino	1	Reported to have been scrapped
1954 Park Avenue	1	Unknown
1954 Firebird I	1	Wrecked and rebuilt, still owned by GM
1955 "50 millionth" GM automobile	1	Bel Air Sport Coupe with Anniversary Gold paint and gold-plated trim, exists
1955 Biscayne	1	Under restoration, in Bortz Auto Collection
1955 Strato-Star	1	Unknown
1955 Eighty-Eight Delta	1	Unknown
1955 Wildcat III	1	Strongly believed to have been scrapped
1955 Eldorado Brougham	1	Probably destroyed
1955 La Salle II Sedan	1	Needs restoration, in Bortz Auto Collection
1955 La Salle II Roadster	1	Undergoing restoration, in Bortz Auto Collection
1955 L'Universelle	1	Unknown
1956 Impala	1	Probably scrapped
1956 Club de Mer	1	Rumored to exist
1956 Golden Rocket	1	Rumored to exist
1956 Centurion	1	Displayed at Alfred P. Sloan Museum in Flint, Michigan
1956 Eldorado Brougham	1	Probably destroyed
1956 Eldorado Brougham Town Car	1	Restored, sold in early 2006 at RM Auctions
1956 Firebird II	2	Both exist and are owned by GM, display chassis also built
1958 Firebird III	1	Owned by GM, shown again at 1961 Motorama, display chassis also built
1961 Tempest show car	1	First production Tempest modified with tilt body, show-quality finish throughout, probably scrapped
Various production show cars with special paint, trim, upholstery	Many built	A few are known to still exist, See Chapter 11

Appendix B: Motorama Show Dates and Locations

1949 (Transportation Unlimited)

Jan. 20–27
Waldorf-Astoria, New York City, NY

Apr. 9–15
Convention Hall, Detroit, MI

1950 (Mid-century Motorama)

Jan. 19–27
Waldorf-Astoria, New York City, NY

1953

Jan. 17–23
Waldorf-Astoria, New York City, NY

Feb. 11–17
Dinner Key Auditorium, Miami, FL

Apr. 11–19
Shrine Convention Hall, Los Angeles, CA

May 1–7
Civic Auditorium, San Francisco, CA

May 16–24
Fair Park, Dallas, TX

June 6–14
Municipal Auditorium, Kansas City, MO

1954

Jan. 21–26
Waldorf-Astoria, New York City, NY

Feb. 6–12
Dinner Key Auditorium, Miami, FL

Mar. 6–14
Pan Pacific Auditorium, Los Angeles, CA

Mar. 27–Apr. 4
Civic Auditorium, San Francisco, CA

Apr. 24–May 2
International Amphitheatre, Chicago, IL

1955

Jan. 20–25
Waldorf-Astoria, New York City, NY

Feb. 5–13
Dinner Key Auditorium, Miami, FL

Mar. 5–13
Pan Pacific Auditorium, Los Angeles, CA

Mar. 26–Apr. 3
Civic Auditorium, San Francisco, CA

Apr. 23–May 1
Commonwealth Armory, Boston, MA

1956

Jan. 19–24
Waldorf-Astoria, New York City, NY

Feb. 4–12
Dinner Key Auditorium, Miami, FL

Mar. 3–11
Pan Pacific Auditorium, Los Angeles, CA

Mar. 24–Apr. 1
Civic Auditorium, San Francisco, CA

Apr. 19–29
Commonwealth Armory, Boston, MA

1959

Oct. 16–22, 1958
Waldorf-Astoria, New York City, NY

Nov. 8–16, 1958
Commonwealth Armory, Boston, MA

1961

Nov. 3–11, 1960
Waldorf-Astoria, New York City, NY

Jan. 7–15, 1961
Civic Auditorium, San Francisco, CA

Jan. 28–Feb. 5, 1961
Pan Pacific Auditorium, Los Angeles, CA

Stars of an All-Star Cast
PRESENTED BY
GENERAL MOTORS
AT THE CANADIAN NATIONAL EXHIBITION

MIAMI DAILY NEWS
FRIDAY EVENING FEBRUARY 5 1954
GM Motorama 1954

Dream Cars

BUICK'S *Wildcat II*

PONTIAC'S *Bonneville Special*

CADILLAC'S *El Camino*

OLDSMOBILE'S *Cutlass*

CHEVROLET'S *Corvette Nomad*

Los Angeles Motorama EDITION
SUNDAY, MARCH 6, 1955

GENERAL MOTORS Presents:
DREAM CARS of 1955

CADILLAC ELDORADO-BROUGHAM

PONTIAC STRATO-STAR

BUICK WILDCAT III

OLDSMOBILE "88" DELTA

LA SALLE II SEDAN

CHEVROLET BISCAYNE

PAN-PACIFIC AUDITORIUM
MARCH 5-13, INCLUSIVE

General Motors

On Stage
General Motors presents
"LOOKING AT YOU"

Produced and directed by
Richard and Edith
BARSTOW

Music written and conducted by
VICTOR YOUNG
with lyrics by EDWARD HEYMAN

Costumed by Raoul Pené du Bois

Choreography and special lyrics by
Richard Barstow

Introducing for the first time
on an American Stage . . .
Mme. Liane Dayde
Premiere Danseuse of the Paris Opera

The Broadway Singing Stars
Priscilla Gillette
David Atkinson

The Ashtons
THE CABOTS
THE FISHER BODY GIRLS
THE SINGING VIOLINS AND
THE PARK AVENUE FASHIONETTES
in Couturiere Originals
created for the Motorama by
SOPHIE OF SAKS FIFTH AVENUE

motorama
of 1955

Waldorf-Astoria   Jan. 20-25
NEW YORK CITY

CHEVROLET • PONTIAC • OLDSMOBILE • BUICK • CADILLAC
BODY BY FISHER • CHEVROLET AND GMC TRUCKS • FRIGIDAIRE • GM DIESEL

1955 G.M.
motorama

LA SALLE II SEDAN

LA SALLE II SPORTS COUPE

GMC L'UNIVERSELLE

PAN-PACIFIC AUDITORIUM   MARCH 5-13

We cordially invite you
to see GENERAL MOTORS'
GREATEST MOTORAMA

Greatest cars ever—cars of today and tomorrow! See the 1956 Chevrolet, Pontiac, Oldsmobile, Buick and Cadillac in the largest, most colorful display of this year's General Motors cars ever assembled! See the gas turbine Car of Tomorrow, the Firebird II. See 5 boldly contoured Dream Cars!

Greatest exhibits ever—the electronic Highway of Tomorrow in Technicolor on a giant screen—the Aerotrain of Tomorrow exhibit—the breath-taking Kitchen of Tomorrow. More exhibits than ever, a fascinating scientific show!

Greatest entertainment ever—the first combined VistaVision and Stage Show!

General Motors Presents
"KEY TO THE FUTURE"
A Thrilling Musical Prediction of Things to Come
Produced and Directed by MICHAEL KIDD
Lyrics by Jack Brooks

Featuring the Car of Tomorrow on the Highway of Tomorrow

The most advanced engineering concept of a safety-highway comes to life on stage and screen for the first time.

ADMISSION
FREE
GM MOTORAMA
of 1956
PAN-PACIFIC AUDITORIUM, Los Angeles
March 3 thru 11

GENERAL MOTORS
1961 MOTORAMA

The San Francisco
Civic Auditorium, January 7 thru